מסורה

ArtScroll® Series

Rabbi Nosson Scherman / Rabbi Gedaliah Zlotowitz
General Editors
Rabbi Meir Zlotowitz ז״ל, *Founder and President*

A LIFE WORTH

Published by

Mesorah Publications, ltd

ונקדשתי בתוך
בני ישראל

LIVING

Stories and ideas for
constant Kiddush Hashem

RABBI SHRAGA FREEDMAN

FIRST EDITION
First Impression … January 2019

Published and Distributed by
MESORAH PUBLICATIONS, LTD.
4401 Second Avenue / Brooklyn, N.Y 11232

Distributed in Europe by
LEHMANNS
Unit E, Viking Business Park
Rolling Mill Road
Jarow, Tyne & Wear, NE32 3DP
England

Distributed in Australia and New Zealand
by **GOLDS WORLDS OF JUDAICA**
3-13 William Street
Balaclava, Melbourne 3183
Victoria, Australia

Distributed in Israel by
SIFRIATI / A. GITLER — BOOKS
POB 2351
Bnei Brak 51122

Distributed in South Africa by
KOLLEL BOOKSHOP
Northfield Centre, 17 Northfield Avenue
Glenhazel 2192, Johannesburg, South Africa

ARTSCROLL® SERIES
A LIFE WORTH LIVING
© Copyright 2019, by MESORAH PUBLICATIONS, Ltd.
4401 Second Avenue / Brooklyn, N.Y. 11232 / (718) 921-9000 / www.artscroll.com

ISBN 10: 1-4226-2276-2 / ISBN 13: 978-1-4226-2276-6

Typography by CompuScribe at ArtScroll Studios, Ltd.

Printed in the United States of America by Noble Book Press Corp.
Bound by Sefercraft, Quality Bookbinders, Ltd., Brooklyn N.Y. 11232

Table of Contents

Introduction

A Life of Meaning and Purpose

There are some people in the world who live with a sense of mission. By and large, these are the people who are the happiest, most satisfied, and most successful in life. They are driven and passionate; nothing stops them or prevents them from striving toward their goal. In addition, they are not consumed by all the minor mishaps or even major hardships of life. Because they feel that they are living for a purpose that is much larger than themselves, the bumps and bruises that are part and parcel of living do not distract them or interfere with their dedication. And they are also the people who create an eternal legacy through their actions and accomplishments in life.

All of us could benefit from finding a way to add meaning to our lives, and the way to do that is to understand our mission in this world. The more meaning and purpose that we can infuse into our daily lives, the more enthusiastic, motivated, and fulfilled we will be.

For some people, there is even more of a reason to seek a sense of meaning in life. There are many people in the world who are dealing with a wide range of challenges, who would definitely appreciate some insight into the meaning of their struggles. There are many people, ranging from prestigious Torah scholars to ordinary youths, and encompassing many in between, who feel they are nothing but numbers in *frum* society, and who wish they could feel that they are making a special contribution to the Jewish world. There are *baalebatim* who work hard to make a living, who wonder how they can find meaning and purpose in a life with severely limited hours for Torah study. There are the people who are dealing with children or relatives who suffer from physical or emotional ailments, and who struggle to understand the purpose of their suffering. There isn't a single person in the world who couldn't benefit by finding a way to add a greater sense of meaning to their life, and that meaning comes from understanding our mission in this world.

The Mission

In *Shaarei Teshuvah* (3:158), *Rabbeinu Yonah* tells us that every Jew has a special mission: "The reason that Hashem chose the Jewish nation, elevated them above the rest of the nations of the world, and sanctified them with His Torah and mitzvos, is *solely so that they would fear Him and sanctify His Name.*"

I first heard this statement of *Rabbeinu Yonah* about 20 years ago in a *shmuess* from Rav Mattisyahu Salomon, when I was learning in Bais Medrash Govoha of Lakewood. The idea simply blew me away. I had always known that kiddush Hashem is a very important mitzvah, but I had never realized that it is the ultimate purpose of every Jew's existence, and that the entire Torah and all of its mitzvos are tools to help make it happen.

A Paradigm Shift

As I continued to learn about this mitzvah, my entire perspective on Yiddishkeit was transformed. It connected all the aspects of *avodas Hashem* and made everything, from Yamim Tovim to donning *tefillin*, much more meaningful. It took all the different pieces of the puzzle that is Jewish life, and fused them into a much larger picture that was beautiful and complete. It was the thread that connected it all. It added extraordinary balance and harmony to my life as a Jew.

And it became my purpose and my mission.

Before long, I realized that this mission is not exclusive to me. It is actually the mission of our entire nation, a calling that was meant to be carried out over the course of our entire history. And it is also the mission that every individual must carry out over the course of his or her lifetime.

No matter who you are or what your occupation is, no matter what your strengths and weaknesses are, you have your own unique mission to create a kiddush Hashem in a specific way. There are endless ways to live a life of kiddush Hashem, and each and every Jewish person has his own individual way to excel in doing so. For all of us, for every Jew, a life of kiddush Hashem is a life worth living.

The First and Second Books

This is the theme that I explore in this second book on kiddush Hashem. There are many different ways for a Jew to be *mekadeish Shem Shamayim*, and each of these forms of kiddush Hashem has many practical applications. These ideas are illustrated by many true stories, stories that could happen to any one of us.

This book is not meant to rehash the contents of my first book, *Living Kiddush Hashem*, nor is it a substitute for that book. The first book provides a broad understanding of the way kiddush Hashem works and how it connects with all the Yamim Tovim and other aspects of Yiddishkeit. I was touched by the responses I received from the many people who read that book, who described the life-changing impact that it had on them.

In this book, I attempt to transition the material discussed in my previous book to fruition, to make it real and practical for every reader. The purpose of this book is to take the concept of kiddush Hashem out of the realm of theory and to put it into practice. In addition, in the second to last chapter of this book,

I explore the approaches to kiddush Hashem that can be learned from the examples of several *gedolei Torah*. As you will see, there are many aspects of their behavior to which even simple Jews can relate. In the last chapter of this book, you will be introduced to many special people and organizations whose examples may change our perspectives on life, and open new horizons in our efforts to create kiddush Hashem.

Make Your Own Kiddush Hashem Mission Statement

I hope that everyone who reads this book will take it upon themselves to make kiddush Hashem their mission in life in some way.

What follows is a template for creating your own personal kiddush Hashem mission statement. As you read through this book, use the template to write down the ideas that resonated with you and that you feel are a good fit for your own personal values and strengths. You can then use those ideas to develop a mission statement that will keep you focused and will guide you through life. Your mission statement is meant to be fluid, and you can expect it to change as you yourself change. You may also have one mission in your home, another at work, and a third for your dealings with the community. Every few months, review your mission statement and adjust it. Make a copy, and keep it in a visible place.

Every one of us can make a difference by making our own personal kiddush Hashem. With our individual missions, all of us can change the world, one person at a time.

Here is a template you can use to create your mission statement:

"My mission in life is to live each day with [insert up to three values or principles] so that [identify what you will accomplish by living with those values]. I will do this by [list the specific behaviors you will use to live by those values]."

Here is an alternative version:

"In order to [identify what you want to achieve, do, or become] so that [list the reason/reasons why it is important], I will do the following [list the specific behaviors or actions you can use to achieve that goal]."

The Living Kiddush Hashem
Mission Statement

Living Kiddush Hashem was founded with the goal of imbuing every Jew with a powerful sense of mission: the mission to be mekadeish Shem Shamayim in his or her own unique way. We strive to accomplish this by raising awareness of the paramount importance of the mitzvah of kiddush Hashem and its centrality in everything we do.

Preface

Attitude Changes

Over the many years that I have been teaching and writing about the topic of kiddush Hashem, many have spoken to me about the paradigm shift that they experienced after learning about it. Here are some of the essential thoughts and attitudes that are developed by a focus on kiddush Hashem, as they were expressed to me by many students and readers.

It gives me a sense of meaning and purpose. It is incredibly motivating to feel that I have a unique mission to carry out in the world, based on my own individual strengths. No matter what I am involved in, there are always ways to serve Hashem by creating a kiddush Hashem. I can contribute to this great cause whether I spend my life in the *beis medrash* or in the working world. Even the most mundane activities — driving, shopping, cleaning, gardening, grooming, and the like — can be elevated into efforts to give rise to kiddush Hashem. Challenges and suffering can also take on new dimensions of meaning. Every action, great or small, can be infused with a focus, a goal, and a vision when it is channeled into the creation of a kiddush Hashem.[1]

I can make a difference in other people's lives. I do not have to be a highly influential or successful person in order to create a kiddush Hashem that will affect others. In a world of darkness, even a tiny ray of light can make a major difference. There are always many opportunities to make an impact and accomplish something positive. I recognize that even without being

---

1 *Michtav MeEliyahu,* Vol. 1, p. 22.

a professional *mekareiv*, I have a role to play in bringing other *Yidden* who are not yet religious closer to Hashem.

I have more respect and sensitivity for other people. I have learned to be more sensitive to others around me, and to be less absorbed in my own agenda. I think about the effects that my actions have on others, and I am conscious of their feelings. I know that a smile, a greeting, or a show of gratitude can have enormous power. I recognize that every human being was created to honor Hashem and was endowed with the potential to serve Him in his own unique way. I know that we can make a difference and even stave off anti-Semitism.[2] I also recognize that the *mitzvos bein adam laMakom* and the *mitzvos bein adam lachaveiro* are of equal importance and share the same goals. Both types of mitzvos are necessary in order to create kiddush Hashem, and one will not suffice without the other. In fact, if we do not take proper care in our dealings with others, our Torah may be worthless, and we may actually create a chillul Hashem.[3]

I am very careful to be honest in all my monetary dealings. I am not satisfied with fulfilling the letter of the law. I operate *lifnim mishuras hadin*, with the goal of fulfilling the underlying intent of the Torah's monetary laws. I do not take advantage of loopholes or engage in aggressive business practices, and I have no tolerance for *sheker*. I am careful to abide by the *dina d'malchusa* with regard to taxes and government programs, and I do not take advantage of or abuse airline and credit-card promotions, sales, and return policies.

My mitzvos *bein adam laMakom* have been greatly improved. Focusing on kiddush Hashem has helped me develop a stronger relationship with Hashem. My *avodas Hashem* has become more heartfelt and sincere; I serve Hashem in order to bring honor to Him, not merely to check off items on a list of obligations that I perform by rote. I am proud to be holy and different. I recognize that my mitzvos reflect Hashem's *kedushah* in addition

2. *Netziv, Sefer She'air Yisrael.*
3. *Mesillas Yesharim, perek* 11.

to His attributes. I have also found more meaning in our oft-repeated *tefillos* (such as *"asei l'maan shemecha"* or *"yehei shemeih rabba"*), and I have a deeper connection and commitment to Rosh Hashanah and its emphasis on the Kingship of Hashem. I also feel a much more powerful connection to the concept of eagerly awaiting the *geulah*, which I have come to understand as the ultimate manifestation of *kevod Shamayim*.[4]

I make a constant effort to avoid chillul Hashem. My pride in being a Jew does not cause me to look down on others. On the contrary, I am proud to be part of the nation that is tasked with bringing honor to Hashem. I realize that even if an act of insensitivity seems small and insignificant, it can become one of many tiny actions that contribute to a wave of chillul Hashem. Therefore, I train my children and myself to be constantly respectful and considerate of others. My children are courteous toward their non-Jewish teachers and to their classmates who are on different levels of Yiddishkeit. I myself have been able to forge more peaceful relationships with my neighbors through regular communication; by avoiding misunderstandings, I have reduced the potential for friction between us. I am especially cautious because I realize that the danger of chillul Hashem is especially great in our modern era, when pictures and videos can be transmitted in seconds and circle the globe, impacting thousands or even millions of people. I know that modern technology magnifies the potential for both kiddush Hashem and chillul Hashem many times over, and every action I take can have enormous repercussions.

Spreading the Word

It is my hope that these attitudes will continue to spread and take root, and that all of Klal Yisrael will remain constantly

---

4. *Mesillas Yesharim, perek* 19.

aware of the central place of kiddush Hashem in our lives. I encourage my readers to start a *chaburah* to learn this topic with others, and to bring it to their *shuls*, schools, camps, and other venues. It would be an excellent idea to create neighborhood committees for the purpose of fostering mutual respect and understanding between our communities and our neighbors. And there are many other ways to enhance and encourage a global commitment to kiddush Hashem.

May we all be successful in this mission, and may we be *zocheh* to greet Mashiach and be able to proclaim that we have done our part to hasten his arrival.

Available for free download is the Sefer Mekadshei Shemecha Hamekutzar and 4 booklets of Curricula developed and distributed in conjunction with Zechor Yemos Olam of Torah Umesorah. Please email LivingKiddushHashem@gmail.com or visit LivingKiddushHashem.com to receive these files and other resources.

Acknowledgments

I owe tremendous *hakaras hatov* to my editor, Rabbi Dovid Sussman, who has been my partner in this endeavor for the last seven years. He has been able not only to read and understand my material, but to read my mind and heart as well, and express all of my ideas beautifully on paper.

I am grateful to the ArtScroll team for seeing the potential of this project, and for providing valuable guidance along the way in order to make this book as professional and impactful as possible.

A special thank-you goes to Rabbi Pinchos Lipschutz of *Yated Ne'eman*, who gave me the opportunity to write the column on kiddush Hashem from which most of this material was gleaned.

A special thanks goes to my beloved children, who have sacrificed so much to allow me to have the *menuchas hanefesh* to delve into this topic and pursue this project, and who have shown tremendous enthusiasm for the mitzvah of kiddush Hashem.

Last but not least, I must also thank my wife, who has been a constant source of support and inspiration through rain and shine, and whose greatest dream is to see an enhancement of *kevod Shamayim*.

It has now been three years since we moved to Cincinnati, a city with an exceptional degree of energy and growth that is truly a jewel in Hashem's crown. We are grateful to Hashem for the incredible journey on which He has guided us, and for the many *berachos* He has showered on us. May He continue to guide us and enable us to be *mekadeish Shem Shamayim*.

Foreword
by Rabbi Moshe Tuvia Lieff

The Essence of Our Existence

Kiddush Hashem is the essence of our mission in this world; it is the reason for the Jewish people's existence. *Ramchal* (*Maamar Hachachmah*) teaches that the entire human race was created to honor Hashem, to serve Him, and to bask in His glory; this comes about through the Jewish people's service of Hashem. When we learn Torah and observe its precepts, we become the vehicles through which Hashem's existence and honor are revealed to the entire world.

Our mission of kiddush Hashem is pivotal to the existence of the world itself. *Rashi* (*Bereishis* 1:1) quotes *Chazal*, who state that the world was created *"bishvil Yisrael shenikre'u reishis* — for the sake of the Jewish people, who are called 'the first.'" We generally understand this to mean that everything in the world was created to assist us in serving Hashem; however, the *Shelah HaKadosh* (in his classic *tefillah* for parents) explains this *maamar Chazal* to mean precisely the opposite: The Jewish people exist in order to serve the world, not vice versa. Through our service of Hashem, we become the force that brings the entire world to perfection and leads it to achieve its purpose.

Satellites of His Will

How does a nation as tiny as ours, which makes up such a small percentage of the world's population, lead the rest of mankind to recognize Hashem and become worthy of receiving His goodness? As you read this book, you will find that there are many ways that Klal Yisrael can fulfill this mission; however, I would like to share with you how Rav Naftali Amsterdam, the renowned *talmid* of Rav Yisroel Salanter, asserted that he would achieve this. One of Rav Naftali's students once discovered a note that Rav Naftali had written to himself, in which he committed to cause the entire Jewish nation to return to Hashem. The student was surprised by his *rebbi*'s statement; he was certain that no human being could accomplish such a feat. He gathered the courage to approach Rav Naftali and to reveal that he had read the note, and then he asked his *rebbi*, "How do you think you will be capable of changing the entire Jewish people?"

Rav Naftali replied, "That resolution means that I will fulfill all the halachos in the *Shulchan Aruch*. By doing that, I myself will become a manifestation of the Will of Hashem."

The Gemara states that since the destruction of the *Beis HaMikdash*, Hashem was left with only one place in the world: the *daled amos shel halachah* ("four cubits of halachah"). Rav Tzaddok HaKohen explains that the observance of halachah is the means by which Hashem's Presence and Will are broadcast to the entire world. Of course, it stands to reason that during the hour that a working man spends learning in the *beis medrash*, Hashem will always be with him. But what happens when he leaves the confines of the *beis medrash* and spends the following nine hours in the working world? Even then, he requires Hashem's guidance and protection, and that is achieved through the observance of halachah. If a Jewish person runs his business in accordance with the *Shulchan Aruch*, abiding by all the laws in *Choshen Mishpat*, he will be living within the *daled amos shel halachah*, and Hashem will be with him at all times. He may be engaging in business dealings in Hong Kong, but he will still be in the company of the *Shechinah*. And when a businessman demonstrates patience and *derech eretz* in his dealings with his employees, clients, and customers, he will increase the degree of *kevod Shamayim* in the world. Thus, every person who remains faithful to the Torah, wherever he goes, actually serves as a "satellite" of the Divine Presence, for the *Shechinah* will always accompany him in all of his endeavors.

This is how the tiny Jewish people have such an incredible impact on the entire world. In China, in Canada, in Israel, and in countless other places — even on the World Wide Web — there are hundreds of thousands of representatives of G-d's Will, who bring honor to Him through the simple fact that they are meticulous about observing His laws.

We Are Public Figures

As Jews, we cannot avoid this responsibility; we cannot escape from the fact that we represent the Master of the Universe. No matter how hard we try, it is impossible for us to go unnoticed. We are always in the spotlight; one way or another, we are bound to be in the news. That is the nature of our existence, and it is what Hashem desires of us. Let us make our impact as positive as we can.

Rabbi Bentzion Lopian, the son of Rav Elya Lopian, was a *talmid* in the famed yeshivah of Kelm. He once described an exchange that he overheard in the market in Kelm between a non-Jewish lumber merchant and a Jewish customer. The merchant was demanding immediate payment for his merchandise, insisting that he did not trust the Jew to pay him at a later date, but the Jewish customer wanted to purchase the goods on delivery. Their argument was soon interrupted by another non-Jew, who asked his friend, "What is the matter? It's Elul now; you can trust him!" The influence of Elul was obvious to the non-Jews of Kelm. Our mission is to recreate that same impression within the world of which we live today.

Beneath Our Dignity

There is another important attitude that can make a huge contribution to our fulfillment of our mission. Rav Yitzchak

Eizik Sher, the *rosh yeshivah* of Slabodka, always taught that holiness is attained *"lo mitoch prishus ela mitoch chashivus* — not through abstinence, but rather through [a sense of] dignity." The Torah commands us to bring honor to Hashem and to develop ourselves into holy people; however, we are not meant to be motivated by fear of punishment. We should not be telling ourselves that we must divorce ourselves from *gashmiyus* in order to avoid falling to the lowest depths, absorbing harmful influences and suffering the punishment of Gehinnom. That is not the attitude that will propel us to become vehicles for *kevod Shamayim.*

Rather, we must train ourselves to feel that we are too noble and respectable to act in a sinful or crass fashion, that our *neshamos* are too precious for such behavior. It is beneath our dignity to make a chillul Hashem. If this is the guiding principle of our actions, then we will be elevated in countless ways. We will not pounce on the food at a smorgasbord like gluttons, because we will have too much self-respect to demean ourselves in that fashion. We will not be tempted by questionable business deals or other dishonest practices, because we will view ourselves as *ehrlicher Yidden*, members of the *mamleches Kohanim* and the Chosen People, which makes all of us important dignitaries. This is how a person becomes a constant living kiddush Hashem: by remembering that sinful behavior is beneath his dignity.

We are the royalty of the world. We are princes and princesses. If we think of ourselves as royalty, if we always remember what we represent, then we will act accordingly.

Dressing with Dignity

A ceremony was once held in Lower Manhattan to mark the opening of a park dedicated in memory of the British nationals who were killed in the 9/11 terror attacks. The event was held on a very hot day in July, and many people arrived in highly immodest clothing. However, there was one distinguished woman who was dressed in the most regal fashion: Her sleeves extended past her elbows, her dress reached below her knees, and she wore an elegant hat. When it was her turn to speak, she strode purposefully to the podium with her head held high, and she delivered her remarks to a crowd that reacted with awe and respect. This woman was the queen of England.

As religious Jews, we do not dress modestly because we are frightened of the evil in the world or paranoid about the results of exposing ourselves. Rather, we dress in this way because we are dignified; we take pride in our level of humanity and our *tzelem Elokim*. We are people of stature; we know that we represent Hashem Himself, and that is a status that elevates us.

For the same reason, we will never be ashamed to carry out the Will of Hashem, even when it is not popular or it is not appreciated by the world around us. If we have the right attitude about our role in the world, then we will exude confidence in the correctness of our actions even when others disapprove of them.

Over 20 years ago, a serious concern arose about the permissibility of wearing a *sheitel*, when it was discovered that many *sheitels* were made of hair that came from India and might have been donated in *avodah zarah* ceremonies. When this first came to light, Rav Elyashiv ruled that women should refrain from wearing *sheitels* until the issue could be clarified. The next day, thousands of professional women showed up at their places of work wearing hats or *tichels*. Their coworkers could not believe their dedication; they were astonished that these women had sacrificed their professional appearance in order to observe the halachah. It was a major kiddush Hashem.

Explain Politely When Possible

However, there is a qualification to this idea, and that is my next advice regarding kiddush Hashem. Although we must always follow the dictates of halachah in every situation, even if our actions seem strange or even distasteful to others, we must always try to show sensitivity. We should never rub our actions in other people's faces. Whenever possible, we should explain the reasons for the actions we do.

The power of a few words of explanation is illustrated by the following incredible story. The residents of the neighborhood of Ezras Torah were once perturbed by a stranger who deliberately shattered the peace and calm of their Shabbos. Week after week, the same car would be seen in the streets of the neighborhood, driving around in circles solely in order to disturb the Shabbos-observant residents. Some of the people began loudly protesting the intrusion, but Rabbi Hershel Zaks, who was equally disturbed by the chillul Shabbos, decided to take a different approach. When the car appeared, he memorized its license-plate number. After Shabbos, he was able to use the number to find out the man's address, which was in the neighborhood of Ramot.

Accompanied by a companion, Rabbi Zaks went to Ramot and knocked on the door of the man's home. The door was opened by a little boy, who looked the visitors up and down and then called over his shoulder, "*Hashechorim higi'u* — The black ones are here!" From somewhere within the apartment, his father shouted back, "Give them a *shekel*!"

"We aren't here for money," Rabbi Zaks told the child. "We want to talk to your father."

The boy disappeared into the house, and then his father came to the door. "What do you want from me?" he demanded. Rabbi Zaks gently explained that the Jews of Ezras Torah were pained by the appearance of a car driving on their streets on Shabbos. The man replied, "You are crazy, but you are right. I will not drive on your streets."

A year and a half later, Rabbi Zaks received an invitation to a *bar mitzvah* in Ramot. When he arrived at the *simchah*, the father of the *bar mitzvah* boy asked him, "Rabbi, do you recognize me?" Rabbi Zaks admitted that he did not. "About two years ago, you came to my door to ask me not to drive in Ezras Torah on Shabbos," the father said. "Today, I have become *shomer Shabbos* because you cared enough to come to see me and explain the situation. I sent my child to a religious school because I want him to learn how to emulate you, who took the time and made the effort to explain yourself to me."

Of Handshakes and Respect

At the beginning of the intifada, the Federation invited me to join a mission to Israel to give *chizuk* to our suffering brethren. After consulting with the Moetzes Gedolei HaTorah I agreed. This mission was joined by 23 members of my *kehillah* in Minneapolis. I encouraged my congregants to wear their black hats throughout the trip, so that the people we visited would see that "black-hat Jews" care about them.

On the third day of the trip, we visited an affluent kibbutz. As soon as we entered the dining hall, the woman in charge of the facility barked at me, "Don't go into the kitchen to check anything out! Just sit at the places with the words 'glatt kosher.'" I greeted the woman in my most cordial tone, "*Aleichem shalom*", and she extended her hand. I explained that I do not shake hands with women, and she said archly, "Oh, you are one of *those* people."

"Yes," I replied. "Do you know why we don't shake hands with women?"

"It's because you are afraid of me," she said.

I opened my wallet to reveal a picture of my wife. "I am happily married to this lady," I said. "Do you really think I am afraid of you? Do you want to know the real reason that I won't shake your hand?" She shakes her head in the affirmative. "The reason I won't shake your hand is that I respect you; it is a sign of honor."

The woman was genuinely surprised; she confessed that it was the first time she had ever heard such an explanation for this religious practice. With that, her entire demeanor changed, and she proceeded to take me on a private tour of the kibbutz and to attend to all of our needs. As we were about to leave she requested to take my picture and then she asked me, "Do you want to know why I got so angry when I saw you? I grew up in Meah Shearim, and at the age of 17 I ran away from it all. Whenever I see people like you, I know that I was supposed to be like you, and I become angry at myself."

The tragic aspect of this woman's story is that Yiddishkeit was never explained to her in a way that she could appreciate. It might have made a major difference in her life if someone had taken the time to help her achieve even a modicum of understanding. After all, even the smallest ray of light can repel an immense amount of darkness.

Under Close Scrutiny

The prohibition of chillul Hashem appears in *Parashas Emor*, in the *pasuk* that states, "*Lo sechallelu es shem kodshi* — Do not desecrate My holy Name." Immediately before this *pasuk,* the Torah states, "*Ushmartem es mitzvosai va'asisem osam* — You shall guard My mitzvos to do them." The *Chasam Sofer* understands this *pasuk* as referring to studying the Torah for the sake of having the knowledge necessary to observe the mitzvos. In these *pesukim*, the Torah warns us that a person who learns Torah must be very careful not to cause a chillul Hashem; he must make sure that his actions only bring honor to Hashem.

Rav Yerucham Levovitz, the revered *mashgiach* of the Mir yeshivah in Europe, used to stress that a person who learns Torah must excel at loving other people. Kiddush Hashem means much more than not fighting for a parking spot and making sure to speak nicely to others; it means excelling in the mitzvah of *v'ahavta l'reiacha kamocha*. Kiddush Hashem means being a master of treating other people with respect and speaking to them with pleasantness. It means being such an elevated person that other people will marvel at the character traits of a person who is known to study Torah.

The *pasuk* that commands us to study the Torah uses the

term "*v'shinantam*." In a literal sense, this means that a person should "sharpen" his understanding of the Torah. *Chazal* teach us that a Torah scholar must be fluent in the Torah, so that when he is questioned about the material he has learned, he will be able to answer accurately and with confidence. The reason this is important is that a person who engages in Torah study is a person who represents the Torah; he is meant to be an expert on the Torah, and if he is unable to give a clear answer when he is questioned about it, then others may be led to denigrate the Torah itself.

Imagine a professor who is an expert in a specific field, who has written many scholarly papers on the subject and has devoted his entire life to that area, but finds himself unable to answer the questions posed to him at a presentation. In the audience's eyes, this will cast doubt on all of his knowledge and theories; it will show a fundamental lack of confidence in his discoveries. The same is true of us; as religious Jews, we are seen as experts on the Torah way of life. The Torah promotes exemplary *middos* and character refinement, but if the world does not see that in us, then the entire Torah lifestyle may be discredited in their eyes. If a religious Jew gives others the impression of being coarse or corrupt, it will not merely reflect negatively on him as an individual; rather, it will cause others to look askance at the entire Torah way of life. Not everyone will appreciate the depth of *lamdus* or the beauty of a Brisker *chakirah* or an intricate *pilpul*, but everyone appreciates being spoken to with respect. A Torah scholar is judged by the world based on the way he behaves, which is seen as the measure of how the Torah affects and shapes him as a person.

Anyone who learns Torah must excel in showing love for other people, even non-Jews. A student of Torah must show honor and respect to all other human beings. As religious Jews, we all have the obligation to live up to this standard. And the more a person is perceived by others as having studied and absorbed the Torah, the greater is his obligation to be a model of proper interactions with other people.

Impatience Can Destroy

I was once in a kosher supermarket in Minneapolis, where I watched as a *yarmulke*-wearing customer was greeted by a worker behind the counter who spoke a broken English. In response to her question of "What can I do for you?" the person snapped, "You could learn how to speak English!"

I was deeply perturbed. "My friend," I wanted to rebuke him, "you should take off your *yarmulke*! I don't care if you go to *seder* or that you wear *tzitzis*; people need to see that you are kind and patient."

A Rude Encounter

Rabbi Eliezer Sorotzkin, the director of Lev L'Achim, told me a fascinating story. A resident of Chol HaYam, a secular kibbutz, had traveled to Yerushalayim to visit the Kosel. He donned a paper *yarmulke* and then stood in the Kosel plaza, watching in awe as a group of five hundred children sang and danced with great passion. Upon making some inquiries, he was told that the children were students in the schools of Lev L'Achim. That sight alone was enough to inspire him to seek a connection of his own to the Torah.

At the man's request, a *yungerman* from the Haifa branch of Lev L'Achim was sent to the kibbutz to learn with him. When the *yungerman* arrived at the kibbutz, he found the entrance gate locked, and the security guard in the booth beside the gate ignored his presence. The visitor knocked on the window, and the guard opened it and barked, "We don't want your kind here. You don't belong here!" The visiting *yungerman* whipped out his cell phone and called the man with whom he was assigned to learn. He explained the situation and handed the phone to the guard, and a fierce argument ensured. Although the kibbutz resident demanded that his visitor be admitted, the guard was just as adamant about barring him from the kibbutz. "We don't want these people here! Absolutely not!" he said vehemently. Finally, a compromise was reached: The *yungerman* would be permitted to enter the community only if his learning partner drove to the gate to pick him up in his own car. This became the regular arrangement between the two men.

Today, the same *yungerman* delivers a *shiur* to a group of 18 residents of Chol HaYam, and there is even a *minyan* on the kibbutz. Most amazingly, the same security guard has become the organizer of the *shiur*! This is a change that came about gradually, over the course of more than a year. The *yungerman* from Lev L'Achim came to the kibbutz every week and the same scene repeated itself time and again: The *yungerman* would call his learning partner, who would come to pick up his visitor in his own car. Every week, while the visitor from Lev L'Achim waited for his host, he would engage in small talk with the guard. Those pleasant conversations eventually led the guard to decide to join the learning himself. This was an achievement that was made possible only by the *yungerman's* ability to keep his cool. In spite of the guard's behavior, he never allowed himself to become angry or indignant. Rather than responding in kind when he was insulted, he remained kind and pleasant, using the Torah as his guide, and the results were remarkable.

Small Changes

Another important guideline for working to create a kiddush Hashem is to view even the smallest amount of progress as a tremendous mitzvah. If you manage to reduce other people's hatred for the Torah, that alone is a huge accomplishment.

The Chofetz Chaim used to expend significant time and energy arranging kosher food for the Jewish soldiers who were stationed on several of the czar's army bases. Someone once remarked to the Chofetz Chaim that his efforts were a waste of time; the soldiers were eating the kosher food he had arranged for them, but then they were consuming *tereifeh* food as well.

The Chofetz Chaim replied, "If these Jewish boys eat a little less *treifos* because they are somewhat full from the kosher food, that makes it worthwhile as well." Even causing a slight reduction in an *aveirah* is a mitzvah in its own right. This is a very important concept that should be taught to every religious Jew.

When Your Life Is on the Line

A certain Jewish man owned a nursing home in Baltimore, in which all of the residents were not Jewish. Due to the makeup of its clientele, the nursing home served nonkosher meals. One day, however, the owner discovered that one of the elderly women living in the home was indeed Jewish. He arranged for kosher food to be served to her, but the woman refused to accept the meals; she insisted on being served the same nonkosher fare that was provided to all the other residents. The case was brought to court, and the judge ruled that if the resident did not begin receiving the meals she wanted within thirty days, the entire facility would be shut down. The owner called Rav Noach Weinberg and begged him for a *heter* to serve nonkosher meals to the woman, but Rav Weinberg ruled that it was forbidden.

Several months later, Rav Weinberg encountered the man and asked him how the story had ended. The nursing home owner replied, "We figured it out. She agreed to eat kosher."

"How did you do that?" Rav Weinberg exclaimed.

"We made her *shomer Shabbos*," the man replied.

The *rav*'s incredulity grew. "How did you do *that*?" he demanded.

"My life was on the line," the owner said simply. "I was in danger of losing the facility and my entire livelihood, and I had no choice: I had to figure out how to get her to become religious."

All of us must realize that our lives are on the line as well; our entire existence revolves around our obligation to create a kiddush Hashem. If we understand that, then we will make any sacrifices that are necessary — giving up time, money, or anything else that is required — in order to carry out our mission and achieve the purpose of our existence.

With every step we take, every breath we breathe, every word we speak, and every action we perform, we represent Hashem. Kiddush Hashem is the purpose of the world's creation, and it is likely the paramount mitzvah of our generation. In this era, we are no longer in survival mode; we live in a land of freedom and liberty, and that gives us the opportunity to excel at kiddush Hashem perhaps more than at any other time in history. That is our obligation; let us do it right.

CHAPTER 1

WORDS AND DEEDS

A group of yeshivah bachurim are playing basketball in the park, while other boys are waiting their turn to play against the winners. The game is becoming intensely competitive, as the scores of the two teams are very close. People are seated on benches in the park, watching the children at play. As the game goes on, the typical shouts can be heard: "Pass it here!" "That was a foul!" "Look out!" But there is something different about the way these boys call out to each other; there is something unusually pure and wholesome about their language. Even when one teenager is knocked to the ground as he tries to take a shot, there are no shouted obscenities or harsh words; the boys simply stop the game and crowd around to help their friend. Another boy gives away his spot in the game to allow someone who has been waiting a turn to play. The adults in the park cannot help but be impressed. This is something they have never witnessed before.

The Power of Empathy

Rav Yechezkel Abramsky was once walking in Yerushalayim, deep in conversation with another *rav* about a matter of great importance, when he passed a young girl who was crying. Another man might not even have noticed her, but Rav Yechezkel interrupted his conversation, bent down, and asked the child what was wrong. The girl told him that another child had made fun of her, telling her that her dress was ugly. Rav Yechezkel assured her that it was truly beautiful, and the child left with a brilliant smile. To his companion, Rav Yechezkel explained, "The *navi* says, '*Umachah Hashem dimah me'al kal panim* — Hashem will wipe away the tears from every face.' We are commanded to emulate Hashem's *middos* and 'wipe away' everyone's tears, even those of a child."

The mitzvah of having *middos tovos* (proper character traits) is derived from the verse *"v'halachta b'drachav"* (the commandment to emulate Hashem, which literally means "you shall walk in His ways"). The Torah tells us to mirror the ways of Hashem so that we represent Him properly in this world. By behaving in a praiseworthy way, we bring honor to Hashem and show the world that His servants are fine and virtuous people.

This is the message of the *pasuk* (*Yeshayah* 43:7), *"Kol hanikra bishmi u'lichvodi barasiv* — All those who are called by My Name are created for My honor."* A person who is "called" by the Name of Hashem is a person who displays the attributes of Hashem; thus, when we adopt His traits, we bring honor to Him.[1]

The Thirteen Attributes of Mercy, which we recite many times during the *Yamim Noraim*, share a common theme: They are all based on the trait of empathy. In order to display Hashem's *middos* and to create a kiddush Hashem, we must master the art of empathizing with and caring for others. This is a key component of our mission to promote *kevod Shamayim*.

The biography of Rav Eliezer Geldzahler[2] relates a remarkable

---

1 *Michtav MeEliyahu, chelek* 1, pg. 138.

This is why, as *Rashi* tells us in *Sefer Bereishis* (17:22), the *tzaddikim* are called Hashem's "chariot." A chariot takes its rider wherever he wishes to go, and the Shechinah similarly "rides" on the *tzaddikim*, since every one of their actions and movements is intended solely to do Hashem's Will. By living purely to serve Hashem and emulate the traits He has revealed to us, *tzaddikim* advance *kevod Shamayim* everywhere they go, spreading the recognition of His Kingship throughout the world.

There is also another way that the Jewish people's kindness and empathy bring honor to Hashem. The nations of the world sometimes recognize the existence of a Supreme Being and the need to serve Him, but they often have distorted understandings of what He expects of His creations. Throughout history, their warped perceptions of religious devotion have caused untold pain and suffering to millions of innocent human beings. When the Jewish people conduct themselves in an elevated, refined way, the rest of the world is shown an example of Hashem's true ways. Thus, for instance, the *Prishah* explains (in the beginning of *Choshen Mishpat*) that *gemillas chassadim* is one of the three things that sustain the world because it creates awareness that Hashem Himself is kind and merciful, and in fact, that is why He commanded us to do *chessed*.

2. *Reb Leizer: The Life and Legacy of Rabbi Eliezer Geldzahler,* Yisroel Besser, Judaica Press, 2014.

story about the power of empathy: A few months after Rav Eliezer's passing, his daughter drove into a gas station where the attendant on duty was a midget. As the man began washing her windows, he noticed a large portrait of her father, which she had left on the front seat of the car, and he became excited. "Do you know this man?" he asked. "I've been waiting for him to come back here for a long time. Where is he?"

The daughter gently told the attendant that Rav Lazer was her father and had passed away, and he began to cry. "I must tell you what your father did for me," he said. "This is one of the few jobs I can do, and most people here look away when they see me. But one day, your father came and greeted me warmly. He told me that I am an inspiration because I don't act like a victim even though I have a handicap, and I get up every morning and work to make an honest living. He even said that he was going to speak to the students in his school about what they can learn from my example. Ever since that day, I have looked forward to seeing him come here. He always made me feel tall."

Empathy is an important trait to use in our dealings with others, but it begins with our relationships with our families. We must ask ourselves if we have truly mastered this trait in our relationships with the people who are closest to us. Do we give enough consideration to the emotional needs of our spouses and our children? Are we concerned about their feelings? If our children are secure in the knowledge that we care about the way they feel, then they will learn from our example to be empathetic toward others as well.

Takeaway

When we show concern for the feelings of others, we emulate the middos of Hashem, which are rooted in empathy. This is the key to representing Hashem in the world.

Goodwill Through Gifts

The launch of America's new health care system spelled disaster for many Americans. Many people suddenly found themselves without any health insurance, struggling to find new plans in a system that was plagued by glitches. Mrs. Silverstein (name changed), a *frum* woman, spent many days working with Steve, a nonreligious insurance broker, to find a plan that would meet her needs. After expending much time and effort, Mrs. Silverstein ended up on the phone with the manager of an insurance company, who finally managed to get the online system working and to find a plan that was suitable for her. The manager urged her to grab the opportunity and sign up immediately for the plan.

Mrs. Silverstein was in a quandary. While this might be her only opportunity to get the health plan she needed, she would effectively be depriving Steve of a commission by signing up through the company. After all of his efforts on her behalf, she felt uncomfortable doing that. She asked the manager to stay on the line and called Steve to explain the situation. He assured her that she should register for the plan.

Mrs. Silverstein still felt that some show of appreciation was due to her hardworking broker, and she had a cake delivered to his office, along with a check for 100 dollars. Steve called her back immediately, overwhelmed by the gift. He was so moved by her actions that he decided to donate the money to her children's school. "I love working for religious Jews," he added. "They are always so appreciative."

A gift can be an incredibly potent tool to create a kiddush Hashem or to help defuse tensions or hard feelings.[3] The power of gifts to cultivate patience and understanding is illustrated by a powerful story told about a noted *maggid shiur* in Montreal who lived next door to a triplex occupied by three non-Jews, one of whom was known for his hostility toward the *chassidim* in the neighborhood. The *maggid shiur* made a practice of going out of his way to greet the man, and he even purchased large boxes of chocolates once a year for each of his three neighbors.

The *maggid shiur*'s friendly overtures later turned out to have far-reaching effects. A prominent *rav* in Montreal was once

---

3. When giving gifts to a non-Jew, however, one must be careful not to violate the Torah prohibition of "*Lo sechaneim* — Do not show them favor" (*Devarim* 7:2), which forbids giving a *matnas chinam*, a "free gift," to a non-Jew (*Yoreh Deah* 151:11). A gift can foster a relationship between the giver and the recipient, and a Jewish giver might be corrupted by the values and lifestyle of a non-Jew to whom he gives a gift (*Sefer Hachinuch, mitzvah* 426). With a proper understanding of when it is permitted to offer a gift to a non-Jew, we can add this to our repertoire of techniques for generating kiddush Hashem.

One case in which it is permissible to give a gift is a situation of *darchei shalom:* when the purpose of the gift is to avoid hurt feelings or show remorse for inconveniencing the recipient. Another case is if the giver will receive something in return. This includes giving a gift to receive better service; for example, presenting a gift to an employee so that he will put more effort into his work. This is permitted even if someone other than the giver himself benefits from the gift, such as if the worker is later employed by another Jew. One may also give a gift to a non-Jew as payment for a service when basic decency calls for it, even if one will not have an opportunity to benefit from the non-Jew in the future. A gift of this sort is not considered a *matnas chinam,* since it simply fulfills the requirements of basic *mentschlichkeit*.

seeking a male voice therapist, and one of Quebec's *askanim* searched far and wide for a suitable practitioner. The field was apparently dominated by women, though, for only one male voice therapist could be found, and he claimed to be too busy to take on additional patients. After a while, the therapist agreed to add the *rav* to his packed schedule. This therapist turned out to be none other than the hostile neighbor whom the *maggid shiur* had gone out of his way to appease, and he made it clear that he had taken the *rav* as a patient out of appreciation for his gracious neighbor.

Often, the good will generated by a gift may benefit others even if the giver himself does not experience the results. The Bobover Rebbe, Rav Shlomo Halberstam, was very kind to a non-Jewish painter who painted his house. The Rebbe served the painter a hot breakfast every day, and when the job was completed, the Rebbe gave him a hefty tip, far beyond the standards of that time. The painter's next customer was another *frum* Jew, whose house was in dire need of painting, but who had only enough money to paint a single room. Warmed by the Rebbe's generosity on his previous job, the painter insisted on applying his tip from the Bobover Rebbe to cover the cost of painting the entire house.[4]

Of course, a gift is sometimes necessary simply for the sake of common decency. One should always make certain to tip a waiter, taxi driver, barber, or other such worker for a job well done. In situations where it is customary to give a tip, failure to do so would actually lead to a chillul Hashem, since it would create the impression that religious Jews lack good manners or appreciation for others. But even when a gift is not expected, the power of a gift to touch the hearts of others makes it a valuable tool, when used appropriately, for the creation of a kiddush Hashem.

---

4. This story was shared by Rav Yaakov Shlomo Meisels, the Liminover Rebbe, in an interview with *Binah* magazine

Giving a gift or a token of appreciation is a way to demonstrate respect to others, which always touches people's hearts.

Making It Practical

- Give a gift of appreciation to someone from whom you have benefited.
- Make sure to tip a worker generously whenever it is expected. Even when it is not expected, offer a tip when feasible.

⇒•◇•⇐

The Circle of Gratitude

Rav Shimshon Brodsky *zt"l*, a renowned *rav* and *marbitz Torah*, passed away in 2011 after a brief period at Leisure Chateau, a nursing home and rehabilitation center in Lakewood. After the *shivah* ended, Rabbi Brodsky's children felt the need to express their gratitude to the staff at the facility. For that purpose, they presented the staff with a framed letter of appreciation thanking them profusely for their dedicated care, along with a small picture of their father.

It wasn't long before the director of Leisure Chateau, himself a *frum* Jew, called to congratulate them for the kiddush Hashem they had created. "The staff went wild when they received your letter!" he exclaimed. The letter was placed on the wall next to the nurses' station, where it has been on display ever since. Over the years, many others have followed the Brodsky family's example, and their letter is now surrounded by an array of other poems and letters of thanks.

While no one chooses to be in such a situation, there are many people who have close family members in hospitals, nursing homes, and rehabilitation centers. When family members are visible in such facilities, they are invariably noticed by the staff — and with a little effort, this opportunity can be used to make a kiddush Hashem.

Hakaras hatov is both appropriate and beneficial in other situations as well. For instance, Mrs. Batsheva Perlstein (name changed) was a regular customer at a dry cleaning establishment located just outside the Jewish community of Cleveland Heights, Ohio. Once, when Mrs. Perlstein came to pick up quite a number of garments before Pesach, she realized that she did not have sufficient funds in her bank account to cover the payment. "I'm sorry, Mike," she told the proprietor, "but I don't have the full amount right now. You'll have to hold onto some of the clothing until I do."

"No, it's all right; you can take it all," Mike replied graciously. Mrs. Perlstein later repaid his kindness with a piece of advice to help boost his business: She suggested that he place an advertisement in a local Jewish publication. Mike accepted her suggestion, and before long found himself serving a large Jewish clientele. To this day, when Mrs. Perlstein brings him her clothes, he returns the garment with the words "0 dollars — good deed" written on the receipt. He has also come to donate generously to various causes in the Jewish community.

True *hakaras hatov* emanates from a desire to be kind and give to others. Rav Chaim Friedlander *zt"l* (*Sifsei Chaim, Middos V'Avodas Hashem* I, p. 323) refers to the trait of *hakaras hatov* as the *shoresh hachessed* — the root of all kindness. In *Tehillim* (63:4), David HaMelech states, "For Your kindness is better than life; my lips shall praise You." *Malbim* explains that the purpose of life itself, and of all the good that Hashem gives us, is for us to praise Him and give thanks for His kindness. Thus, Hashem's kindness is "better than life" because it enables us to achieve the purpose of life: to sing His praises.

The blessings we possess are worth far more than all the treasures ever amassed by all the most affluent people in the world. Let us learn to appreciate the gifts we receive from others and from Hashem, and we will certainly enrich our own lives and the lives of all those around us.

Takeaway

Hakaras hatov toward Hashem causes us to sing His praises, and expressing gratitude to the people around us causes others to praise Him as well.

Making It Practical

- On a regular basis, write a note to a spouse, parent, relative, or teacher to express your appreciation and gratitude for all that they have done for you.

In a Manner of Speaking

The *bachurim* of Yeshivas Toras Chaim of Denver were frightened. For weeks, a local gang had been harassing them, shouting threats and calling them names, and hateful graffiti had been scrawled on the yeshivah building on many occasions. After the situation had persisted for a while, the *hanhalah* decided that it was time to call in the police.

A police officer arrived at the yeshivah and asked to hear a detailed account from the *bachurim* of their experiences. "Depending on what the gang members have been saying, their actions might be classified as a hate crime," he explained. "That is a much more severe crime than a simple conflict between teenagers." But when the policeman questioned the *bachurim*, he was surprised to find that one *bachur* after another could not bring himself to repeat the profanities that the gang had hurled at them. Each *bachur* simply replaced every expletive with a "beep." The policeman threw up his hands in exasperation. "How am I supposed to write a police report like this?" he exclaimed. "I can't report to the judge that those boys called you 'beep, beep, beep Jews'!" Then his tone softened. "But the truth is that that's why we like you boys so much," he admitted. "Because of your refined speech, you seem much more human than other teenagers on the street."

The *Chovos Halevavos* states that the mouth is the "quill" of the heart; it gives expression to the thoughts and feelings buried within a person's heart, exposing them for the world to see. Through our speech, we reveal the *tzelem Elokim*, the Divine spark hidden within each of us. When a religious Jew speaks with refinement, with respect for others, or in a way that demonstrates his elevated moral standards, he reveals the workings of his heart.

Our power of speech contributes to kiddush Hashem in another way, as well. *Ohr Gedalyahu* (*Parashas Beshalach*) teaches that the purpose of the power of speech is to reveal not only what lies within *us*, but also what is hidden within the world around us. "The purpose of man's ability to speak," he states, "is solely so that he can give testimony about the world and reveal the Divinity that lies within creation, through which Hashem's honor will be revealed. As the *navi* states (*Yeshayahu* 43:21), '*Am zo yatzarti li tehilasi yesapeiru* — This nation that I have created for Myself shall relate My praise.' This means that the very purpose of the Jewish people is to reveal Hashem's praises in all of creation."[5]

Takeaway

We create a kiddush Hashem not only through our actions, but also through our words. The way we speak and the words that we say have the ability to reveal what is in our hearts. This is the true manifestation of the tzelem Elokim within us, which makes our speech a powerful tool for revealing Hashem's existence.

Making It Practical

- Make sure to speak in a refined way that expresses the sanctity of our lifestyle.
- Always ask yourself if you are speaking in a manner that is befitting for royalty.

———⟫◈⟪———

---

5. In *Sefer Tehillim*, David HaMelech speaks in many places about the importance of giving public praise to Hashem. For instance, he states (*Tehillim* 26:7-12), "To proclaim thanksgiving in a loud voice and to recount all Your wondrous deeds... in assemblies I will bless Hashem." *Malbim* explains that the primary way to give thanks to Hashem is to talk to other people about His wonders, which will cause them to recognize His greatness. Several *perakim* later (Ch. 34:2-4), David HaMelech goes on to say, "I will bless Hashem at all times; always shall His praise be in my mouth... Declare the greatness of Hashem with me, and let us exalt His Name together." Some sources cite this last *pasuk* as the source of the requirement to recite *birchas hagomel* upon being saved from certain dangerous situations. That *berachah*, in essence, asks the congregation to join in praising Hashem.

The Right Words

There are countless ways to use our power of speech to be *mekadesh Shem Shamayim*. Speech provides us with the power to reveal the G-dliness within ourselves, within others around us, and within the world. When we speak in a refined manner and show truthfulness, good character, and *kedushah*, we give expression to the *tzelem Elokim* within ourselves.

We can also use our speech to show our recognition that others possess the same spark of Divinity. When we relate to other people with respect, it often leads them to become aware of their own G-dliness.[6] This, in fact, was the catalyst for a marked metamorphosis in the behavior of Baruch Schwartz (name changed), a young man who had earned a reputation in his school as a troublemaker. One day, Baruch was sent to the principal's office for the umpteenth time, where he sat through the principal's usual lecture about the importance of behaving properly, having values and goals in life, and so forth. The next day, Baruch underwent a miraculous change. Suddenly, he became far more cooperative and well mannered, and before long he had become a model student. The entire faculty was curious to know what the principal had said that had affected him so deeply, but the principal admitted that he had no idea what had caused the change.

Finally, the teachers decided to ask Baruch himself what had brought about his transformation. "I wasn't really paying attention to a word the principal said that day," the boy confessed. "But in the middle of our conversation, his intercom buzzed,

---

6. In *Pirkei Avos* (1:12) Hillel states, "Be among the disciples of Aharon, loving peace and pursuing peace, loving people and bringing them close to Torah." *Avos d'Rabbi Nosson* explains that whenever Aharon encountered a wicked person, he would greet the person. The next time the person was about to sin, he would remember the greeting he had received from Aharon and be too ashamed to commit a sin. Thus, Aharon's practice of greeting everyone he met served to "bring them close to the Torah."

and the secretary told him he had a phone call. 'I can't talk now; I'm in a meeting with someone very important,' the principal told her. When I left his office, those words kept echoing in my mind. The principal thought I was very important! It made me feel so wonderful that I decided to buckle down."

The human capacity for speech can also be used to reveal Hashem's Presence in the world around us. When we praise Hashem for His kindnesses, when we recite *berachos* on the food we eat,[7] and when we speak about the beauty of His creation, we reveal the depths behind the material world; we strip away the mask of nature to expose the Divine Providence that lies beneath it. We can create this type of kiddush Hashem with our speech in many more ways as well: by teaching others about *emunah*, by praising those who serve Hashem,[8] and even by learning His Torah. Moreover, the *Ramban* teaches us (in *Parashas Bo*) that the purpose of having *shuls* where we gather to *daven*, and of lifting our voices in prayer, is to make a public declaration that we are Hashem's creations and servants, which also creates a kiddush Hashem.

Our job is to strengthen the spiritual dimension of our existence, revealing the hidden spark of holiness that lies within every human being and within the world as a whole. By doing this, we will reveal Hashem's ultimate Kingship over the world.

Takeaway

With our speech, we have the ability to bring out the full potential in others by helping them feel important. We can also use the power of speech to raise awareness of the Divine Providence that governs the world around us.

---

7. Rav Yerucham Levovitz (*Daas Chachmah U'Mussar*, Vol. 2, *maamar* 86).
8. Rabbeinu Yonah (*Shaarei Teshuvah, shaar* 3 par. 148).

- Use your words to give great respect to other people. When you succeed in making another person feel important, ask yourself what words you used to have that impact, and keep that in mind for the future.
- Set aside time with your family to discuss Hashem's *hashgachah* and the blessings He bestows upon you. Enthusiastically share your observations with your family and friends.

Beyond the Norm

In the year 2014, the city of Detroit was hit with major floods. In many homes, basements were ruined and furniture destroyed. With many uninsured families staggering beneath the burden of the sudden financial loss, not to mention the scale of the cleanup job, a group of young men came together to launch the Detroit Chessed Project. The group managed to obtain new furniture and mattresses to replace those that had been lost by many families, and to recruit volunteers to clean out the flooded basements. Since that time, the project has gone on to provide assistance, financial and otherwise, to people contending with countless needs.

On *Chol Hamoed Succos*, the group met for a small but festive *simchas beis hashoevah*. The delectable food, excellent music, and spirited singing created an atmosphere of tangible *simchas hachag*.

A participant suggested that the members of the group each share a brief account of what each committee had accomplished.

The revelations were astounding, even to the participants them-selves. One member of the project related that his committee had recruited sponsors for a huge quantity of clothing donations over the course of the year. Another had arranged with a large retail chain store to donate a truckload of bedding, lamps, and accesso-ries each month. A professional caterer then stunned the group by revealing the number of food packages he distributed each week. Suddenly, the rest of the attendees began volunteering to sponsor the costs of the food packages over the upcoming months, one after another. In a completely spontaneous development, thou-sands of dollars were pledged in the span of a few minutes. Once the impromptu fund-raising session had ended, the singing began again and the festivities continued until late in the night.

At the conclusion of the event, as the musicians began pack-ing up their equipment, the host approached the non-Jewish sax-ophone player, who lived an hour's drive away, to thank him for his time and effort. "I appreciate you agreeing to stay so late," he said. "How much do we owe you for tonight?"

Visibly moved, the musician said, "Please, take the money and put it toward your wonderful program. I have never seen a display of such generosity and joyful giving in my life. You are the most incredible group of people I have ever seen."

As Jews, we are charged with behaving in a way that will earn us the world's admiration and lead others to recognize the great-ness of Hashem. In order to accomplish this, we must go beyond ordinary human behavior. We must learn to display positive character traits that are so incredible that they are clearly rec-ognized as being G-dly in nature. It must be clear to the world that our positive attributes are not the result of our being nice people, but rather are due to our service of Hashem. As Rav Shimon Schwab often commented, "Where *mentschlichkeit* ends its achievements — at that place, Yiddishkeit begins."[9]

9. The *Yerushalmi* (*Bava Metzia* 8a) relates that when Rabbi Shimon ben Shetach returned a precious diamond to its non-Jewish owner, the non-Jew exclaimed in awe, "Blessed is the G-d of Shimon ben Shetach!" Rather than praising Rabbi Shimon ben Shetach himself, the non-Jew expressed respect for Hashem. This

The story has been told of a restaurant employee in New York City who began distributing leftover food from the restaurant to a group of homeless people who frequented the streets nearby. Although most of the people were grateful for his kindness, one homeless woman refused to touch any of the food he offered. After several days, his curiosity overcame him, and he asked her why she would not accept his gifts. "I would rather starve to death than accept food from a Jew!" she replied.

Surprised, the man exclaimed, "But I'm not Jewish! Why would you think I am?"

"Only Jews are capable of this type of generosity," she insisted.

When the man shared this story with his mother, he was shocked by her reply. "You aren't going to believe this, but the truth is that you *are* Jewish," she admitted. "Your father is a non-Jew, but I am a Jew, and that makes you a Jew as well." This incredible revelation eventually led the man to Eretz Yisrael and a life of full Jewish observance.

The homeless woman's perception in this story highlights the very goal that we must all strive to attain. As Jews, we must be not just *gomlei chassadim*, but practitioners of *chessed* on such a level that the rest of the world will see it as unmistakably Jewish. We must rise beyond the norm and show the rest of the world that we are connected to the Master of the Universe — and by doing so, we will surely bring great honor to His Name.

Takeaway

We must not be satisfied with living up to the standards of etiquette of the society around us. As Jews, we have a higher responsibility; we must represent Hashem's attributes on a much higher level. Our character traits must mark us as servants of G-d Himself.

is the level of *tzidkus* to which we must aspire: a level at which observers praise Hashem for our actions, recognizing that our deeds transcend human nature to such an extent that they must mark us as *avdei Hashem*.

Humility and Arrogance

Some people are blessed with extraordinary charisma or persuasive powers, which they use to change the lives of others. But there are other people who have a profound effect on others even without the same magnetic personalities. My grandfather, Rabbi Avrohom Abba Freedman, was one such person. He was not a powerful speaker, and he did not have any special charisma, yet he somehow managed to be *mekarev* hundreds of people. People were never able to turn him down, whether he was convincing parents to send their children to a Jewish day school in the early years of Detroit's Jewish community, or he was bringing busloads of Russian Jewish immigrants on an inspirational trip to New York. Somehow, he managed to exert a magnetic pull, ostensibly without possessing any magnetic qualities. What was the secret of his success?

I believe that the answer lies in a passage in the *Orchos Tzaddikim* (*shaar* 2). The *Orchos Tzaddikim* states that a person who is humble and unassuming will wield a powerful influence over others. People will naturally accept whatever such a person does or asks, and he will inspire others to emulate him. Ultimately, he will be able to bring greater honor to Hashem.

Rabbi Freedman lived solely for the sake of serving Hashem. He was not motivated in the slightest by pride or self-interest. At the *bar mitzvah* of one of his grandsons, he dozed off during a speech. He woke up when the speaker mentioned his name, but as soon as he realized that the speaker was praising him, he fell asleep again; compliments from others meant nothing to him. His son, who was the executive director of Bais Yehuda in Detroit, once posted an article on the school's bulletin board that described Rabbi Freedman's pivotal role in the establishment of Detroit as a *makom Torah*. Before long, the article disappeared, and every time he replaced it with a new copy, it was removed again. Finally, the principal told the younger Freedman, "You may as well give up; you may be stubborn, but your father is much more stubborn. He is the one who keeps taking down the article, and he even wants to call the editor to object to it as a distortion of the truth." Because Rabbi Freedman had no ulterior motives at all, everyone could sense that his messages were pure, unadulterated truth.

Rabbi Avrohom Abba Freedman once convinced a young man to learn in yeshivah rather than attending college, much to the dismay of the young man's father. The furious father said, "I have a younger son who is much smarter than the older one, and I certainly won't send him to your yeshivah! You may have gotten the older one, but at least *I* will get the younger one!" The younger son, however, begged and pestered his father until the father relented and sent him to the yeshivah, as well. The next time the father encountered Rabbi Freedman, he was seething with anger. "I see you got both of them," he snapped.

"No," Rabbi Freedman replied calmly. "They are neither mine nor yours. They belong to the *Ribbono shel Olam*."

Just as humility is one of the greatest factors that contribute to kiddush Hashem, the opposite of humility—arrogance—can be one of the greatest causes of chillul Hashem. The *Orchos Tzaddikim* condemns the trait of *gaavah* (arrogance) in the strongest terms: "An arrogant person desecrates the Name of Hashem and causes people to sin. He is like a carcass that has been cast in the marketplace, that causes every passerby to cover his nose until he has passed it. Similarly, the prideful person disgraces the Torah and those who study it and drives people away from the Torah, for they say, 'What benefit is there in the Torah if those who study it are bad?' As a result, they leave the Torah."

Arrogance may perturb not only nonreligious Jews, but *frum* Jews as well. When a person who represents the Torah demonstrates haughtiness or conceit, it may lead even other *frum* Jews to lose some of their appreciation for the value of the Torah. It should be clear that cultivating the trait of humility is a vital part of our mission to bring honor to the Master of the Universe.

Takeaway

Humility is another trait that has tremendous potential to create kiddush Hashem. When a person is humble and it is clear that he has no ulterior motives or personal agendas, others will naturally trust him. The magnetic pull exerted by humility is the pull of the truth.

MAKING IT PRACTICAL

- When you are about to perform a *chessed* or to teach students, take a few minutes to remove any personal agenda or self-centered motivation from your mind. Instead, bear in mind that your actions be completely *l'Shem Shamayim.*

Discussion Points:

❖ How does one create a kiddush Hashem through positive *middos* like empathy and kindness?

❖ How can we create a kiddush Hashem by following a certain standard of behavior, when many other societies have their own concepts of etiquette? What is special about the Jewish approach to interpersonal dealings?

❖ How can we impact the honor of Hashem through the way we speak?

CHAPTER 2

A HEALTHY BALANCE

Yankel, a Jewish salesman, enters a store seeking to sell some jewelry to the owner, Bob. Bob is impressed by the merchandise, and a discussion ensues about Yankel's company. The storeowner asks to see the company's website so that he can view other products that they sell. Yankel apologizes and explains that his company does not use the Internet. "We stay away from the Internet, in order to avoid being exposed to the many inappropriate sites and to all of its pitfalls. It may be feasible to use strong Internet filters, but we want to avoid any issues completely."

Bob is intrigued by the company's high moral standards, but he seems to be confused or troubled by something. After some coaxing from Yankel, he reveals that he has had some interactions with the company in the past, as well as with several others in the Jewish companies, and he felt that they were not always as scrupulous in their business practices as they were about avoiding inappropriate sights. "Isn't that a kind of contradiction?" he asks pointedly.

A Package Deal

Rav Yosef Zimbal, a *rav* in West Gate in Lakewood, once shared a story of an interaction he had with Rav Shmuel Kamenetsky at a wedding. Before the *chuppah*, Rabbi Zimbal had a lengthy conversation with the *rosh yeshivah*, yet after the *chuppah* was over, when Rav Shmuel passed him again, he greeted Rabbi Zimbal effusively as if he were seeing him for the first time. Rabbi Zimbal respectfully pointed out that they had already spoken.

"I know that, of course," Rav Shmuel replied, "but there are many more people here now who did not see us talking earlier. I wouldn't have wanted all of them to think that I simply walked by without greeting you."

There is much we can learn from the example of Rav Shmuel

Kamenetsky, one of the greatest Torah luminaries of our time, who excels in striking the balance between the mitzvos of *bein adam laMakom* and *bein adam lachaveiro.*

It can be a great challenge to achieve the proper balance between these two areas of the Torah. Although each category of mitzvos is important, there is a prevalent tendency for people to emphasize one at the expense of the other. In some circles, the proper observance of *mitzvos bein adam laMakom* is heavily stressed, but this results in a lack of attentiveness to the laws of interpersonal conduct. In other circles, the opposite is true: Great emphasis is placed on *mitzvos bein adam lachaveiro*, but as a result, people tend to fall short in their practice of other mitzvos. Keeping the proper focus on *both* aspects of the Torah requires a constant struggle.[1]

How do we achieve this balance? How does a person make

---

1. At the beginning of *Sefer Yeshayah* (1:27), the *Malbim* has a fascinating insight: He notes that when the *navi* addressed *Shevet Yehudah*, most of whom lived outside of Yerushalayim, his words of rebuke focused on their neglect of *mitzvos bein adam laMakom*, because that was the area in which they generally fell short. When Yeshayah turned his attention to the people of Yerushalayim, though, he stressed their failings in the realm of *bein adam lachaveiro*, since the residents of Yerushalayim generally kept the *mitzvos bein adam laMakom*, and their shortcomings lay in their conduct toward other people. The *Malbim* adds that this is the meaning of the *pasuk*, "*Tzion b'mishpat tipadeh v'shaveha b'tzedakah* — Tzion will be redeemed through justice, and those who return to it through righteousness": The *navi* emphasizes that the inhabitants of Yerushalayim will merit the redemption when they improve their interpersonal conduct, represented by "justice," while "those who return to it" — i.e., the Jews living outside Yerushalayim — will be redeemed when they demonstrate "righteousness" in their relationship with Hashem. Only when both aspects of Torah observance are perfected will the Jewish people be worthy of redemption.

The Torah tells us that the *Aseres Hadibros* were inscribed on two *Luchos*, and *Rashi* states that the two *Luchos* were identical. Rav Shamshon Raphael Hirsch (*Collected Writings*, Vol. 1, pp. 279-281) notes that *Chazal* also teach us that the writing on the *Luchos* could be read from either side. The symbolism of this, he explains, is that a Jew must bear the "writing of G-d," so to speak, in such a way that it can be "read" from every side. It is not sufficient for a Jewish person to act as a servant of Hashem, reflecting His Divine qualities and His commandments, only in some ways, while other aspects of his behavior do not bear the mark of Divinity. Rather, the effects of *Kabbalas HaTorah* must completely permeate a Jew's personality, defining him in every way. His relationships with both Hashem and his fellow man must be shaped by the Torah; every part of his life must be geared to follow the Divine Will with the same degree of care and dedication.

sure that he will devote the proper emphasis to *both* categories of Torah commandments?

If we keep in mind that our overriding goal is to create a kiddush Hashem, we will remember that both aspects of the Torah are of equal importance. Neither aspect can be emphasized without the other, because if we lose either dimension of the Torah, we will be left with nothing at all. If we set our sights on kiddush Hashem, then we will recognize that both forms of *avodah* are indispensable for us to achieve that goal.

The Gemara states (*Yoma* 86a) that if a *talmid chacham* does not treat others properly, he creates a great chillul Hashem. The Gemara also implies that a person who treats others admirably but does not learn Torah is also incapable of creating a kiddush Hashem. A person may be respected for his character and kindness, but if he is not known for his Torah knowledge, then that respect will bring honor only to him as an individual, not to the Torah or Hashem. In order to create a kiddush Hashem through his actions toward others, a person must also be a Torah scholar and *eved* Hashem. As the *Navi* states, Hashem declares, "*Avdi atah, Yisrael asher becha espaar* — You are **My servant**, Yisrael in whom I take pride." In order for Hashem to "take pride" in us, we must truly be His "servants."

The only way to accomplish our ultimate goal — being *mekadesh Shem Shamayim* — is to pursue both aspects of the Torah with equal zeal, by recognizing that the Torah is a single, all-inclusive package deal.

Takeaway

When a person displays both character refinement and kedushah, it becomes apparent that his character traits are a reflection of his service to G-d. Keeping our focus on kiddush Hashem is the way to make sure that we will give equal importance to both aspects of the service of Hashem.

- Put effort into demonstrating *derech eretz* and relating to other people positively by greeting others in a friendly way. While you are doing this, remind yourself that your purpose is to bring honor to Hashem as His servant, not to increase their respect for you as an individual.
- Say the words *"hineni muchan l'kadeish Shem Shamayim"* before interacting with others. This will help you maintain your *kedushah*, as well as the balance between the two components of Yiddishkeit.

—————>◆<—————

A Potent Combination

Rabbi Moshe Tuvia Lieff boarded an El Al flight and found himself seated in an aisle seat next to two middle-aged women, one Israeli and the other American. The women's facial expressions made it obvious that they were not pleased to be seated next to a religious rabbi. Rabbi Lieff greeted them politely and made small talk for a few minutes in both Hebrew and English. Then he said, "Ladies, I am sitting in the 'excuse me' seat." They both looked at him quizzically. "That means," he explained, "that it is a seat that is a privilege, but it also comes with great responsibility. If you need to get up, just ask me to excuse you, and I will be happy to let you through as many times as you need. Please feel free even to wake me up if you need to get up."

The flight passed uneventfully. After disembarking, Rabbi Lieff was waiting in the parking lot for his rental car when a loud shriek echoed from behind him. He turned around just in time to see a car come to an abrupt halt beside him. Inside the car was his Israeli seatmate, along with a tall paratrooper who was clearly her son. *"Zeh harav! Zeh harav!"* she was shouting excitedly in Hebrew. "This is the rabbi I told you about! If more people acted like him, we would have no problems!"

Kedushah and good *middos* are the two ingredients for the creation of a kiddush Hashem. Together, these two make a potent combination that can bring incredible honor to the Master of the Universe. Neither one, however, can be effective without the other. A person who is steeped in holiness and religious dedication must develop his character as well, or he will not succeed in fostering a kiddush Hashem.

We have all heard the adage of *derech eretz kadmah l'Torah*; however, this is a concept that requires explanation. How is it possible for *anything* to take precedence over Torah? Rav Mattisyahu Salomon explains that the entire purpose of Torah study is to bring about *kiddush Shem Shamayim*. A person who lacks *derech eretz* cannot create a kiddush Hashem. His Torah study would be in vain if its ultimate purpose is not realized.[2] Therefore, Torah without proper *middos* cannot create a kiddush Hashem.

---

2. Prior to receiving the Torah, Hashem instructed the Jewish people, "You shall be My treasure from among all the nations, for the entire land is Mine. You shall be for Me a kingdom of Kohanim and a holy nation for Me." The *Keren Orah* (*Taanis* 20a) explains why this is an introduction to the Giving of the Torah: "The main purpose of the Giving of the Torah was not merely to benefit Bnei Yisrael, but rather to perfect all of Hashem's creations, and to make the deeds of all people be pleasing to Him.... Hashem's main desire was that through the study of the Torah, all people would be perfected, and they would all call out in the Name of Hashem." The *Keren Orah* goes on to explain that a person who learns Torah must be a positive influence on others; if he sets a poor example for others, then his own Torah study will not achieve its ultimate purpose. In other words, Bnei Yisrael were given the Torah in order to bring about kiddush Hashem.

In the words of *Mesillas Yesharim* (Ch. 11), "It is honorable for the Torah when a person who engages in copious Torah study also excels in uprightness and in proper character traits. If these things are lacking in a person who learns much Torah, it causes disgrace to the learning itself, and that would be, Heaven forbid, a desecration of the Name of Hashem, **Who gave us His holy Torah and commanded us to study it in order to achieve perfection.**" See *Netziv* (*Ha'amek Davar*), in his introduction to *Sefer Bereishis,* where he explains that Hashem desires *talmidei chachamim* only if they are *yesharim*. See also *Ramban* ad loc., 6:18.

Rav Shimon Schwab once spoke out strongly against the "audacity" and "shame" of Jews who observe mitzvos such as Shabbos and *kashrus* meticulously, yet who engage in dishonest business dealings. "A Jew cannot choose to follow one set of halachos and disregard another," he declared, condemning the "ugly traits" of "gross materialism, blatant selfishness, insatiable love of wealth and brazen disregard for common decency" even when they are accompanied by "excessive charity and benevolence." Rav Schwab ended his speech with the rousing call, "Let us proclaim, loud and clear, that we shall have no part of such sickly 'Yiddishkeit.' Our aim is to strive for kiddush Hashem, and in order to reach this goal we shall band together and march together, we and our children, with clean hands and pure hearts, toward the dawn of *geulah*, speedily in our days."

Takeaway

If a person's Torah learning and mitzvah observance are not accompanied by proper middos, his Torah will lack the power to be mekadesh Shem Shamayim. In fact, the Torah he learns may become a chillul Hashem rather than a kiddush Hashem. Torah and middos are a "package deal"; one cannot exist without the other.

Making It Practical

- In your learning or Torah classes, make sure to include some focus on growth in *derech eretz* and *mitzvos bein adam lachaveiro.*
- Devote some time to studying the halachos of monetary matters.

Keeping Consistent

Refoel Levin (name changed) was in his dormitory room on the campus of Hebrew University when the sounds of a heated argument from the corridor outside reached his ears. It did not take him long to identify the two parties to the dispute: At the time, in 1971, there were only three Arab students in the university, and they were arguing heatedly with a group of Israelis over who possesses the true rights to the Land of Israel. One of the Israeli students insisted that the Land belongs to the Jews, as descendants of Avraham Avinu; an Arab countered that Yishmael, their progenitor, was also Avraham's son. Another Jewish student cited the Holocaust and the unwillingness of many other countries to accept Jewish refugees; the Arabs responded that thousands of their own brethren were living in refugee camps with nowhere to go. A third Israeli student argued that by international law, if an aggressor loses a war, the winning country may keep the conquered territory. "Then we can start another war and take the land back!" one of the Arabs shouted.

The young man listening from his dormitory room was surprised when the group suddenly came to his door. "You answer us, Refoel!" one of the Arab students insisted. "Tell us who has the rights to this land!"

Refoel was another unique figure on campus. As a religious student in the school, he knew that his peers watched him curiously every day as he ate kosher, wore *tzitzis*, *davened*, and learned Torah. He had even earned the respect of the Arab students by making sure to greet them regularly, even though they were generally shunned by the other Israelis. Now, it seemed, his standing in the college had made him responsible to voice his own perspective on a longstanding feud.

With a good deal of trepidation, Refoel opened a *Chumash* to the first *pasuk* in *Bereishis* and read aloud from *Rashi's* commentary, "If the nations of the world tell Bnei Yisrael, 'You are robbers, for you have stolen the land of the seven nations,' they can say to them, 'The entire earth belongs to Hashem; He created it and He gave it to whomever He saw fit. He chose to give it to them, and He chose to take it from them and to give it to us.'"

The Arab gazed at Refoel intently. "Is this a holy book?" he asked.

"Yes," the young man replied.

"Is it true? Is everything in it true, from beginning to end?"

"Yes," Refoel confirmed again.

"Does it say to wear *tefillin*? Do you wear *tefillin*? What about *tzitzis*? What about kosher food? What about Shabbos?" The Arab rattled off a list of mitzvos, and when he was satisfied that Refoel observed the mitzvos of the Torah, he announced, "Since you fulfill all of the commandments in this book, I can accept this answer from you, because you are consistent. But I cannot accept this answer from the other Israelis. They do not observe the laws in this book, and that means that they do not believe in this truth. Why should they be entitled to the Land?"

This dialogue points to the importance of maintaining absolute consistency in our behavior. Our mission of kiddush Hashem places us in a position in which we represent the Torah to the rest of the world. In that capacity, it is crucial for us to make sure that all of our actions are in line with our goals. People in positions of leadership are always under scrutiny, and if the slightest inconsistency is detected in their behavior, others may reject everything they stand for.

Thus, it is not sufficient to be exacting only in the observance of some of the Torah's mitzvos. In order to be consistent in our observance, we must dedicate ourselves to stringency in all of its commandments — including the *mitzvos bein adam lachaveiro*. The *sefer Yachel Yisrael* (3:1) warns that a person who deals with others in a way that is not commensurate with his spiritual standing is guilty of a chillul Hashem, and that the Midrash (*Pesikta d'Rav Kahana* Ch. 22) accuses such a person of violating the third of the *Aseres Hadibros*, "You shall not take the Name of Hashem your G-d in vain." He may pride himself on representing the Name of Hashem by learning the Torah and observing Hashem's commandments, but his failure to deal with other people in a fitting manner makes all of that "in vain."[3]

When we seek to influence others — as parents, as educators, or simply as observant Jews trying to create a kiddush Hashem — we would do well to remember a powerful statement that was once uttered: "What you *do* speaks so loudly that what you say I cannot hear." If our actions, or even some of our actions, are not consistent with our words and values, then we cannot hope to have a positive influence on others. But if we embody that crucial trait of consistency, then we can indeed have a major impact on the rest of the world.

Takeaway

One of the prerequisites for influencing others is being consistent in one's own actions. To borrow a common expression, it isn't enough for us to "talk the talk"; we must also "walk the walk."

Making It Practical

- When you take on a kabbalah or a stringency in halachah, resolve to adopt a stringency in the halachos of monetary matters as well. This way, you will grow in both areas at the same time.

---

3. In this vein, the Kotzker Rebbe makes a fascinating comment on David HaMelech's statement, "I am a worm and not a man." David was pursued and oppressed by numerous foes, including Shaul HaMelech, Doeg and Achitofel, and Avshalom, his own rebellious son. Many of his enemies were men of tremendous spiritual stature, some of the greatest *talmidei chachamim* and leaders of the *Sanhedrin* of his generation. The Kotzker Rebbe explains that this *pasuk* is a powerful condemnation of those enemies. "You are so exacting in your observance of *mitzvos bein adam laMakom*," David declared, "that if you saw a worm in a plate of food, you would never allow yourselves to eat the food, lest you inadvertently ingest the worm. Yet when it comes to me, you are ready to devour me alive! If only you would be as stringent in the way you deal with me as you are careful to avoid consuming a worm."

Chessed in Yeshivos

Yehuda Bernstein (name changed), a *yungerman* from Lakewood, was worried. His three-year-old son, Sholom, had been feeling ill, and Yehuda feared that his symptoms might indicate a serious condition. On a Friday afternoon, he found himself in the office of a well-known pediatrician. The doctor examined the results of Sholom's blood tests and grimly ordered the father and son to report to the hospital. As Shabbos began that evening, Yehuda stood at his son's bedside in the pediatric emergency room in a Philadelphia hospital, his head spinning as he was bombarded with grim diagnoses and unfamiliar medical terms. In a matter of minutes, his entire life had been turned upside down: His child had been diagnosed with cancer.

The Bernstein family's ordeal continued over the course of an entire year. Sholom underwent grueling treatments and even a bone marrow transplant. One of Yehuda's greatest daily challenges was coaxing Sholom to take his medication every morning . Naturally, the child resisted the nurses' efforts to give him medicine and resented the hospital, which he viewed as a place of suffering. One Friday, when the situation was particularly difficult, help arrived in the most unexpected way.

The child was in the midst of refusing to take his medication when the door to the hospital room suddenly opened , and a group of *bachurim* from the Yeshiva of Philadelphia entered the room. Within seconds, the sounds of guitar music and song filled the air, as the *bachurim* erupted into a spirited dance, drawing Sholom into their circle to dance to a series of lively tunes. A broad smile spread across the boy's face, and the *bachurim* sat down to play with him, encourage him, and cheer him on as he swallowed his medication with pride. The nurses watched in astonishment, wondering how these teenagers could develop such a rapport with the child, and how they had known to arrive exactly when they were needed.

"Most teenagers are concerned only with themselves and

have a hard time empathizing with others," a nurse remarked to Yehuda. "It is remarkable that these boys are able to connect with a three-year-old child and show him such care and compassion . Mr. Bernstein. You are lucky to be a part of the Jewish family!"

Recently, there was a major conference of *mesivta rebbeim* who met to discuss how to promote *derech eretz*, positive *middos*, and concern for the laws of *bein adam lachaveiro* among yeshivah students. If other *bachurim* followed the example of that group from Philadelphia, the impact could be enormous. The administrations of our yeshivos can certainly find opportunities in their respective cities for *bachurim* to perform *chessed*; of course, making certain not to allow it to detract from the boys' learning or their *kedushah*. This can involve many types of activities: making *minyanim* at *shivah* homes, visiting the elderly in nursing homes, shoveling snow for the elderly or infirm, or learning with children in need of assistance. Aside from what the recipients will gain, the *bachurim* themselves will also benefit from the experience by absorbing the value of helping others and developing a sense of communal responsibility.

Rav Shmuel Yeshaya Keller, the *menahel* of the Yeshiva of Telz in Chicago, shared an anecdote that he had heard from his grandfather, Rav Lazer Levine, who was an eyewitness to the incident: The Chofetz Chaim once asked a *bachur* for a favor, but the *bachur* refused, claiming that he did not wish to take away time from his learning. The Chofetz Chaim later repeated his request, but the *bachur* turned him down again. A few days later, the *bachur* approached the Chofetz Chaim with a question on a *Tosafos*. "What is your *Tosafos* worth if you can't do a *chessed*?" the Chofetz Chaim rebuked him.

Rav Reuven Feinstein once received an effusive letter from a non-Jew, who praised the *bachurim* of his yeshivah for their respect and courtesy. This letter is a testament to the power of a yeshivah *bachur* to create kiddush Hashem. With the proper blend of *kedushah* and *derech eretz*, the yeshivah students who are our pride and joy can have an outstanding impact on others.

Rabbi Feinstein,

I was so impressed with the young bachurim of the Staten Island Yeshiva of which you are the head, that I must write this email to you.

In February of last year, I drove a frum friend of mine, Rabbi Eli Beane, from Lakewood, NJ to upper Staten Island for therapy on his knee.

Rabbi Beane needed to daven the afternoon prayers and determined that your yeshivah was a convenient place to do so. That February day was cold and snowy. I helped Eli up the icy steps to the yeshivah and waited in the hallway while he prayed. I watched the students as they traversed the halls. I cannot help but be in awe of the dress code, the demeanor and the courtesy, shown to me a stranger—a non-Jew.

I live in a non-Jewish world—a world in which people are low in respect for teachers, parents and themselves. The lexicon, the revealing clothing, and the shameful "sewer" mouths are to me an abhorrence to the Almighty. I am not a predictor of the future but I say that without a belief in an Almighty (Hashem—Eli's word) and a judgment we all must face, the non-Jews that I live among are doomed—and they don't know it or couldn't care less. What a terrible, short-sighted, selfish view!

Rabbi Beane remarked to me once that without a high degree of morality the world sinks into cannibalism and savagery. The world is there.

The only hope I see, if any, is the islands of bachurim studying Torah and Talmud, living its commandments and influencing others.

May the Almighty bless you, the yeshivah, the rabbis and your students. May your yeshivah be an example of what humanity should be!!

Shalom,
Gerry Mullen

PS: Rabbi Feinstein, may I suggest you do more Talmud Torah!!

Yeshivah bachurim are the visible embodiment of Torah learning. When they give some of their time for chessed, their sensitivity to others becomes sharpened and developed, and the impressions they create can last for a lifetime.

Making It Practical

- Find opportunities for your children to volunteer for a cause that has value to the community.

- Fridays and Motzaei Shabbos are times that might be suitable to set up *chessed* opportunities for teenagers who are busy with their studies during the week. It goes without saying that *chessed* performed at home is also *chessed* of the highest degree. For those teenagers whose input is not necessary on erev Shabbos then a weekly *chessed* program may broaden the students' sense of responsibility and empathy for others.

- Encourage yeshivah *bachurim* to volunteer some of their spare time to learn with younger or less privileged students.

Within and Without

The Gemara states (*Shabbos* 114a) that a *talmid chacham* who wears a stained garment is liable to the death penalty. While this ruling may sound extreme, *Rashi* explains that a person who has a reputation for Torah wisdom must maintain a distinguished appearance at all times. Otherwise, people may come to disrespect him and, by extension, lose respect for Hashem.

Rav Dov Katz, the author of *Tenuas Hamussar*, writes at length about the Beis HaTalmud of Kelm, the yeshivah of the legendary Alter of Kelm, Rav Simcha Zissel. Much of the information he presents is attributed to Rav Elya Lopian, who learned there in his youth. According to Rav Elya, one of the values emphasized in the Beis HaTalmud was the importance of cleanliness and order. The *talmidim* were always particular to present a neat and organized appearance; their clothes were always spotless, their shoes were shined, and they carefully adhered to all the rules of modern etiquette. Rav Simcha Zissel considered this part of their responsibility to promote kiddush Hashem and to increase the general sense of respect for *bnei Torah*.

Once, Rav Simcha Zissel saw a *talmid* from a wealthy family purchasing an inexpensive suit. "You are burying the Torah," he said to the *talmid*, implying that it was an affront to his Torah knowledge for him to cheapen his appearance. At the same time, he was also known to rebuke *talmidim* who he felt devoted too much attention to their external appearances for reasons other than to bring honor to Hashem. The *maskilim* of the day used to live by the motto, "Be a Jew in your home and a man when you go out." Rav Simcha Zissel had his own version of that motto: "Be a Jew *and* a man in your home, and a Jew and a man when you go out." In his view, the ideal image of a Jew was that of the most exalted possible man.

Beis HaTalmud did not hire a paid cleaning staff; instead, maintaining order and cleanliness in the yeshivah was the job of the *talmidim*. Different *talmidim* would be assigned to keep the yeshivah's premises organized, to sweep and scrub the floors, and to draw water from the river. It was considered an honor to be assigned one of these tasks; occasionally, the coveted assignments were sold on Rosh Hashanah, and the competition was intense.

Rav Elya himself faithfully followed the teachings of his *rebbe* until the very end of his life. Even at the age of 83, when he was blind in one eye, he always dressed immaculately. Although he lived in an area plagued by fierce winds and a high dust content in the air, which left layers of dust on most people's clothing, his own garments were always spotless.

The Gemara teaches that the gift of *nevuah* is granted only to a person who possesses wisdom, wealth, and physical strength. Why should wealth and strength have any bearing on whether a person is fit to be a *navi*? *Derashos HaRan* (*derush* 5) explains a *navi* is supposed to influence other Jews, and in order to accomplish that, he must appeal to every type of person within the nation. Some people are more impacted by a person who is wealthy, while others are more easily influenced by one who is blessed with wisdom or with physical strength. Even a tall person is considered to have a certain advantage in influencing others.

People are naturally attracted and influenced when their environs are neat and organized. When our neighborhoods are kept clean and orderly, people will conclude that there is cleanliness and order within our homes as well. When our homes, our lawns, and we ourselves appear well maintained, we will radiate the self-respect and pride that contribute to kiddush Hashem.

In the summer, in particular, we spend a good deal of time in full view of the outside world. As the nation that reflects Hashem's royalty, we must take care to dress and act with dignity in order to preserve His honor. With our large families and camps, this means that we must take care to clean up after any visit to a park, a store, or any other public area.

A cashier at a 7-Eleven convenience store once asked a *bachur*, "Are you part of the religious school across the street?" When the boy replied that he was, the cashier smiled. "I like the boys from that school," he said. "They never leave a mess behind. Whenever they spill a drink, they make sure to clean up after themselves. They are the only boys who do that!"

The Midrash relates (*Vayikra Rabbah* 34:2) that Hillel *Hazakein* would tell his *talmidim* before he visited the bathhouse that he was on his way to perform a mitzvah. When they asked him how bathing could be considered a mitzvah, he would point out that cleaning the statues made in a king's likeness was considered a most honorable job; certainly, cleansing the human body, which is created in the image of Hashem, is a great mitzvah as well.

We are not accustomed to devoting much attention to externals; the emphasis of our lives tends to be on the purity of our *neshamos* and creating a beautiful "home" for our souls in the Next World. As the above sources show us, though, it is important to pay attention to externals in this world as well, both for their effects on others and because of their impact on ourselves.

Takeaway

Focusing on kiddush Hashem gives us a sense of balance, ensuring that we devote the right amount of attention to our spiritual concerns as well as to our physical appearance and needs.

Making It Practical

- Take extra care to ensure that the clothing you and your family wear is clean and presentable.
- Be careful to keep your home and yard orderly and pleasant looking.

Discussion Points:

❖ How do we teach our children to attach equal importance to mitzvos *bein adam lachaveiro* and mitzvos *bein adam laMakom*? How do we avoid focusing on one category of mitzvos at the expense of the other?

❖ How do both categories of mitzvos — both *bein adam lachaveiro* and *bein adam laMakom* — contribute to kiddush Hashem?

❖ Why must we display *kedushah* in order to create a kiddush Hashem? Why isn't it sufficient simply to show positive *middos*?

❖ If a person attains a high level in his learning and *kedushah*, can he be content with that achievement even if his *middos* are lacking? Is this enough to create a kiddush Hashem?

CHAPTER 3

SMALL ACTIONS BIG OPPORTUNITIES

Chaim is rushing through the airport, in a hurry to get home after a long flight. As he passes a stand where a man is selling sunglasses, he suddenly hears the vendor shout "Shalom!" in an unmistakable Israeli accent. Turning around, Chaim sees a smiling nonreligious Israeli who is happy to have attracted someone's attention, and the vendor quickly begins to approach him with a few pairs of sunglasses.

Within seconds, Chaim's mind cycles through all the possible reactions that are available to him. He can ignore the vendor and hurry away to avoid the interaction. Alternatively, he can smile and excuse himself politely, explaining that he is in a rush. But there is a third possibility: He can strike up a conversation with this fellow Jew who has appeared in the most unlikely place, inquiring about his move from Israel to America and showing some interest in his well-being. Perhaps his brief conversation will even have some impact on the stranger.

Dazzling the Judge

It was an exciting day at Camp Chayos Hakodesh, a summer day camp in Denver A trip had been scheduled to the local courthouse, where the campers would have the opportunity to watch an actual criminal trial. When they arrived, a police officer explained the workings of the court, and then they settled down to enjoy the proceedings.

The trial was very exciting for the children. A woman with a veil covering her face was brought into the court by a policeman. She was accused of having robbed a store at gunpoint. The attorneys for the prosecution and the defense made their cases, and each side brought a witness to testify and be cross-examined. After fifteen minutes, it became clear that each of the two witnesses had given a different description of the accused; one claimed that she was dark skinned, while the other maintained that she had a fair complexion. The judge ordered her to remove her veil, and she shook her head to indicate her refusal.

At the judge's request, a police officer approached the woman and pulled the veil off her head. The campers gasped in shock, as the "defendant" turned out to be not a woman at all, but one of their counselors, with his face painted blue and green. "Color war!" the counselor shouted, surprising and delighting the children.

The judge, the attorneys, and the police officers, all of whom were real, had graciously agreed to stage a mock trial for the boys as part of the color war breakout plan. "Order in the court!" the judge called, banging his gavel, as he produced a new sheaf of papers. The counselors had provided him with a short speech to read on the topic of *sur mera* and *aseh tov*; each of the color war teams was to represent one of the two concepts, and the campers were charged with learning about each of them and understanding the need for both. "It isn't enough to stay away from evil," the judge read aloud. "One must also contribute to goodness."

The police officers later complimented the counselors on the campers' excellent behavior during the mock trial, offering to repeat the performance in a future summer. But perhaps the most fascinating reaction was that of the judge himself. When the head counselor thanked the judge for his involvement, the man replied, "Actually, I should be the one to thank you for asking me to do this, because I really learned a lot from it. When I was explaining the themes and speaking about how a person must constantly evaluate his actions, making sure to avoid evil and constantly do good things, it caused me to realize that I should be examining my own life in the same way. I never thought about life in this sense, and I thank you for enlightening me."

A week later, Rabbi Chaim Sher, the owner of the camp, received a surprising call from a non-Jewish woman. The caller explained that her son had been caught shoplifting, and the judge had sentenced him to sixteen hours of community service. The judge, who had presided over the color war breakout, suggested that his service should be done for Camp Chayos Hakodesh, a religious camp where the children are taught and practice high standards of behavior, in the hope that the campers would exert a positive influence on him. The mother asked, with a hint of desperation in her voice, if the camp had any work that her son could perform.

The concepts of *sur mera* and *aseh tov* are basic Torah concepts. Nevertheless, to a judge in the American court system, a man whose entire career revolves around justice and moral values, these elementary ideas were incredibly eye opening.

Takeaway

The simplest Torah values can be eye opening to those who live in the darkness of the modern world.

Making It Practical

- Develop a stronger appreciation for the simple Torah values that we sometimes take for granted.
- At your Shabbos table each week, share a *dvar Torah* on the *parashah* that you appreciate and that highlights a basic Torah value. This practice will bring out the beauty of the Torah way of life.

Tiny Sparks of Light

Rav Yitzchok Zilberstein (in his *sefer Barchi Nafshi*) shares the story of a *talmid chacham* who accidentally struck a parked car while driving to Meron. The man left a note on the windshield of the damaged car with his contact information, promising to pay for the repairs, and proceeded on his way.

Several hours after he returned home, someone knocked at the door. He opened the door and was startled when the visitor, a complete stranger and obviously irreligious Jew, held up a camera and snapped a picture of him. "I am the owner of the car you hit," the stranger said. "I was so astonished by your actions that I simply had to come and take a picture of you. You must be the only person in the world who would leave a note so he could pay for damages when he could easily have avoided doing so!"

Several weeks later, the man showed up at the *talmid chacham's* doorstep again. This time, he said, "My wife and I have decided that if this is the way a religious person behaves, we want to be part of your community!"

Rav Eliyahu Dessler (*Michtav MeEliyahu*, Vol. 4, p. 301) raises a fascinating question: If the Jews of previous generations, who lived on such an exalted level of *kedushah*, were unable to generate the *kevod Shamayim* necessary to bring about the *geulah*, how can we hope to do so in our own spiritually impoverished generation? He explains that since the darkness in the world around us has grown so intense and pervasive, and the world has experienced such a massive spiritual decline, even a small amount of spiritual light can have a much greater impact. In today's world, even the smallest actions we perform cannot be taken for granted. As the moral and spiritual fiber of the society around us frays and crumbles, our opportunities for kiddush Hashem become that much greater.

A striking example of the world's moral decline is the dramatic change in the behavioral issues that are named as rampant problems in public schools. In the 1940s, the top discipline issues in public schools were children chewing gum, making noise, running in the hallways, stepping out of line, violating the dress code, and leaving trash on the floors. By the 1980s, the list had changed to include drugs, alcohol, licentiousness, robbery, and assault.

In a society that has fallen so far, the tiniest sparks of *kedushah* can generate enormous spiritual illumination.

Not long ago, a religious Jew by the name of Isaac Theil became a worldwide sensation as a result of the smallest, simplest act: He was riding home on the subway when the man sitting next to him fell asleep and leaned his head on Theil's shoulder. Rather than wake his slumbering seatmate, Theil sat quietly and allowed the man to continue sleeping. An onlooker snapped a picture, which was posted on social media and quickly attracted the attention of over a million people, making a profound impact on thousands.

To create a kiddush Hashem, we do not have to be extraordinary people or Torah giants. In this time of overwhelming spiritual darkness, let us do our best to create as many sparks of light as we can, as small as they may be, and we will surely reap the fruits of our efforts.

Takeaway

The greater the darkness, the greater the light produced by even the tiniest spark of kedushah. In a world steeped in decadence, even an ordinary person can create an enormous impact with a trivial act.

Making It Practical

- Try to demonstrate kindness or sensitivity to others with at least two simple acts every day.
- While you are driving, shopping, in shul, or involved in any other ordinary activity make an effort to find two opportunities to perform even the most minor acts of kindness.

Sowing the Seeds

*Note: The names of the individuals and places
in the following story have been changed.*

It was a busy erev Succos morning. At 10 a.m., Reb Shlomo Greenwald, a *yungerman* in Beis Medrash Govoha of Lakewood, was shopping in Torah Treasures, a local *sefarim* store, when a bareheaded man wandering about the store caught his attention. Shlomo approached the stranger and asked if he could be of any help. "No thanks. I'm just waiting to pick up the *succah* I ordered," the man replied.

In the ensuing brief conversation, Shlomo learned that the man — whose name was Michael — had recently moved from Utah to nearby Toms River, with his wife and four children. He was Jewish, but he was not religious. "My family enjoys having guests," Shlomo said. "Would you like to join us for a meal during the holiday?"

That *Chol Hamoed* meal was a turning point for Michael and his family, marking the beginning of a long journey back to Yiddishkeit. Over the coming months, Michael began learning with Shlomo once a week, attending shul every Shabbos, and keeping kosher. For Michael's wife, Linda, who had undergone a Reform conversion, the transition was somewhat more difficult, but she soon took a liking to a *frum* woman she met at a Lakewood supermarket, and she gradually began to emulate her husband's progress. Soon enough, the family began to contemplate moving to Lakewood.

But their steady progress came to an abrupt end just as they were on the verge of purchasing a house in Lakewood. A family in the community was graciously hosting them for a Shabbos meal, when Linda made an inadvertent blunder: As the father of the family began singing a *zemer*, she unthinkingly began singing along. The sound of her voice elicited an expression of shock from the hostess. Mortified, Linda decided at that moment that she had had enough of Yiddishkeit. At the first opportunity, she presented Michael with an ultimatum: She was returning to her former life in Utah, and if he did not want to go along with her, then they would simply have to get divorced.

With that, Michael and his family vanished from the Lakewood community. Shlomo Greenwald was mystified by their disappearance; Michael did not even return his calls. Months went by, and it became painfully clear that Michael and his family were gone.

Eight years later, Shlomo received a call from his cousin Yaakov, who lived in Baltimore. "Do you know a man from Utah named Mordechai, who used to call himself Michael?" Yaakov asked.

"Of course!" Shlomo exclaimed. "But I haven't seen him in years. Where is he?"

"He's sitting right next to me!" his cousin trumpeted.

Michael took the phone and recounted the events that had occurred since his departure. He had hoped to persuade his wife to continue their religious growth, perhaps at a slower pace, but his efforts were of no avail. Their differences ultimately led them to divorce, and Michael continued his determined progress in pursuit of religious Judaism. Eventually, he married a *frum* girl from Baltimore and settled there. Yaakov, another member of the community, had happened to ask "Mordechai" how he had become *frum*, and when he learned that his journey had begun with an encounter with a *yungerman* named Greenwald, he grew excited. "I had to call you and tell you that the effort that you made, the fact that you did not let an opportunity slip away, ultimately bore fruit, even though it took a long time for you to see the results," he told Shlomo, who was moved by the revelation.

Thousands of other *baalei teshuvah* have similar stories to tell about the way their return to Yiddishkeit began. Almost invariably, an irreligious Jew's interest in Yiddishkeit will be sparked by a seemingly minor incident: receiving an offer of help from a *frum* Jew, witnessing a *frum* Jew do something that impresses him, and so forth. The initial inspiration quite often does not come from *kiruv* experts and their inspiring classes; rather, it is a minor, seemingly trivial encounter with an ordinary person that ignites an interest in learning more about Judaism.

Takeaway

Kiruv is not an endeavor for the professionals alone. In fact, the kiruv professionals need our help. When a nonreligious Jew becomes interested in attending classes or engaging in dialogue, it is generally because his interest was sparked by small positive interactions with ordinary frum Jews. It is up to all of us to create that spark of interest.

Making It Practical

- If you see someone who seems to be lost or in need of help, use it as an opportunity to reach out and show that you care.

Small Impressions

In an article in the January 2001 edition of the *Jewish Observer*, Rabbi Yonason Rosenblum shared the story of how three *baalei teshuvah* became *frum*. The trio of friends had all been enjoying successful careers in the film industry in Hollywood, when they had a life-changing experience. As they sat in a restaurant one Shabbos morning, they watched as a *frum* family passed by on their way home from *shul*. Each of the men was struck by the sight of that family; something about it touched a chord within them, making them realize that their lives of glamor and material success were somehow lacking. Today, years later, all three are fully observant. Incredibly, Klal Yisrael merited three additional religious families from something as simple as the sight of a family with children calmly walking home from *shul* on Shabbos morning.

Each of us, too, can achieve what that family achieved; undoubtedly, without even realizing it. We are not all experts on *kiruv*, and we cannot all deliver illuminating lectures on the philosophical underpinnings of Judaism, but all of us make up the collective face of the Jewish people. If we demonstrate the pleasantness and sweetness of the Torah way of life, then we, too, can have a positive impact on our lost brethren — even through the tiniest gestures. When a secular or non-Jewish person sees religious Jews acting graciously, dressing modestly, or having respectful children, when they see teenagers who can play ball without spewing profanities, or large families of well-behaved and happy children, or religious Jews leading a disciplined and moral life, the impact can be far greater than we can even imagine.

At the same time, the reverse is also true: Even a minor false move, especially in the early stages of an irreligious person's progress toward Yiddishkeit, can have devastating consequences. Even the slightest chillul Hashem can cause a person to shut down completely, losing all interest in pursuing a connection with Yiddishkeit. The journey to Yiddishkeit can begin *and* end based on a small impression.

Kiruv experts have noted that the number of participants in *kiruv* classes and programs — meaning, in effect, the number of irreligious Jews interested in Judaism — has dwindled over the years. One *rav* has attributed this decline to the few unfortunate instances of widely publicized chillul Hashem over the past decade, which have made many irreligious Jews reluctant to be part of the religious world. While we ourselves were not the perpetrators of those misdemeanors, he declared, we are all responsible to rectify the situation by practicing good *middos* and demonstrating integrity, thus combating the chillul Hashem with an equally powerful kiddush Hashem.

Takeaway

The beginning of a non-religious Jew's journey toward Yiddishkeit is an extremely critical and delicate time. At that time, even the minutest impressions can have inestimable consequences. An interaction with a religious Jew, no matter how trivial it may seem, can whet his appetite for Yiddishkeit, or can drive him away from his religion.

Making It Practical

• When you interact with a *baal teshuvah* or a *ger*, make sure to be extra sensitive to their feelings. Especially at the beginning of their journey, even a single word can make a tremendous difference.

Be on the Lookout

Not long ago, Rabbi Moshe Schwartz (name changed) took his class on a camping trip in a state park. As anyone who has taken such trips is well aware, there are many rules governing the use of campsites, and the park rangers strictly enforce those rules; every group of campers is virtually guaranteed to receive at least one visit from a ranger. Sure enough, the class had barely been there for five minutes when the telltale rumble of a car engine signaled the arrival of a park ranger. A middle-aged woman in uniform arrived and clambered out of her car to greet the *rebbe*. "Hi there!" she said congenially. "Are you a rabbi? Are you from Chabad?"

Preoccupied with the numerous matters demanding his attention, Rabbi Schwartz answered the ranger's questions briefly and listened as she listed the rules, making no effort to take the conversation further. It was only after the ranger had left that he began to regret his failure to seize an opportunity.

Fortunately, Rabbi Schwartz was given a second chance. At about 9:30 that night, the *bachurim* were seated in a circle around the campfire, enjoying a hearty *kumzitz*, when the park ranger reappeared. When she greeted the class with the words "*Erev tov*," Rabbi Schwartz pounced on the opportunity.

"Are you Jewish?" he asked.

"Oh yes," the ranger replied. "In fact, I was religious just five years ago; I was even married to a rabbi who was a chaplain in the Navy." A wistful note crept into her voice. "I get quite lonely out here," she admitted, "and I don't see many Jews. I recognized all the songs you were singing: *Ani Maamin, Ko Amar,* and all the others. They brought back such fond memories for me. You see, I am not bitter, and I had no quarrels with my ex-husband, whom I really respect. I simply needed to find myself and enjoy the outdoors...."

"We are from a Jewish community only about 45 minutes away," Rabbi Schwartz told the woman. "If you would like to visit our community for Shabbos, I would be pleased to have you as a guest."

Tears suddenly glistened in the park ranger's eyes. "I would enjoy that very much," she said.

Eventually, the conversation turned to the reason she had come, and she informed the rabbi that the height of their fire was above the permitted limit. He promised to lower it, and she drove off again.

Even on his trip to the mountains, Rabbi Schwartz never lost his focus on kiddush Hashem, and as a result, his eyes were wide open when an opportunity came his way. That is an important concept for all of us to remember: We must constantly be on the lookout for opportunities to create kiddush Hashem, for we can never know when such opportunities will come our way.

For Rabbi Avrohom Weinrib, the *rav* of Congregation Zichron Eliezer of Cincinnati, Ohio, a stroke of *hashgachah pratis* on a flight out of Cincinnati brought him an unexpected opportunity. It began when Rabbi Weinrib found himself seated on a plane next to an elderly man who identified himself as Jeremy. After the rabbi greeted him politely and introduced himself, Jeremy asked, "Do you live on Farm Acres?" Farm Acres is a street in the Jewish neighborhood in Cincinnati and is, in fact, where Rabbi Weinrib lives.

"Actually, I do," the rabbi said in surprise. "How did you know?"

The older man revealed that he had lived on the same street years earlier. "I am Jewish but not religious," he added, "and I know that a lot of Jews live on that street."

The two men spent the next hour chatting about the neighborhood and the way it had changed. "By the way," Jeremy asked suddenly, "do you know Mark Moskowitz?"

"Certainly, Rabbi Weinrib replied. "I learn with him as a study partner regularly."

Jeremy was astounded. "Then you are the rabbi whom Mark always talks about!" he exclaimed. "He is always begging me to come learn with him and his rabbi, and now here we are, sitting together on a plane. This is too much of a coincidence to be random!"

Of course Rabbi Weinrib graciously invited the older man to join his regular learning sessions, and within a few weeks he took the rabbi up on his offer.

The odds of those two men finding themselves in adjacent

seats on the same flight were probably about as low as the average person's odds of winning the lottery. But we do not live in the world that follows the laws of probability; our *emunah* teaches us that nothing in this world happens by chance. Whenever we cross paths with someone or find ourselves in a particular place, it may very well be a Divinely sent opportunity for *kiddush Hashem*. If we remain on the lookout for those opportunities, we will be able to make the most of them when they arise.

Takeaway

If we go about our daily lives robotically, then it is indeed unlikely that we will have many chances to create a kiddush Hashem. But we can choose to live in a different way. If we keep our mission of kiddush Hashem at the forefront of our minds, we will find that many opportunities come our way to make a difference. All we need to do is seize those opportunities when they present themselves.

Making It Practical

- Prepare a sentence or a greeting to utilize when someone makes it obvious that he is Jewish and seems to be trying to connect: whether it is a Shabbos invitation, a suggestion of a resource for more information about Judaism, or something else of the sort.

Kiddush Hashem in the Age of Connectivity

One of the hallmarks of the contemporary era is the speed at which information spreads. The Internet, with its constant connectivity and instantaneous exchange of information, has created a world in which stories, ideas, perspectives, and news reports spread like wildfire, reaching thousands — or even millions — of people within seconds. The results are dramatic: Passions can quickly be stirred, social movements can gain momentum rapidly, and even governments can be brought down by the worldwide sharing of news and ideas.

One of the major ways in which technology has changed our lives is the fact that nowadays, everything that we do or say, no matter how trivial, is liable to be public knowledge. Private conversations or interactions are a thing of the past; pictures and videos are constantly being taken and transmitted to countless people, often without the subjects' awareness. Under the circumstances, the potential for chillul Hashem is magnified many times over by this phenomenon. At the same time, these technological developments have created an opportunity for kiddush Hashem like none that we have experienced before.

Consider the following true story: The host of a television show with millions of viewers recently decided to conduct a social experiment of sorts. He recruited a man to dress up as a cartoon character and then to "trip" and land on his back on a busy sidewalk, where he begged passersby to help him up. The point of the experiment was to see how long it would take until someone would come to his aid. A hidden camera recorded the scene as the man lay on the sidewalk for six minutes, begging for help as hundreds of people passed by, looking at him curiously but refraining from offering him a hand. "This isn't a joke! Please help!" the odd-looking character insisted as a runner leapt over him, a dog sniffed him curiously before its owner hurried past, and numerous other pedestrians barely gave him a glance. Finally, a group of yeshivah *bachurim*, whose attire clearly marked them as religious Jews, came across the man and helped him up. All of this was caught on camera and watched by millions of Americans.

That incident led to many positive impressions, but the Internet is also a hotbed of negativity. Countless books, articles, and blogs are being used by Jews who have left the fold to air their anger and resentment and to defend their lifestyle changes. But while it often seems that negative sentiments are much more likely to be shared than positive ones, there is still much that we can do about this.

A *chassid* from Montreal once wrote the following to me:

"Robert Davis (name changed) is a secular Jew who lives near the *chassidish* neighborhood in Montreal. He is a filmmaker with definite left-wing leanings; a few years ago, he produced a film about Jewish boys and girls who have gone 'off the *derech*,' portraying Orthodox Jews in a very negative light. I met him once in a kosher supermarket on erev Yom Kippur, when he was looking for a *yahrtzeit* candle, and we struck up a conversation and eventually developed a relationship. Since then, he has visited my home many times on Shabbos, Succos, and other such occasions. Although he is still far from *frum*, he joined a Thursday night *chaburah* two years ago and has completely changed his view of religious Jews."

The letter went on to relate that Robert Davis had sent his *chassidish* friend an e-mail with a copy of an article written by a Modern Orthodox Jew who had moved to Williamsburg. The author related that when he first arrived in his new community, he was terrified to appear in *shul* on Shabbos. With his strikingly modern appearance and attire, he feared that he would be instantly judged, denigrated, and branded an outsider. "After all," he wrote, "it seemed like every week I had read another horror story regarding their community and their insularity."

To his surprise, though, when he arrived in a *shul* on Shabbos morning, he was treated to a warm welcome as the *mispallelim* hastened to supply him with a *tallis*, *siddur*, and *Chumash* and to find him a pleasant seat, as well as honoring him with an *aliyah*.

After an inspiring *tefillah*, he attended a *kiddush* where he was deeply impressed by the *shul*'s hospitality and congeniality.

"They redefined for me what Jewish hospitality — *hachnassas orchim* — should look and feel like," the writer declared. "With small and intentional gestures, the great divide between us seemed insignificant." He concluded his account by noting that they had reminded him of the Baal Shem Tov's teaching, "Be careful when you pass judgment on another. It is really yourself whom you may be judging."

Along with the article, Robert Davis included a brief note: "Great story. Very similar to what I experienced with you!"

One can imagine that Robert Davis's next documentary about Orthodox Jews is likely to be a source of kiddush Hashem, rather than the opposite. And there is no question that his newfound *chassidish* friend, along with the members of the *shul* in Williamsburg, deserve the credit for that.

Takeaway

Modern technology has given us a tool that can enable any kiddush Hashem to spread and reach many more people than was ever possible in the past. At the same time, the risk of chillul Hashem has also been magnified a thousandfold. Due to the advances in communication, we are all essentially on stage, in the public eye, at every moment of every day.

Making It Practical

- Think of every human being you encounter as far more than just an individual. The impression you make on him will spread to his family and his social media friends very quickly. Every individual has a platform and a voice to spread every experience that he has. Keep that in mind in all of your interactions!

Discussion Points:

❖ If I don't have the charisma of a professional *kiruv* worker and I do not interact regularly with non-religious Jews, is there any way for me to make a difference in the outside world?

❖ Centuries ago, there were Jews who lived on a much loftier spiritual plane than our own lowly generation. If they were unable to generate the *kevod Shamayim* necessary to bring about the *geulah*, how can we, with our puny spiritual stature, hope to do so?

❖ Is kiddush Hashem only for great people? If I am not an outstanding *tzaddik* or prominent *talmid chacham*, can I truly make a kiddush Hashem?

CHAPTER 4

AVOIDING CHILLUL HASHEM

The Golds are among several kollel families who have just moved into a neighborhood that is home to a budding Jewish community. They are excited about their new environment and the tremendous potential for growth in the community, but it does not take long for them to realize that the situation might not be as rosy as they imagined. During the weeks following their arrival, they begin to notice that their neighbors are not exactly pleased with the changes taking place in their neighborhood. The first unpleasant incident takes place when Rabbi Gold is walking to shul with his children on Shabbos and is pushing his double stroller in the street because the sidewalk is not wide enough to accommodate it; as a car passes them, the driver shouts angrily, "Why can't you stay on the sidewalk?" A few days later, the Golds find an anonymous note posted on their front door, asking them to take better care of their yard. They begin to feel terrible about the animosity, and they wonder if there is anything that they can do about it.

Opening the Lines of Communication

Alaska Airlines Flight 241 was *en route* from Mexico City to Los Angeles when panic suddenly struck. Three men had fastened odd-looking black boxes to their foreheads and arms, tying them in place with strange black straps, and the three were now standing in their seats and murmuring to themselves in an unfamiliar language. The flight attendants noticed the passengers' suspicious behavior and notified the security crew on the plane, prompting them to lock the cockpit and order a security alert on the ground. When the plane landed, it was met by fire crews, foam trucks, FBI agents, Transportation Security

Administration workers, and police. The three passengers were taken into custody and questioned before being released.

To those in the know, the explanation for the men's "strange" behavior is obvious: They were Orthodox Jews *davening* Shacharis while wearing their *tefillin*. But to their fellow passengers on the plane, their actions were alien and frightening. When a non-Jew encounters unfamiliar Jewish practices for the first time, it can often result in confusion and misunderstandings — even if the results aren't always quite so dramatic.

Many of those misunderstandings, however, can be avoided with proper communication. Explaining the reasons for our "strange" behaviors, even briefly, can turn a potentially uncomfortable encounter into an experience of mutual understanding and respect. At the beginning of a flight, for instance, an Orthodox Jewish passenger might consider explaining to his non-Jewish seatmate why he will have to leave his seat several times during the flight to wash his hands.

On a larger scale, this is the idea behind the efforts of Rabbi Tzvi Steinberg, the *rav* of Congregation Zera Avraham of Denver, Colorado. Rabbi Steinberg was well aware of the potential for misunderstandings between the police and the members of his own community. Even something as simple as a traffic stop on a Friday afternoon, when a Jewish driver might answer a police officer abruptly and anxiously as he watches the minutes before Shabbos ticking away, can lead to potential problems. Anticipating such scenarios, Rabbi Steinberg met with the entire police force in order to help them understand the culture of religious Jews. He then worked together with a number of police officers to put out a pamphlet that would educate the police on what to expect when dealing with religious Jews. The police officers in Denver have now learned that a Jew may refuse to sign papers on Shabbos, that a Jew may try to wave down an officer in the street on Shabbos because he is not permitted to use the telephone, and that a Jew may turn down a handshake from a female officer without meaning to insult her. And, of course, if a Jewish driver has been pulled over on a Friday afternoon and is acting anxious and rushed, even begging the officer to ticket him as quickly as possible, it is not because the driver has something to hide; he is simply trying to get home in time for Shabbos. Without the benefit of this pamphlet, the police officers might have interpreted all of these actions as rude, disrespectful, and even suspicious. Rabbi Steinberg's goal was to prevent ill will between the police and Jewish citizens.

Education about Jewish culture can be the key to developing a good rapport with non-Jewish neighbors as well. While the typical *frum* Jewish family does not disturb their neighbors with the ruckus of the parties and loud music that are common in the secular world, there is still a certain amount of disturbance that their neighbors will have to tolerate. Many *frum* children do not entertain themselves by watching television or playing video games, and as a result, they can often be found outdoors for many more hours than the average child today. Often, our children spend that time riding noisy toys on the sidewalk or otherwise making a commotion. A *frum* family's lawn may also not be as well tended as those of their neighbors, and a family with many children may generate much more noise than the average household. It is only natural for a non-Jewish neighbor to be irritated by these things, but greeting neighbors regularly and having an occasional conversation with them can be highly effective in dispelling these negative feelings.

In all of these situations, positive interaction and communication are the key to good relations. If we act indifferent to the people around us, then we shouldn't be surprised if they become resentful or hostile toward us. On the other hand, if we show them that we are aware that they exist, and that they are worthy of our attention, our apologies, and our explanations, then we can create much more positive feelings, and that will contribute to our goal of kiddush Hashem.

Effective communication is a vital tool for relieving tension and clearing up misunderstandings. If we learn to communicate properly with others, our relationships with the people around us may improve drastically.

Making It Practical

- Choose one person (a neighbor, an employee, or anyone else) with whom you feel that you have some tension, and take the time to explain a little about our culture to them. They will certainly appreciate your efforts to communicate.
- If you are about to do something that may appear strange to others and might disturb them, make sure to give a short explanation of what you are doing. They won't understand completely, but the effort you make will go a long way.

Coexistence in Outremont

In the past, when Jewish communities were smaller, it was much simpler for Jews in *galus* to go about their business without the general society taking much notice of them. But today things have changed. Thanks to the many blessings Hashem has showered on us over the years, our society has grown. Many *frum* Jews now live in large, highly visible communities, with schools catering to hundreds of students and with many other communal institutions. And with the increase in the size of our communities, our needs have increased as well.

Many *frum* communities today walk a very fine line. On the one hand, there are needs that must be met, and in order to fulfill those needs, we have to tap into the resources and benefits that are rightfully due to our large schools and other institutions. On the other hand, we live in insular communities and tend to be seen as outsiders by the society around us — and that leads them to envy and resent us even when we simply stand up for our own rights. What can we do to stem the tide of resentment?

The community of Outremont, Montreal, is an excellent model of positive relations between a group of Jews and their non-Jewish neighbors.

Outremont, especially the neighborhood of Hutchison Street, is a densely populated area that is home to a few hundred families including a large *chassidish* community whose relations with its non-Jewish neighbors haven't always been peaceful. The *frum* community, which accounts for the majority of the local residents, shares a limited living space with its non-Jewish neighbors, and the neighborhood has been the scene of conflict after conflict over the years. For a long time, every issue that could possibly create tension — whether it was a *shul* expansion, the construction of an *eiruv*, public transportation, or any of a wide range of other matters — was blown out of proportion by people who wanted to create misery for the Jewish community. One councilwoman actually appealed to a court to force the Jewish community to take down their *eiruv*, claiming that it denied her the right to fly a kite. Another local blogger worked for years to delegitimize the *frum* community, attacking every politician who dared to express support for them. And his efforts paid off; to a large degree, he was able to intimidate many local politicians and community members into avoiding doing anything to assist the Jewish community.

In the midst of all this tension, a group of *chassidim* decided to act to save their community's reputation. The time had come, they felt, for their neighbors to hear their side of the story.

They began by opening a blog and printing flyers aimed at their non-Jewish neighbors, notifying them in advance about each of the Jewish holidays and what they could expect to see during that time. Open meetings were held so that issues of concern — such as how to deal with the extra garbage generated by the *frum* community's large families, or how their yards should be tended to satisfy their neighbors — could be discussed in a respectful fashion. At the same time, of course, the people behind this initiative urged the members of their own community to be more sensitive to their neighbors' feelings.

In short order, the *chassidim* found an unexpected ally. Another group, calling itself "Friends of Hutchison Street," was soon established with the goal of replacing the hostility toward the *frum* community with mutual respect and understanding. Leila Marshy, the founder of the group, is a non-Jewish woman of Palestinian descent born in Canada. Although she had always been devoted to the Palestinian cause, she had lived on Hutchison Street for many years and had come to admire and appreciate her Jewish neighbors, and she took offense at the slander that was often directed at the community.

The two groups — Friends of Hutchison and the Outremonthassid.com blog — now work hand in hand to promote peace and mutual understanding in the neighborhood. Their work has received many positive responses.

"It's always nice to see life and vibrancy on the street, and it allowed me to discover a festive side to my Hassidic neighbors that I haven't seen before," one local resident wrote in a letter to the *chassidish* group. "I want to thank you for the good public relations work you have done with the two letters that you distributed in mailboxes. In the 23 years I've been living in the area, this is the first time I've seen an effort by the Hasidic community to inform us about an event."

Another non-Jewish neighborhood resident once wrote to Friends of Hutchison to share his own positive experience: His car had been damaged in its parking spot in front of his home, and he was surprised to find a note from the *chassidish* driver who had caused the damage. The note identified the driver, who took full responsibility for the damage and provided his phone number so that he could be contacted to pay for repairs. The owner of the damaged car was deeply impressed. Based on past experience, he would never have expected anyone to come forward and identify himself in such a scenario, and he was pleasantly surprised to find that his expectations were wrong.

He was even more impressed by the *chassid's* response to his surprise and gratitude: "But you cannot do unto others what you would not want done to yourself!" In his letter to Friends of Hutchison, the car owner wrote enthusiastically, "If we all thought and acted as he did, we would live in the most beautiful area of the world! One year after moving here, I feel more and more in harmony with my Hasidic neighbors."

There is much we can all learn from the community of Outremont. As our communities expand, we have every right to make sure to receive everything that we are entitled to: government funding, rights, and so forth. At the same time, as legitimate as our actions may be, we must be sensitive to the way they are viewed by others. Whether we are leaders or ordinary members of our communities, we must make sure that kiddush Hashem is always among our top priorities.

Takeaway

Friction between a growing Jewish community and its non-Jewish neighbors is not inevitable. It is possible to listen to our neighbors' concerns and to create solutions that will satisfy everyone. A small amount of effort to cultivate mutual respect, along with the occasional sacrifice on our part, can go a long way toward promoting peaceful coexistence.

- Try to identify the sources of friction in your own neighborhood, and come up with changes that can be made to improve your community's relationship with its neighbors. And once you have an idea, get involved in making it happen!
- Pay attention to the lifestyle and standards of cleanliness in the neighborhood where you live. This includes finding out your neighbors' expectations about when to put out garbage for collection and how to maintain your lawn and keep your property clean. It is simple *derech eretz* to abide by the standards of the area where you live.

Breaking the Silence

Reuven was surprised when Shimon, a casual acquaintance, approached him and asked with a hint of trepidation, "Reuven, are you upset with me over something?"

Reuven, who did not feel the slightest ill will toward his friend, was quick to reply, "Not at all! Why would you think that?"

"Because," Shimon replied, "you haven't said anything to me in a while...."

This is a fairly common scenario, which many of us have surely experienced. When two people stop communicating with each other, negative feelings often take root. Even if they were not at odds in the past, the silence might cause one to suspect that the other is angry or displeased. And when the two were already in conflict, the effects can be far worse: A lack of dialogue can aggravate tension that already exists, turning even a minor misunderstanding into major tension. Before long, the two people may find themselves trapped in a conflict with no resolution — all because they failed to talk to each other.

Talking is important in any relationship: between a husband and wife, parents and children, teachers and students, employers and employees, and so forth. Any form of communication, even small talk, can do wonders to dispel tension and to create an atmosphere of caring, camaraderie, and respect.

This idea is illustrated by a halachah concerning the exile of an inadvertent murderer. The halachah states that a person who kills someone inadvertently is sentenced to *galus* in an *ir miklat* (city of refuge) only if he did not feel enmity toward the victim. This is derived from a *pasuk*, which states that the murderer "did not hate him [i.e., the victim] yesterday and the day before." But how can a *beis din* know whether the killer felt hatred toward the victim? The *Ralbag*, in his commentary on *Sefer Shmuel II* (*perek* 21, *toeles* 50), teaches that anyone who did not *speak* to his victim for a period of three days is considered to have despised him. An unwillingness to speak to another person is considered a sign of hatred.

One of the areas in which it is crucial to remember this idea is in our relationship with irreligious Jews. There will always be a certain degree of tension between different circles within the Jewish people; it is almost unavoidable. And it is understandable that irreligious Jews might feel uncomfortable or be easily offended when they are dealing with religious Jews. It is only natural for a nonreligious Jew to worry that observant Jews feel superior to him, or to feel inconvenienced or not trusted by Jews who follow halachah. However, if we fail to engage in dialogue with other Jews, if we simply treat them to silence, then those natural tensions might erupt into full-scale hostility.[1]

1.Some people make the mistake of believing that it is permissible to harbor ill will toward an irreligious Jew. After all, the Gemara (*Pesachim* 113b) states that it is permitted to despise a person who is steeped in sin. But the *Chazon Ish* (*Yoreh Deah* 2:28) explains that this ruling applies only to a sinner who was warned not to sin and was informed that his actions would incur a punishment mandated by

This doesn't mean that we must speak with irreligious Jews specifically about the issues that divide us. Any type of dialogue, formal or informal, about any subject, can create a sense of closeness between people and can help calm any tensions that may develop. Even simply greeting other Jews we meet in the streets, on buses, and in stores can be an important first step toward creating a positive relationship.

The activists of Lev L'Achim in Eretz Yisrael have all heard the story of a religious Jew who struck up a friendship with a man from an irreligious kibbutz and agreed to learn with him once a week. When he arrived at the kibbutz, to his surprise, the guard refused to permit him to enter; an official kibbutz rule barred religious Jews from entering its grounds. The man telephoned his friend, who came out of the kibbutz to meet him. Thus began a weekly routine: Every week, the religious Jew would arrive at the entrance to the kibbutz and wait for his friend to meet him. While he waited, he would often have a brief conversation with the guard, chatting about the weather or any other subjects that came to mind. After a few months, the guard, once a hardened *chiloni*, began to display signs of softness toward religious Jews. Eventually, he became a full-fledged *baal teshuvah*.

Takeaway

With minimal effort, we can create a kiddush Hashem by being more communicative with the people we meet. Whether it is a neighbor, a friend, a storekeeper, or even a seatmate on a plane, it often takes just a brief conversation to turn a strained relationship into a pleasant one. We can achieve incredible things if we choose to break the silence, instead of allowing the suppressed tensions to fester.

the Torah. In today's generation, we are no longer capable of delivering *tochachah* (rebuke) properly, and it is therefore forbidden for us to hate Jews who do not keep the Torah. On the contrary, we must reach out to them and try to engage with them; above all, we must communicate with them.

Guests in a Foreign Land

If you ever visit the city of Prague, you may be shocked at the sight that will meet your eyes at the Charles Bridge, a 600-year-old bridge that traverses the Vltava River. There, you will find a Christian statue decorated with gold Hebrew letters that spell out the words of the *pasuk* "*Kadosh, kadosh, kadosh Hashem Tzevakos.*" Rabbi Paysach Krohn tells the tragic story behind this inscription: In 1696, a Jew passing by this statue made a show of his lack of respect for it. His actions were observed by non-Jews, who nearly murdered him and launched a pogrom in retaliation. In the end, the authorities ordered the Jewish community to pay for the gold letters that would spell out these sacred words, which were then placed around the statue's neck as a symbolic degradation of the Jewish religion. Today, over three centuries later, those letters are still there.

In this story, Rabbi Krohn sees a powerful lesson: We cannot anticipate the powerful, long-lasting repercussions that can result even from the most trivial actions. Before we do anything, we must remind ourselves that we are in *galus*, we are guests in a land that is not ours, and we must act accordingly.

This is a very important principle for us to keep in mind, especially during the summer, when many of us leave our homes and our communities to go on vacation. During the summer, there is a massive surge in the *frum* presence in many areas that cater to vacationers, and with our large numbers and high visibility, we are noticed. Although we tend to feel comfortable and at home in vacation areas that are familiar to us, we must never forget that we are in *galus*, and are guests in the country where we live. We must always be sensitive to the feelings of the citizens of this country — our "hosts" in exile.[2]

For example, in many state parks, there are very strict rules regarding how campers may make fires and where they are allowed to pitch tents, as well as rules against littering or wandering off the marked hiking trails. A high school *rebbi* who occasionally takes his students on camping trips once remarked to me, "Every time that I go on an overnight trip with my *bachurim*, the park rangers always catch us committing some small infraction. I always wondered how they managed to find out about every violation of the rules, no matter how trivial it was. Did they have hidden video cameras monitoring every square inch of the park? Finally, I realized that there were no cameras at all. Instead, it was all the other visitors to the park, who cared deeply about the state of the park and were bothered enough to report any violation of the rules to the park rangers, no matter how small it was."

To us, the things that concern our neighbors in *galus* may seem unimportant. Nevertheless, we must respect their feelings, and we must recognize that they might consider us rude or even destructive when we do not abide by their rules.

---

2. Some people believe that it is easier for Jews who live in "out of town" communities to develop this outlook. Those of us who live "in town," among large Jewish populations, often feel a sense of ownership in our surroundings; it is only natural to feel a certain degree of entitlement when one lives surrounded by other Jews. For a *frum* Jew who lives out of town, though, in an area where most of his neighbors are not Jewish, it is easier to feel the sense of being a guest in someone else's territory.

In the spring of 2015, Edward Day, the Rockland County Executive, publicized a photograph that was taken of a *frum* family in Haverstraw Bay Park, with one of their children sitting on a 9/11 memorial statue. "As one who responded to the first attack on the World Trade Center," he wrote, "I am personally troubled that these sites, designed for peaceful, quiet reflection, are increasingly being used as jungle gyms." Day's comment sparked a deluge of scathing condemnations of religious Jews. That wave of hostility was an important reminder that we are living in a society in which every action is seen, and everything we do can have repercussions.

In *Tefillas Haderech*, we ask Hashem to give us "charm, kindness, and mercy in Your Eyes and in the eyes of all who see us." Today, more than ever, we must *daven* for this with the greatest possible intensity. Every time we set foot outside our homes and our communities, we must remember that every one of our actions may be seen by more people than we could ever imagine. Let us hope that we will never do anything, *chas v'shalom*, that tarnishes Hashem's honor even for a moment, much less for hundreds of years.

Takeaway

We are living in galus, and that means that we are guests in countries where the majority belong to other nations. As long as we remain guests in their lands, it is our responsibility to follow their rules and respect their sensitivities.

Making It Practical

• When you are traveling or on vacation, make sure to find out and abide by the regulations that the local residents take for granted. Show sensitivity to the people around you, and make sure to behave like a good guest.

The Raindrops and the Flood

There was a time when my family and I lived on a block where there was only one other Jewish family. As long as we were surrounded by non-Jews, we felt that we weren't overly visible. If our children left a riding toy or two on our lawn or in the driveway, it wouldn't make much of a difference in the overall appearance of the block. When we neglected to mow our lawn, or we left the garbage bins out for longer than usual after the sanitation workers came, the neighbors barely noticed. But then things changed.

As more *frum* families arrived in the neighborhood and the Orthodox presence grew, the little things that had once been unobtrusive became more widespread. Suddenly, it wasn't just one family leaving a couple of toys outside; it was several families. And now a number of houses, rather than just one, were surrounded by patches of overgrown grass.

Frum parents with many children may be too preoccupied with their families' needs to worry about tidying up outdoors, but for the typical family in American suburbia, keeping the street presentable is a top priority. On that block, our neighbors came to resent the fact that the occasional minor eyesore had turned into a major disturbance, severely disrupting the orderly appearance of the block.

As an old saying goes, no single drop of rain believes it is to blame for the flood. When there is a "flood" of chillul Hashem, it is often the cumulative effect of many people's irresponsible actions. These are actions that might have gone unnoticed individually, but combined to create a flood of bad impressions. When one person throws a candy wrapper out of his car window, parks or drives irresponsibly, or commits some other minor infraction, he may be tempted to rationalize his actions as trivial and meaningless. "What's the big deal?" he may reason. "Who cares if I bend the rules just this once? What harm can it possibly do?" But in reality, even if that one act causes no harm on its own, the potential for chillul Hashem is enormous when there are countless other people doing the very same thing. And when one person commits that kind of act, he must realize that it is very likely that he is not the only one to do so.

It wasn't too long ago that the *frum* community in America was small, and the actions of Orthodox Jews often went unnoticed. Today, though, we have been blessed with an explosion of growth, and this is no longer the case. Our communities have grown, our schools and organizations have expanded, and our presence has become much more noticeable within society as a whole. In this context, even a tiny "drop" of chillul Hashem can contribute to a massive flood. One need only look at the huge crowds of *frum* Jews filling amusement parks and other recreational areas during *Chol Hamoed*, and at the flurry of letters about kiddush Hashem or chillul Hashem that often follow a Yom Tov, in order to recognize this. The way we act — children and adults alike — no longer goes unnoticed by the society around us, and we must be constantly aware of that fact.

Moshe (name changed), a *yungerman* in Lakewood, received a startling reminder of this idea when he took advantage of a mail-in rebate offered by an office supply chain to customers who ordered three boxes of paper. A few days after he placed the order, he looked out his window to find the mail truck parked outside his house and the mailman, a man in his fifties, unloading the paper from his truck, one box at a time, and dropping it on the sidewalk. The mailman was clearly exhausted from the effort, and Moshe hurried outside and offered to take the boxes to his front door. The mailman was relieved, but he grumbled, "Paper, paper, and more paper! Every single house is suddenly getting paper, and not just one box but three! What is going on?"

This is not a chillul Hashem and no one is at fault for the impression it created, but it illustrates just how careful we must be to anticipate the effects of our actions. In our close-knit communities, news of attractive sales and special deals tends to spread like wildfire. When it is legitimate to take advantage of the deals, this can be a wonderful thing, but when many people begin using questionable loopholes, it does not go unnoticed. Let's not delude ourselves: Airlines and credit card companies are aware when a long list of people with Jewish names take advantage of their promotions, and large retailers are familiar with the zip codes of areas with large Jewish populations.

There is plenty to be said about the difference between life in small communities and in areas with large Jewish populations, but one aspect of life in a more heavily Jewish area is the magnified potential for chillul Hashem. At the same time, the reverse is also true: A large Jewish community has a much greater ability to create kiddush Hashem than a small group of individual Jews. An individual can have some impact on others, but it takes a communal effort to truly change the world.

Rabbi Avi Shafran once had an interesting theory as to why there are occasional onslaughts of chillul Hashem and negative stories in the media about Jews, while at other times the world's outlook on the Jewish people seems to be more positive. "I picture a spiritual cloud of sorts, an amorphous mass of minor acts of chillul Hashem," he explained. "Any time a Jew blocks traffic by double parking, or is impatient with a clerk at a supermarket, or cuts corners while doing his taxes, a bit of malign moisture is added to that chillul Hashem cloud. And when it is sufficiently heavy, it rains down on our heads, and into the media, in the form of a large and public desecration of G-d's Name."

At the same time, he added, when there are numerous Jews who are polite, considerate, and honest, their actions create a "cloud" of kiddush Hashem. And when that "cloud" reaches its point of saturation, it "rains" down in the form of a global focus on all that is positive about the Jewish people.

Let us all be cautious with our own actions, making certain that they contribute to Hashem's honor and not, *chas v'shalom*, to chillul Hashem. Let us never fail to remember that while each of us may think we are only raindrops, in truth we are all part of a flood.

Even when we feel that our actions are too insignificant to create a chillul Hashem, we must think about the impression that would be created if many people did the same thing. We are all a part of a group, and we all share responsibility for those actions that lead to a cumulative chillul Hashem.

Making It Practical

- Take care not to litter. Your soda can or candy wrapper might not seem like much of a big deal, but imagine what would happen if everyone else left just one empty can or wrapper in the street.

- Resist the urge to grab an illegal parking spot, even for a short time, and even if it doesn't seem likely to interfere with anyone. If a dozen other people do the same thing, you will be contributing to a clogged street and a major nuisance.

- Before you take advantage of a special sale, store return policy, or a loophole of some kind, double-check to make sure it is perfectly legitimate. Even when it is okay, think about the impact it will have if fifty visibly Orthodox Jews show up to take advantage of it — and if you think that it might make a negative impression, consider the possibility of letting it go.

Stringency with Sensitivity

Rav Shlomo Zalman Auerbach was once seated on a bus when a woman took the seat beside him. Rav Shlomo Zalman remained still until the bus reached its next stop and then disembarked immediately, pretending that he had reached his destination. In his great sensitivity to the feelings of others, the *gadol* had made a quick decision to get off the bus rather than simply switching seats in order to avoid sitting next to a woman. Clearly, he felt that it was better for him to have to walk an extra distance to reach his destination than to cause discomfort to the woman passenger (*Chibur L'haahiv es Hashem*, p. 23).

What should a person do if he finds himself in such a situation on an airplane, where it is obviously not an option to follow Rav Shlomo Zalman's example and disembark early? Even if a person feels that he must change seats, he should make every effort to avoid inconveniencing or offending others. If possible, the arrangements should be made in advance; when this is not possible, a short explanation such as "I am switching seats due to a religious sensitivity; please do not take it personally," can go a long way toward preventing any offense.

There are many situations in life in which the observance of a *chumra*, or even a halachic requirement, must be done with care, to avoid making others feel uncomfortable. This point was driven home to a certain *yungerman* one year on the afternoon of Rosh Hashanah. Minchah had just ended at his yeshivah, and a crowd of hundreds of yeshivah students were making their way to the waterside for *Tashlich*. As they approached the water, an irreligious couple was headed toward them, clearly returning from their own *Tashlich*. The woman was not dressed in keeping with the halachic standards of modesty, and all the *bnei yeshivah*, as one, began moving to the other side of the street.

For a moment, one of the *yungerleit* in the crowd felt his heart swell with pride. "Such *kedushah*!" he murmured in awe. "*Mi k'amcha Yisroel*!" But then another thought struck him: What were the secular couple thinking at that moment? It was as if their very presence was offensive to the *bnei yeshivah*. They must have been deeply insulted. The *yungerman* continued heading straight toward the couple and made sure to wish them a good new year as he passed them. Seconds later, he overheard the wife comment to her husband, in a tone brimming with resentment, "That's the first greeting we've received from these religious men all day!"

Of course, there is room for debate as to the exact way that such a situation should be handled, and how the halachic requirement to avoid immodest sights should be balanced with *derech eretz*. It is not our intention to answer that specific question here. But the lesson we can learn from this incident is that it is important for us to invest effort in determining not only *what* is required of us by halachah, but *how* we should follow it. When it is possible to fulfill the halachah in a way that does not cause discomfort or bad feelings to others, it is certainly our duty to do so.

The Mishnah (*Pirkei Avos* 2:1) give us a guiding principle for our service of Hashem: A person should always choose the path that is "*tiferes l'oseha v'tiferes lo min ha'adam.*" *Meiri* explains this to mean that a person should engage in actions that will be pleasing both to Hashem and to other people. *Maharal* adds that a person must not ignore the feelings of others simply because he is doing a virtuous act; he must see to it that his actions "bring honor to him from people" as well as from Hashem.[3]

Rav Yaakov Kamenetsky often told his students that when they went home for vacation, they should avoid making a show of following certain *chumros* in the presence of people who did

---

3. *Rabbeinu Yonah* notes that this is also the rationale of the concept of *hiddur mitzvah* — having "a beautiful *lulav*, a beautiful *tallis*, a beautiful *sefer Torah*," and so forth. The purpose of *hiddur mitzvah*, according to *Rabbeinu Yonah*, is to evoke the respect of others for one's mitzvah observance. We all appreciate the value of adding *hiddurim* to our mitzvos, even at the cost of additional time and money. In the same vein, we must realize that it is just as important to invest our mitzvos with sensitivity, to perform them in a way that will not cause ill feelings and that will be *tiferes lo min ha'adam* — pleasing to others around us.

not observe those *chumros*. His reason was that the *bachurim* might seem to be denigrating those who did not adhere to their standards of halachah (*Reb Yaakov*, p. 184). When we observe a stringency, we must consider what message we will be giving to others by doing so, and perhaps make our *chumros* unobtrusive in order to avoid the appearance of conceit.[4]

Of course, we must observe all of the Torah's halachos to the fullest, without being deterred by concern over the reactions of others. But this does not diminish the need for us to calculate *how* our actions will be perceived. If there is a way to fulfill the *ratzon Hashem* without having a negative impact on other people, then it is our responsibility to do so.

Takeaway

Even in the course of following halachah, we must give careful thought to the impressions we create with our actions. Whenever possible, we should put effort into keeping halachah in a way that will have a positive impact on the people around us, and avoid causing them discomfort of any sort.

---

4. One factor that must be taken into consideration is the question of whether a specific act is a halachic requirement or merely a *minhag* or *chumra*. On that note, *Mesillas Yesharim* states (Ch. 20), "A person is obligated to observe all the mitzvos in all their details in front of anyone, without being afraid or ashamed.... But a distinction must be made in this as well, for this is said only about the actual mitzvos in which we are completely obligated. For them, a person must be as strong as a stone. But if there is some additional act of piety for which others will mock a person if he does it in front of them ... and he can refrain from doing that thing since it is not absolutely obligatory, it is better for a pious one to refrain from doing it.... The rule is: Something that is an absolute mitzvah should be done even before those who will mock it, but something that is not fundamentally required, and that will cause mockery and derision, should not be done."

Survival Instinct

Have you ever seen an animal cornered by a predator and facing an immediate danger to its life? In such a situation, the animal's natural survival instinct kicks in, and it may be capable of reacting in an extreme way, as it is driven to do everything in its power in order to remain alive.

The drive for survival is not unique to the animal kingdom. Human beings have their own version of the survival instinct, which can kick in whenever a threat is perceived — not only a threat to life, but even other types of threats, such as the sense that one's position, social status, or financial stability is in danger. People in such situations often enter a defensive mode in which they are capable of extreme responses to the perceived threat; the drive to protect themselves and their interests can cause them to lose sight of all other considerations, and there may be no limit to what they might do to ward off the threat. A human being can become so absorbed in his own quest for survival of any sort that he will be incapable of thinking of anything or anyone else. This can lead to behavior that is selfish, socially unacceptable, or even harmful or illegal.

The more a person lives in survival mode, thinking only of himself, the more he will be connected to the animalistic side of his existence. When a person is able to step outside of himself, to give thought to the needs and feelings of others even when they conflict with his own interests, that is when his human qualities emerge.

When Howard Schulz, the Jewish CEO of Starbucks, received the Business Ethics Award from Columbia University, he related that he was once taken by Aish HaTorah, along with a group of other businessmen, to meet Rav Nosson Tzvi Finkel. When they arrived, Rav Nosson Tzvi surprised the men by asking a pointed question: "What lesson do we learn from the Holocaust?" The businessmen were speechless, unable to fathom the *rosh yeshivah's* intent. When Rav Nosson Tzvi saw that they had no response, he revealed the answer: "In the concentration camps, people were crammed into overflowing barracks, and five or six people were forced to share a single blanket. But instead of fighting over the blanket, they spread it out so that it covered them all together. That is the lesson for us: Each of you should use your 'blanket' to cover as many people as you can." Mr. Schulz concluded his story, "That has been my mission statement to this day."

For many years, the nations among whom we lived stole from us, taxed us unfairly, and denied us justice and basic liberties. This placed us in a constant struggle for survival, and the resultant mentality may still be ingrained in us today. Nevertheless, we must keep in mind that we are living in a different era, a time when we have much more freedom and are blessed with lives of plenty. We must view this as a gift from Hashem, an opportunity to look beyond ourselves and consider how our actions affect others — and how they affect Hashem's honor. Therefore, while our innate survival instinct can be used for good purposes, it should be dedicated to preserving our spiritual well-being, and should not be allowed to carry over into the physical and financial aspects of our lives.

As we noted, the tendency to fight for "survival" applies on many levels. Sometimes, a person may feel threatened even by small things. In a crowded city, even the nicest person may lose every trace of civility as soon as he gets behind the wheel of a car, as he finds himself battling traffic and competing with other drivers for a parking space. In more competitive social circles, the survival instinct may drive a person to do everything in his power not only to provide for his family's basic needs, but to keep up with the standards of his friends and neighbors; as a result, he may resort to extremes in order to afford the type of clothes, homes, and even weddings and other *simchos* that are standard in his circles.

There are many pressures in contemporary life, and these pressures can have an untold effect on a person's behavior. Sometimes, the instinct for survival, in any of its forms, can drive us to do things that create a chillul Hashem. Let us make sure that we understand our own motivations in everything we do, so that we can avoid falling into the trap of doing things that detract from Hashem's honor.

Takeaway

In order to avoid chillul Hashem, we must be careful not to go into "survival mode," which might make us act selfishly without considering the repercussions. When we are consumed by stress and tension, we lack the energy to give to others or even to have consideration for their needs.

At times when you feel tense and stressed, don't take action. You cannot think properly under those circumstances, and you might do something unwise. Take a few deep breaths, and act only when you feel calm and rational.

Spiritual Retainers

One of the more pleasurable times in a teenager's life is the day when their braces are removed. Sitting in the orthodontist's chair for what they hope will be the last time, they celebrate as their teeth are finally freed from those irritating appliances. More often than not, however, the orthodontist may add a word of caution to his patients: Without continued intervention, their teeth will likely not remain straight. In order to keep those teeth from becoming crooked again, retainers must be worn. Otherwise, all the years of braces pulling and tugging on their teeth may have no lasting effect.

This is an apt metaphor for our spiritual lives. Take the example of a yeshivah *bachur* who spends his *zman* immersed in growth and personal change, working hard to allow the Torah and *mussar* he learns to "pull at" and shape his personality. When *bein haz'manim* arrives and this young man steps out of the *beis medrash*, he is no longer surrounded by forces that contribute to his spiritual growth. Without putting spiritual "retainers" in place to preserve his accomplishments, he is in danger of slipping back into his old habits.

Spiritual "retainers" can take different forms. A person can take precautions to avoid negative influences, by setting limits on the places he will go, the devices he will have access to, and so forth. He can also set goals for himself to make sure that he doesn't become idle and unproductive. This means scheduling *chavrusas* and deciding on goals in learning, but it may also include keeping himself occupied with other projects and activities. In one family, a very insightful mother found a way to make household tasks such as painting, gardening, and home repairs "suddenly" come up every *bein haz'manim*, which kept her yeshivah-age son occupied throughout his vacations. Years later, that *bachur* appreciated his mother's thoughtfulness and wisdom in keeping him constantly occupied and productive.

In *Alei Shur* (Vol. 1, p. 49), Rav Wolbe exhorts every yeshivah *bachur* to be cautious about two things during *bein haz'manim*: First, he must take care not to lose whatever he has gained during the *zman*.[5] Second, Rav Wolbe warns that a yeshivah *bachur*, even more than anyone else, must be very careful to create only a kiddush Hashem and to avoid chillul Hashem at all costs while outside his yeshivah. Someone who is known as a yeshivah student will be constantly watched and observed by others, and he must assume that even the people who see him on the street will examine his every movement as if with a magnifying glass. When a person identifies as a *ben Torah*, others will automatically hold him to a higher standard, and every one of his actions will inevitably be associated with the Torah he has learned.

This is an important concept to keep in mind even when we work on the issues discussed in this chapter. True, it is important to reach out to the non-Jews around us and to communicate with them effectively, but we must also be careful not to be influenced by the outside world. And as we have seen, this is especially relevant during our vacations, when we visit remote areas and

---

5. The Gemara (*Chagigah* 15a) warns us that the Torah is as difficult to acquire as precious gold and as easy to lose as fragile glass. Rav Wolbe explains that during *bein haz'manim*, a yeshivah student should imagine himself carrying a large, extremely delicate glass object that may fall and shatter if he doesn't hold onto it with the greatest care. This glass object represents the spiritual accomplishments of the entire *zman*; in order to "hold on" to those accomplishments, he must invest tremendous effort and care.

come into closer contact with the rest of society. Nevertheless, whenever we step outside our own communities and interact with other people in an effort to create a kiddush Hashem, we must remember to keep our spiritual "retainers" on, setting up safeguards that will prevent us from being dragged down from our spiritual level.[6]

Takeaway

When we reach out to others to create a kiddush Hashem, we must still be careful to protect ourselves from negative influences. This is especially important to keep in mind during the summer, when we leave our sheltered homes and communities; at the same time that we are taking care to avoid a chillul Hashem, we must also be devoted to maintaining our kedushah.

Making It Practical

- At the beginning of the summer vacation, prepare a schedule for yourself that includes specific goals for your accomplishments during the season. Make sure that those goals include making a kiddush Hashem.
- If you have a vacation at any other time of year, try to think of a way to use it as an opportunity for kiddush Hashem.

---

6. In *Parashas Va'eschanan* (*Devarim* 4:6), the Torah states, "You shall observe and do [the Torah's mitzvos], for it is your wisdom and insight in the eyes of the nations, who will hear all these statutes and say, 'This great nation is but a wise and intelligent people.' ... Just take care for yourself and protect your soul very much, lest you forget the things that your eyes saw, and lest they depart from your heart all the days of your life." Why does the Torah warn us here not to forget "the things that your eyes saw" — i.e., *Matan Torah* and the various miracles Hashem performed for us? *Sforno* explains that the Torah is warning us that even though the nations of the world will consider us wise and intelligent, we must still carefully keep ourselves separate from the non-Jewish nations, in order to protect ourselves from the potentially damaging effects of their influence and ways of thought.

Discussion Points:

❖ How can we truly avoid chillul Hashem? Many times, no matter what we do, there will be misunderstandings that are bound to lead to a chillul Hashem. Is there any way to prevent such things from happening?

❖ Many of the mitzvos we do, such as putting on tefillin, may look outlandish to outsiders. Should we be concerned about the fact that the nations of the world scoff at our religious practices? Are we responsible for the tension that seems to result automatically from our very different culture?

❖ As our communities expand, the people around us tend to feel intimidated and threatened by our growth. Can anything be done to prevent these hard feelings on the part of our non-Jewish neighbors?

❖ As our numbers increase, our need for financial aid and government support grows along with them. How can we advocate for our needs while not giving up our goal of creating a kiddush Hashem?

CHAPTER 5

TRUTH AND INTEGRITY

Shimon has just received a tantalizing credit-card offer in the mail. The credit-card company is running a promotion, and they are offering new customers the chance to earn double reward points for every dollar they spend during the first three months.

This seems like the opportunity he has been waiting for. Shimon has been dreaming about traveling to Eretz Yisrael with his entire family for Succos; he knows that it will be an incredibly uplifting experience, but he cannot possibly afford the airfare. With this new credit-card promotion, though, there is a way to pull it off. The only catch is that he would have to spend an extraordinary sum on the credit card in order to earn enough points to afford the tickets — but he is able to figure out a way to do it. He can create some manufactured spending by making purchases and receiving reimbursement; if he does that on a large scale, he will certainly earn enough points to cover the plane tickets. He hesitates, though, because he wonders if the credit-card company would approve of his idea. Is it dishonest, or is it a legitimate loophole in the system? Even if it is technically valid, does that make it the right thing to do? Could it create a chillul Hashem even though he is only a single customer? And does his intent to spend an uplifting Yom Tov in Eretz Yisrael outweigh the chillul Hashem that might result from this idea?

The Magnetic Pull of Honesty

One of the things that are most detrimental to *kevod Shamayim* is dishonesty. The *Sefer Hachinuch* states that there is nothing in the world as repulsive as *sheker*, falsehood. This is an aversion that is built into the human psyche. For this reason, the Torah warns us to "stay far away" from falsehood ("*midvar sheker tirchak"*); this is an expression that is not used about any other prohibition. Even more than that, *Chazal* admonish us to "stay far away" from anything that even resembles falsehood. It should come as no surprise, then, that Rabbeinu Yonah states (*Shaarei Teshuvah* 1:47) that one of the few ways to rectify a chillul Hashem is to be honest and promote truthfulness and integrity. Even if a lie seems justified or beneficial, a person who cares about Hashem's honor will steer clear of anything that smacks of dishonesty.

When we demonstrate honesty and integrity, we can have a decided impact on other people. The following incident illustrates this: Shmuel Goldberg (name changed) once needed to have an important package shipped from his home in Flatbush, and he failed to make it to the post office before it closed on Friday. On Sunday, when the post office is normally closed, he happened to drive past and noticed that the gates outside were open and a worker was loading packages onto a truck. Shmuel pulled up and asked the man if the office was open, but the worker told him that it wasn't. "We're actually here only because we are doing Sunday deliveries for Amazon," he explained.

"Would it be possible for you to do me a favor and accept this package anyway?" Shmuel asked politely. "It's very important." The worker looked at Shmuel, his gaze coming to rest on his *yarmulke*. To Shmuel's surprise, the worker asked if he knew Reb Abish Brodt. "Of course," Shmuel replied. "Everyone knows him!"

"In that case, I will do you the favor," the worker said. "I worked for Abish and his family for 17 years, and it was an incredible experience that I will never forget. They were the most honest and kind employers I ever had." After praising Reb Abish effusively, the non-Jewish postal worker suddenly launched into a rendition of Reb Abish's famous *niggun* for *Modeh Ani*, singing it with profound feeling.

If we commit ourselves to upholding the truth, then we will have a powerful influence not only on the non-Jews with whom we interact, but also on other Jews who are far removed from the

Torah. If we lead lives of integrity, decency, and honesty, then we will certainly cause other Jews to take pride in being part of such a wonderful nation, for no matter how far they have strayed from the path of Torah, they will still have a natural appreciation for ethical values.

Takeaway

The appreciation for honesty — and distaste for dishonesty — is built into the nature of every human being. When we deal honestly with others, we will gain an inordinate degree of respect. On the other hand, when we are dishonest, any other virtues we possess may lose their luster.

Making It Practical

- Make honesty your top priority. Be prepared to forgo small or even large sums of money in order to stick to your standards of integrity. In the long run it will be worthwhile.
- When you are involved in business dealings, consider it your mission to enlighten the world with your own display of honesty.

Capitalize with Caution

In today's trying economic climate, many businesses are more desperate than ever to generate interest in their products and services. We are all aware of the quantity of deals and promotions from numerous businesses—airlines, credit-card companies, car-rental agencies, websites, and many others—that have flooded the market in an effort to attract customers. And thanks to modern technology, consumers are often able to cash in on many more opportunities, from "special" prices created by computer glitches to bargains and promotional deals that are instantly shared with people all over the world.

While there is nothing wrong with taking advantage of these opportunities in a proper way, we must avoid the temptation to cash in on them in ways that are less than legitimate. The complex system that has been created in today's business world, with its many potential loopholes and opportunities for profit, can be highly alluring to those clever enough to work it to their advantage. For that very reason, though, the danger of chillul Hashem is all too great.

A person must invest careful thought and research to ascertain what business tactics are honest, legal, and *yashar* and are condoned by halachah and *hashkafah*, and to recognize the tactics that are illegal, are tantamount to theft, or wrongly take advantage of others' mistakes. Even if a certain endeavor isn't overtly dishonest, as a *rav* once noted, "Some things that are innocent and permissible when they begin can easily lead to much deceit and falsehood."

In recent years, many large-scale operations have begun offering the public their services to take advantage of the promotions used by large businesses to attract customers. They accomplish this through a number of methods, many of them very creative, that make it possible to reap handsome profits through those promotions, sometimes in ways that the companies offering them never intended.

Our objective is not to offer a definitive halachic ruling on the subject. This is simply a word of caution to consumers: No one should utilize the services of these businesses without proper halachic guidance! And there is another factor, as well: We must always take into account the repercussions of our actions on *kevod Shamayim*. Even if something is technically permissible, if it may result in a chillul Hashem, it should still be avoided at all costs.

Many of these innovative businesses are a sort of ticking time bomb that is bound, sooner or later, to create an explosion of chillul Hashem. Already, some people have suffered when various large companies caught on to these businesses' tactics, and many people have lost their bonus mileage, airline tickets, and so forth. There is a real danger that this may occur on a much larger scale, and if that happens, it may well become an ugly stain on our most prestigious communities and on the pride and glory of the Jewish people.[1]

The *Smag* warns us to take hold of "the seal of *Hakadosh Baruch Hu*, which is truth," and to meticulously refrain from deceiving anyone, Jew or non-Jew.[2] The temptations of the modern marketplace can be a tremendous *nisayon,* but we would be well advised to adopt standards of integrity and business conduct that will only serve to create a kiddush Hashem.

---

1. A number of *rabbanim* signed a letter warning of the potentially disastrous consequences of these business practices, which can create hatred toward Klal Yisrael on such a level that it may even reach the point of *pikuach nefesh.*
2. The *navi* tells us that in the times of Mashiach, "I will be exalted and I will be sanctified, and I will be recognized before the eyes of many nations, and they will know that I am Hashem" (*Yechezkel* 38:23). When Mashiach comes, the entire world will perceive the honor of Hashem with the greatest possible clarity. Which members of the Jewish people will live to experience that revelation of *kavod Shamayim*? The *navi* states (*Tzefaniah* 3:9-13): "The remnant of Yisrael will not commit injustice and will not speak falsehood, and deceptive speech will not be found in their mouths." When Mashiach comes, the only Jewish people who survive will be those who are not stained by corruption, who always display the fullest honesty and integrity.

Why is this the deciding factor? The *Smag* explains that the non-Jewish nations are not capable of perceiving the true value of the Torah and mitzvos of the Jewish people. They can discern the greatness of Klal Yisrael only through our external conduct, by the way we deal with other human beings. If Mashiach were to come for a nation that is not honest and upright in its business dealings, the nations of the world would be shocked; it would seem that the people who are beloved to Hashem are corrupt and disreputable, and this would lead to a massive chillul Hashem. Mashiach's arrival, with all of the wonders and miracles that will accompany it, must therefore be delayed until the Jewish people conduct themselves in a way that will lead to a proper kiddush Hashem.

*Using a loophole to game the system, even if it is
technically permitted by halachah, is strictly forbidden
if it would cause a chillul Hashem. When we take
advantage of sales and promotions, we must be extra
cautious to avoid anything that has the appearance of
dishonesty or exploitation.*

Making It Practical

- Before taking advantage of a promotion, sale, or other offer in a questionable way, ask yourself a few questions: *Am I being truthful? Am I fulfilling the criteria for this offer? If the company knew about what I am doing, would they be upset? If many other Jews are found to be doing the same thing, would it cause a chillul Hashem?*

- Even if the company offering the promotion is so large that your actions will probably go unnoticed, don't be too quick to assume that there is nothing wrong. Even if there is no issue of chillul Hashem, exploiting a promotion wrongfully could be considered a sin of *geneivah, geneivas daas,* or *sheker.*

Avoiding Ill-Gotten Gains

Aharon Margalit, the author of the autobiographical work *As Long as I Live*, was once offered a position representing the public on the judicial panel of the Beer Sheva Labor Court.

In order to decide whether to accept the position, he went with a friend to consult with Rav Shmuel HaLevi Wosner. Aharon's friend presented the various sides of the question to the renowned *posek*, pointing out that if he took the position, Aharon would be able to help other people who appealed rulings concerning benefits from the National Insurance Institute and other issues.

As soon as he heard this, Rav Wosner recoiled. He understood this to mean that Aharon would take advantage of loopholes in the law, a possibility that he could not tolerate. In his book, Aharon relates that the *rav* was opposed to him taking any actions that could even be perceived as dishonest. Rav Wosner warned him in the strongest terms to be careful never to cause a chillul Hashem and never to bend the law, even slightly. "Your mission will be to make a kiddush Hashem," Rav Wosner told him. "Always try to reach a compromise" (*As Long as I Live*, pages 224-225).[3]

The Gemara relates that the first question asked of a person in the *Beis Din shel Maalah* is, "Were you honest in your business dealings?" The *Pri Megadim* (*Orach Chaim* 156:3) questions this statement: We are taught that *talmud Torah* is equivalent to all the other mitzvos. Shouldn't the first question asked of a person be whether he has set aside time to learn Torah? The *Pri Megadim* answers that if a person does not act with integrity in his financial dealings, then if he is a *talmid chacham* who has amassed much Torah knowledge, it will actually make his sin worse. A learned person who is dishonest would be guilty of an

---

3. Rather than exploiting loopholes, in fact, *Chazal* strongly advise us to deal with others in a way that is *lifnim mishuras hadin* — beyond the letter of the law. The Gemara states (*Bava Metzia* 30b) that Yerushalayim was destroyed because of the Jews' failure to practice this ideal. Rav Mattisyahu Salomon explains that in Yerushalayim, the holy city of Torah and *tzaddikim*, acting *lifnim mishuras hadin* is not merely a virtuous thing to do; it is an actual obligation. The pious Jews of Yerushalayim are required to constantly bring honor and glory to Hashem's Name, and the failure to act *lifnim mishuras hadin* may often lead to the exact opposite: the grievous sin of chillul Hashem. Rav Mattisyahu adds that this is true today for *bnei Torah* everywhere: There is a mandate to go beyond the letter of the law in order to avoid any possibility of chillul Hashem.

even greater chillul Hashem than that created by a person who is not as well versed in the Torah. Therefore, even before a person is judged on his learning, he must be judged on his integrity.

People often rationalize their acts of dishonesty or exploiting legal loopholes with justifications that seem excellent, even commendable. Some might feel the need to make extra money to support their families and pay tuition; others might wish to earn extra airline miles to visit Eretz Yisrael. But to Rav Avrohom Pam there was no greater contradiction than trying to advance a worthy cause through dishonest gain. In the *sefer Moreh Tzedek*, Rav Pam railed against the practice of using deceit for the sake of financial gain. Misleading others in any way, he stressed, is absolutely prohibited. He condemned even those institutions that sought to cut corners or misrepresent some aspects of their programming for the sake of funding. Despite the fact that their intentions were certainly *l'Shem Shamayim* — so that they would be able to continue to teach Torah — that did not justify their actions. "Is there any obligation to spread Torah through behavior that is the antithesis of the Torah?" Rav Pam asked rhetorically, emphasizing that this actually brings disgrace to the Torah.

Moshe Rothschild was an affluent businessman who was known for his honesty. Bankers and investors alike knew that when Moshe gave his word, there was no need for them even to have him sign any papers; whatever he promised or assured them was always carried out. Moshe once shared the following incredible story, which demonstrates the lengths to which a person must go in order to avoid chillul Hashem: At one point, he was facing the threat of bankruptcy, when he realized that he had a way to put aside no less than one billion dollars, in such a way that the banks would be unable to take the money from him. The transaction was completely legal, but it involved taking advantage of a loophole. Moshe consulted a *rav* in Eretz Yisrael to determine whether it was permissible to do it.

The *rav* asked if his actions might ever become public knowledge and be viewed as dishonest or distasteful. Moshe replied that it was indeed possible, and the *rav* ruled that he should not do it. Even the possibility of a chillul Hashem, he stressed, must be avoided at all costs. Even though such a large sum, in the hands of a generous philanthropist like Moshe, could have been put to excellent use for the Jewish people, there is never an excuse to take the risk of causing a chillul Hashem, even for reasons that are purely *l'Shem Shamayim* — because Hashem's honor is far more precious than all the money in the world.

Takeaway

Bnei Torah have a special obligation to act lifnim mishuras hadin, displaying integrity even beyond the letter of the law; if they fail to do this, the benefits of their Torah itself may be endangered. One should never risk a chillul Hashem even for the sake of a very worthy cause.

Making It Practical

- Find a rav who is sensitive to the issues of kiddush Hashem and chillul Hashem, and make sure to consult with him regularly about the issues you confront in business or in your other financial dealings.

Making Hashem's Name Blessed

The words *"yehei shemeih rabba mevorach,"* which are an intrinsic part of every Kaddish, are the embodiment of every Jew's deepest desire: for Hashem's great Name to be recognized throughout the world, and for Him to be honored and respected by all of mankind. In essence, this *tefillah* is our plea for success in our mission to create kiddush Hashem.

Chazal teach us that the *tefillah* of *"yehei shemeih rabba mevorach"* has the greatest power when it is recited *"b'kol kocho"*: with all of one's strength. This does not mean that the words must be shouted as loudly as possible. Rather, it means that one's *commitment* to the ideal should be complete and absolute. When a person says these words, he should recognize that he is pledging to channel everything in his power — all of his energies and material assets — into creating a kiddush Hashem.

Among other things, this includes maintaining honesty and integrity at all times. If we are willing to give up any sum of money or other material possessions in order to avoid dishonesty, then we can achieve an extraordinary degree of *kiddush Shem Shamayim*. This is a virtue that should be emphasized to children even at a young age. When a person is young, he will encounter many small tests of his honesty, but as he grows older, the stakes become much higher. It is therefore important for a person to instill this value in himself when he is young, so that he will be able to resist the much more powerful temptations of dishonesty later in life.

Rav Yaakov Kamenetsky once expelled a *bachur* from his yeshivah for cheating on a state exam, and that young man was quickly accepted by another yeshivah. Years later, he was exposed as having committed a massive fraud, and his picture appeared on the front pages of dozens of newspapers. When that scandal came out, Rav Yaakov commented that the chillul Hashem was the responsibility of the yeshivah that had accepted him immediately, without allowing him to learn the lesson that even "small" acts of cheating can have negative consequences. The minor offenses of his youth paved the way for a descent into much worse criminal behavior later in his life.

We are all familiar with the story of Rabbi Noach Muroff, the *rebbi* from New Haven, Connecticut, who found a whopping $98,000 in a secondhand desk he had purchased, and returned the cash to its rightful owner. Rabbi Muroff once told me that his actions were inspired by a certain Rabbi Adler, a distinguished businessman who had been a *talmid* of Rav Yaakov Kamenetsky and whose top priority in life was honesty. Rabbi Muroff spent a good deal of time with Rabbi Adler in his earlier years, and the older man's example had left an indelible imprint on his own personality. Rabbi Adler himself attributed his emphasis on honesty to the example of his *rebbi*, Rav Yaakov Kamenetsky.

As a child matures into an adult, he will face many tests of his commitment to honesty. Will he try to save money by taking advantage of a sale to which he isn't entitled? Will he abide by the return policy of a store, or will he ignore the fine print when it suits him? Rental cars, mileage points, and credit cards each offer their own enticements to stretch the truth for the sake of financial gain. And a commitment to the truth may mean sacrificing hundreds of thousands of dollars in taxes or benefits from government programs, way beyond the amount sacrificed by Rabbi Muroff. But if we make these sacrifices for the sake of kiddush Hashem, then we will earn enormous *zechuyos* as a result. Let us be the *anshei emes*, the people of truth, who can truly light up the world.

Takeaway

The path to a life of honesty begins with learning at a young age to make small sacrifices for the sake of the truth. When a child is taught to do that, he will be ready to resist much greater temptations later in his life.

Making It Practical

- When you recite the words *"yehei shemeih rabba mevorach,"* have in mind that you are committing yourself to lead a life of honesty and integrity even when it entails financial sacrifice.

Discussion Points:

❖ Why is a person's level of honesty one of the most critical factors in determining whether he will create a kiddush Hashem or chillul Hashem?

❖ What guidelines should one follow with regard to taking advantage of promotions, sales, and store return policies?

❖ Is it acceptable to utilize legal loopholes with regard to monetary matters? What about exploiting a loophole in order to earn money that will be used for a very important cause?

CHAPTER 6

KIDDUSH HASHEM BEHIND CLOSED DOORS

It is late at night, and Rivky is reflecting on the day that has just ended. All in all, she is satisfied with her accomplishments. In the morning, she helped her mother care for her siblings, and she davened quietly in her room with a decent level of kavannah. She also wrote out a large check to an organization from her maaser account. She was very patient with her elderly neighbor, who spent an hour regaling her with stories about her childhood. She takes pride that she overcame the temptation to watch a YouTube video while she was busy with her online schooling. As she prepares to turn in for the night, Rivky congratulates herself on her achievements; she feels that she has proven herself to be very strong and growing in her avodas Hashem, and she is even proud that most of her good deeds that day will remain unknown to anyone else. But then she becomes troubled by a nagging thought: With all of her good deeds, did she play any role in creating a kiddush Hashem? Are any of the wonderful things that she did behind closed doors considered a valuable part of Klal Yisrael's mission in the world?

Kiddush Hashem from Within

Sometimes, even the most mundane object can serve as a powerful *mashal*. Take the case of a thermos, for instance. When the heat of a thermos's contents cannot be felt from outside, it means that it was manufactured well; the thermos traps the heat inside, maintaining the temperature of its contents. A poorly constructed thermos, though, will allow the heat of its contents to escape, and thus to be felt from the outside.

Similarly, Rav Shimon Schwab teaches that the true righteousness and sanctity of a *tzaddik* is never revealed to the outside world. "We only see the tip of the iceberg, never fathoming the depths of the *tzaddik*'s true essence," he states (*Rav Schwab on Chumash*). What we see of the greatness of our *tzaddikim* is only a fraction of the greatness that lies within them; if too much of that inner "warmth" is visible to the world, it may mean that the *tzaddik* is "cooling off" on the inside.[1]

On Shabbos and Yom Tov, toward the end of *Pesukei DeZimrah* in the Nusach Ashkenaz *davening*, we declare, "*B'kerev kedoshim tiskadash.*" We generally understand these words to mean, "Among the holy ones You will be sanctified," but Rav Schwab offers a different interpretation of the phrase: "*From within* the holy ones You will be sanctified." In other words, true kiddush Hashem comes not from any outer display of piety or devotion, but rather from the core of righteousness that exists *within* the *kedoshim*. In order to create kiddush Hashem a person must have a genuine relationship with Hashem: a relationship that exists within his heart and soul. He must feel an emotional connection to Hashem; he must be truly devoted to Him, and not merely serve Him in a superficial way.

One sign of a true connection to Hashem is when a person performs good deeds that are not observed by any other human being. These actions become a secret of sorts between the person performing the mitzvos and Hashem Himself. This was an ideal that Rav Tzvi Michel Shapira of Yerushalayim, a great *tzaddik* and

---

1. Rav Schwab finds support for his statement in an incredible insight: In *Parashas Vayechi*, after Yosef takes an oath that he will bury his father in Eretz Yisrael, the Torah relates that Yaakov Avinu bowed down. Rashi explains that this was a display of gratitude for the fact that all of his children, even Yosef, were righteous. This seems to indicate that it was only at this time that Yaakov recognized Yosef as a *tzaddik*. Why didn't he perceive it earlier?

To answer this question, Rav Schwab suggests that Yosef had kept his righteousness concealed throughout the years until that moment. As the *Targum* tells us (ibid. 49:24), "Yosef's prophecy was fulfilled because he kept his observance of the Torah concealed." We are taught that Yosef is considered the ultimate *tzaddik* and is termed "*yesod olam*" ("the foundation of the world"); this, too, indicates the fact that his greatness was hidden, just as the foundation of a building is mostly concealed by the ground. It was only at the end of Yaakov's life, Rav Schwab concludes, that he recognized Yosef's greatness, for when Yosef took an oath in his presence, his entire body trembled with awe as he uttered Hashem's Name. This is a *tzaddik*'s automatic reaction to taking an oath, and Yosef's involuntary display of *yiras Shamayim* revealed his true nature.

talmid of Rav Yehoshua Leib Diskin, often strove to achieve. Rav Tzvi Michel made a concerted effort to conceal his greatness from others; it was said that while he attached exceptional value to every mitzvah, he considered a mitzvah performed in private to be worth a hundred times as much as one that was done in public. Rav Tzvi Michel made a practice of getting up at midnight, clandestinely immersing in a *mikveh*, and then learning for the remainder of the night, out of sight of his neighbors and friends. If he ever spotted other people in the street at that hour, he would hide in an alley to prevent them from seeing him. As he grew older, it became increasingly difficult for him to catch sight of other people on the street and hide from them before they could see him; instead, the other Jews of Meah Shearim themselves began to hide, to prevent Rav Tzvi Michel from seeing *them*, so that he would not be distressed by the fact that he had been discovered.

The ideal, then, is to perform mitzvos and acts of *kedushah* in private, without being witnessed by others. But even if the actions themselves are kept out of view of others, the sanctity they create will become obvious to others as well, just as Rav Tzvi Michel's neighbors recognized his lofty spiritual level.[2]

Even a non-Jew can sense when a Jew has risen to a high spiritual level. During the Holocaust, a man with blond hair, blue eyes, and a distinctly Aryan appearance was once herded into a cattle car along with many other Jews and deported to a concentration camp. The other Jews in the car questioned why he hadn't passed himself off as a non-Jew to escape deportation, and the man gave a chilling response. "I am a convert, and I want to die with my nation," he explained. "On Motzaei Yom Kippur after *Ne'ilah*, I saw all the Jews leaving the *shuls*, and there was something

---

2. In *Pirkei Avos*, the Mishnah states, "Anyone who is pleasing to the spirit of other people will be pleasing to Hashem." Why does the mishnah emphasize that such a person is pleasing "to the *spirit* of other people"? Rav Yosef Yaavetz explains that the message of this mishnah is that every human being has a spiritual sense that detects when other people's actions are pleasing to Hashem. When a person is genuinely righteous, when his actions in private are worthy of Divine approval, *kedushah* radiates from him and is sensed by the "spirit" of his fellow man.

incredible about them. These were simple working men, whom I knew from my workplace, yet they were glowing like angels after the Yom Kippur *davening*. When I saw that, I knew that I wanted to be part of this nation, no matter what."[3]

Every Jew should keep in mind that the key to kiddush Hashem lies not only in our visible actions, but in the relationship with Hashem that we create *within ourselves*. As we have seen, Hashem is sanctified *"b'kerev kedoshim"* — through the inner essence of His "holy ones." May we have the privilege of being among them.

Takeaway

When we hide some of our righteousness, it ensures that our piety is deeply rooted within our hearts, and that it is real and sincere.

Making It Practical

- Make a habit of performing one mitzvah or *chessed* every day in private, without telling anyone else about it. This will help build your inner relationship with Hashem.

---

3. Many of the Jewish people's great *tzaddikim* have displayed this dichotomy, concealing incredible depths of greatness while still being recognized by others as unique, holy people. Such was the case, for instance, with Rav Yaakov Kamenetsky. Once, a *talmid* who stayed in Rav Yaakov's home for two weeks was asked if he had noticed Rav Yaakov engaging in any unique or unusual practices, to which he responded, "Nothing at all. Everything he did was so simple." It was only later, when that *talmid* learned many of the intricate halachos of *netilas yadayim*, that he recognized that there was tremendous significance even in the way that Rav Yaakov washed his hands. But despite the many lofty calculations that were involved in Rav Yaakov's behavior, he gave no indication of them to others.

At the same time, those who came in contact with Rav Yaakov recognized that there was something unique and holy about him. Rav Yaakov once arrived in Chicago on a commercial flight, which was greeted by a group of 75 schoolchildren in honor of his arrival. When a stewardess, astonished by the crowd, was informed of which passenger the children had come to greet, she voiced her understanding. "I could see from his eyes that he is a great man," she said (from *Rav Yaakov*, by Yonason Rosenblum).

Out of the Limelight

In the previous section, we explained that in order for a person to influence others, he must first have a genuine, heartfelt connection of his own to the Master of the Universe. As we will see, there is much to be learned in this regard from an unexpected somewhat surprising source: the role of women in Yiddishkeit.

The Gemara (*Moed Kattan* 16a) states that a person should always be modest, even in his Torah study. This is learned from the *pasuk* that teaches that one of the things Hashem expects of us is "walking modestly with your G-d." The Gemara points out that the Torah is compared to the human thigh; just as the thigh is covered and hidden from view, so too one's Torah learning should be hidden and should not take place publicly.

Why must we hide our Torah study? The *Maharal* explains that when something is made public, it automatically becomes less real, losing some of its inner meaning. Something that is visible to the world will inevitably become physical in nature and will lose its spiritual qualities. Therefore, there is a danger that it may become an empty shell, devoid of inner meaning. Torah learning that is done publicly may be tainted by ulterior motives; a person may learn Torah simply to compete with others, to develop a scholarly image, or to accommodate other external pressures, rather than as an expression of his own true being.

In order to have a true, intimate relationship with Hashem, a person should perform His mitzvos in a private fashion. The less visible his actions are to others, the more spiritual they will be.

Some people believe that the primary reason women are not given a public role in *davening* and are otherwise kept out of the public eye is to prevent men who see them from having sinful thoughts. In truth, though, there is a much more fundamental reason.

The female nature itself — and therefore the *avodah* of a woman — revolves around the internal. A woman's main power is her ability to internalize; her strength lies in her inner relationship with Hashem. Thus, her *avodas Hashem* takes place quietly; she *davens* behind a *mechitzah* and in a hushed tone, and she does not sport prominent physical signs of her religion that would be comparable to a man's *peyos* or beard. Women are also exempt from many *mitzvos asei* that are performed in a public forum. Because a woman's ability to internalize is her main feature, her function is to internalize all of her husband's accomplishments and spiritual growth, and to make them real. This is the meaning of the *pasuk* "*kol kevudah bas melech penimah* — the entire honor of the king's daughter is within." Every Jewish woman, as a daughter of the King, is "honored" primarily by what she accomplishes "within"; her strength lies in her *pnimiyus*. A woman's *tefillos* are valued, and possibly even more potent than those of a man, precisely because they are not visible to others.[4]

Even a man must practice a degree of privacy in his *avodas Hashem*; he should learn Torah and performing mitzvos without looking for the approval of others, to ensure that his service of Hashem truly has inner meaning.[5] Rav Shimon Schwab's grand-

---

4. As we all know, a boy's *bar mitzvah* is celebrated with a festive *seudas mitzvah*. This is based on the Gemara's teaching in *Maseches Kiddushin* that performing a mitzvah in which one is obligated is a greater act than doing a mitzvah from which one is exempt. Because of this concept, when a boy reaches the age at which he is obligated to observe the mitzvos, a celebration is in order, because all of his mitzvos then become much more valuable. In light of this reasoning, it would seem that a girl's twelfth birthday should also be marked with a *seudas mitzvah*. Why isn't a *seudah* recommended for a girl as well?

Rav Moshe Feinstein (*Igros Moshe*, O.C. II, 97) explains that a boy's transition to adulthood results in visible changes in his life; for instance, he becomes eligible to be counted for a *minyan*. Since the boy's new status as an adult is visible to others, it is also celebrated in a visible way. A girl, on the other hand, makes no outwardly visible changes when she becomes an adult, and the *simchah* of the occasion is also kept private, even though it is an equally joyous occasion.

We can explain Rav Moshe's statement on a deeper level, as well. It is not by chance that a woman's *avodas Hashem* is barely noticeable to others, and that no visible changes in her life occur at her *bas mitzvah*. A woman was meant to serve Hashem on an internal level; that is her defining quality, and her service of Hashem therefore consists of private actions. It would therefore be counterproductive to celebrate her entrance into adulthood with a public *seudah*.

5. Once we have this understanding, it may become even more baffling that the

son once related that when he came home from Eretz Yisrael with many new *chumros*, his grandfather warned him, "If others know about your *chumros*, they will not be worth much at all." It is also said that the Alter of Kelm had certain insights into the Torah that he did not share with others; he kept those ideas to himself as part of a private spiritual inventory.

This is an important message for all of us, but especially for *rabbanim*, *mechanchim*, and *mekarvim*, those who are charged with teaching Torah to others in a more public setting. Even if a person's role in society places him in the public eye, he should always see to it that some part of his *avodas Hashem*, of his learning or mitzvah observance, remains private and internal, and is not meant for others to observe. That is the only way that he will be able to maintain the relationship with Hashem that is a key to influencing and inspiring others.

Takeaway

Before a person can be a leader of others, he must first become a "leader" to himself. The avodah of women is a model of the type of internal relationship with Hashem that all of us, in some way, should include in our lives — and that is a key to creating a kiddush Hashem.

Making It Practical

- If you are a man, even though you generally daven in *shul*, make a point of saying a personal *tefillah* every day in total privacy. That *tefillah* will always remain between you and Hashem.

---

avodas Hashem of a man is as overt as it is. It would seem that a woman's quiet, unobtrusive service of Hashem is superior; doesn't the public nature of a man's religious observance lend itself to performing the mitzvos with ulterior motives? This is not a question that can be answered fully in this context, but we certainly must recognize that the requirement for *tznius* indeed applies, at least on some level, to men as well.

Not Just Tradition

Many years ago, Rav Shimon Schwab was visited by the president of a Conservative synagogue in Baltimore. This took place at the time of the coronation of Queen Elizabeth II of England, and the visitor commented about the media hoopla surrounding the event and the attention that had been focused on the ancient traditions and historic artifacts involved in the process. Pointing to it as a parallel to Conservative Judaism, he challenged Rav Schwab, "I also keep traditional Judaism. I even put on my *tefillin* every day. Why are you opposed to my movement?"

Rav Schwab calmly replied, "I have very little interest in traditional Judaism. In fact, I could do without it entirely. The fact that my father did something doesn't mean that I have to do the same thing."

The visitor was shocked. "But then why do you put on *tefillin* every day, if you aren't interested in upholding traditional Judaism?" he demanded.

Rav Schwab replied, "I wear *tefillin* because Hashem wants *me* to wear *tefillin* at that very moment. I am happy that my ancestors have kept the laws of the Torah for many generations, but that is not the reason I do so. I observe the mitzvos not because of tradition, but because that is what Hashem wants me to do right now" (from *Rav Schwab on Prayer*).

In order for today's generation to withstand the trials of our times, to remain faithful to Yiddishkeit and even to influence others, it is crucial for every person to develop a genuine, personal connection with Yiddishkeit.

A certain *kiruv* professional who is deeply involved in anti-missionary work often delivers lectures to Observant audiences, in which he begs parents to strive to make Yiddishkeit more genuine and meaningful to their children. Otherwise, he warns, they may readily give it up when they are tempted by foolish alternatives. He often tells a chilling story: A mother once called him in hysterics and told him that she had found a copy of a non-Jewish religious book under her daughter's mattress. When she questioned her daughter about it, the young lady admitted that she had become interested in that movement and had become a loyal member. The mother was panicked and begged the *kiruv* worker for help.

The man visited the family and spoke with the daughter. His first step was to ask about how she had become interested in the movement.

"My roommate in college once gave me some materials to read," she explained. "I wasn't interested at first, but one day I was feeling very lonely and dejected, so I started reading them. While I was reading, I came across a verse that touched my soul so deeply and spoke to my feelings so intensely that I felt an immediate, powerful connection. I decided right away that this was the correct path for me, and I have been loyal to them ever since."

"And what was this deeply moving verse?" the *kiruv* worker asked.

The girl's tone grew hushed and reverent. "It said, 'You shall love your G-d with all of your heart and all of your soul.'" Little did she know that this "verse" was actually a *pasuk* from the Torah that she had callously abandoned. Unfortunately, her parents had failed to give her a proper Jewish education, and the results had been disastrous.

As Rav Schwab taught his visitor, a Jew must be faithful to his *mesorah*, but not only because it is his tradition. Every Jew must take ownership of that *mesorah*, recognizing that Yiddishkeit is not merely the religion of his ancestors, but his own personal faith as well.

In *Sefer Tehillim*, David HaMelech states, "*Kol haneshamah tehallel K-ah.*" These words can be understood in two different ways: either that *every* soul in the world will praise Hashem, or that the *entire* soul of a single human being will praise Him. Rav Shraga Feivel Mendlowitz taught that both of these explanations are in fact one and the same: Any person who channels his entire soul into serving and bringing honor to Hashem will succeed in influencing others to do so as well.

It is not enough to rely on our mesorah as a reason to cling to Yiddishkeit. A Jew must develop an intense, personal connection to Yiddishkeit to the point that it fills his entire neshamah. Once that happens, it will certainly spill over to influence others as well.

Making It Practical

- Take one mitzvah that you have always done by rote — whether it is *tefillin, tzitzis,* or Shabbos observance — and make it "yours." This can be done by making your own unique addition to the mitzvah, whether it is a short *tefillah* before you perform the mitzvah or some *chumra* connected to it.

Subtle Impressions

Rabbi Eli Bernstein (name changed) arrived at his first Toastmasters meeting with a degree of trepidation. A friend had pointed out that his public speaking skills could use some improvement and had recommended that he join one of the organization's weekly groups. As he found himself about to meet the non-Jews who would be the other members of the group, Rabbi Bernstein grew nervous. How would they interact with a visibly religious Jew, he wondered, and what sort of impression would he make on them?

Toastmasters is an international organization dedicated to helping its members improve their leadership and public speaking skills. At every group meeting, the participants deliver speeches that are then evaluated in writing by all the other members. One member is assigned to count the number of times a speaker says "ah" or "um," while another listens for grammatical errors. From time to time, one member of the group chooses a topic, and every person is expected to deliver an impromptu speech on that subject for two minutes. Rabbi Bernstein was pleased that he had found a group made up of older people with a sense of moral values, but he was still slightly apprehensive.

Fortunately, the club meetings turned out to be very productive. The rabbi was pleased to find that he had earned the respect of the members of the group, who took an interest in helping him. One of his new friends even became his private mentor, helping him prepare his speeches and offering him tips on how to improve his technique.

Rabbi Bernstein told me that he was surprised by some of the reactions he received from the group's members. Although he made a point of steering clear of any discussion of religion, the rest of the group somehow picked up on his moral and ethical standards. One day, one of the group members used an inappropriate word during a presentation. The very next day, Rabbi Bernstein received the following message by e-mail from the president of the group: "I apologize for Larry's outburst in his Table Topics speech last week. As standing president, I will note that we simply do not use that language in Toastmasters International, as he is already well aware, as an elder in this club. His disrespect for the club is something I can try and address. But the disrespect displayed in front of a holy man is something that may not be able to be redressed once it has occurred."

"I didn't utter a peep when Larry used those words," Rabbi Bernstein told me, "and I don't think I even made a face. Somehow, though, they recognized that it wasn't appropriate to use that sort of language in front of a Yid."

After he had been a member of the group for several months, Rabbi Bernstein became too busy to attend the sessions. After he announced that he was leaving, he received several farewell letters from the group's members. One of the more memorable notes came from his self-appointed mentor. "Dear Rabbi Bernstein," the man wrote. "You are the first Rabbi I have ever met, and it has been a true pleasure to get to know you over the past few months. Your perspective, shown in every thought-provoking speech you have given, is worthy of contemplation. I consider you a holy man, and I have never known anyone else I would place in that category. I am honored to have been able to be in a position to mentor someone I hold in such high esteem. This Toastmasters group was lucky to have had you in our midst every Wednesday. I am so glad that you came to be with us and to learn all that you did. May you hold these speech lessons close. Please know that you have left a sizable fan club behind."

The strongest impressions we make on others are often through nonverbal communication. Our subconscious facial expressions and body language often convey much more than the spoken word. When we speak, others cannot be certain if we are being sincere; even when we talk about certain ideals or moral standards, our listeners cannot always tell that our words reflect our inner essence. But when we reflect our standards and values through subtle signs — as Rabbi Bernstein did — the effects can be enormous. This often takes place without any intention on our part; we are not aware of it, but we radiate the signs of the ideals we have absorbed. We may also never even be aware of the extent of the impact we have made, until we come to the Next World, where we will be pleasantly surprised by what we have accomplished.

Our task as Jews is not only to "talk the talk" but also to "walk the walk." When we are the same virtuous people both in the privacy of our homes and in our dealings with the outside world, then even our subtlest actions or mannerisms will demonstrate the beauty of our religion.

Making It Practical

- Start noticing if your behavior toward others is the same in private and in public. Make sure that you relate to your wife and children in the same way you would act with an important client.

- Make an effort to be consistent in your attitudes at home and in the outside world. Write down some of the differences that you notice and choose one area to improve upon each week.

Spiritual Radiation

On April 26, 1986, an explosion took place at the Chernobyl Nuclear Power Plant in the town of Pripyat, Ukraine, which was then part of the Soviet Union. The explosion filled the air with massive quantities of radiation, whose devastating results would be felt for years to come. Countless people suffered and contracted severe illnesses from the effects of this invisible radiation; even thirty years later, the degree to which it contributed to cancer and other diseases had not been fully determined.

Thanks to modern science, we are all aware of the ability of invisible, almost undetectable particles or rays to wreak havoc on our bodies, our environment, and our lives. But what many people do not realize is that this concept has a parallel in the spiritual world: Just as there are forms of physical radiation that can harm or even kill, there is a sort of spiritual "radiation" in the world that can even lead to grave sins.

A man once confided in the Chazon Ish that he felt a constant desire to listen to radio programs. "I know it's not good for my children's *chinuch*," he added, "and I don't want them to be exposed or affected by it. I have therefore taken it upon myself never to listen to the radio in their presence. I turn on radio programs only when I am in private, and no one else can hear."

If the man expected the *gadol hador* to be impressed, he was certainly disappointed by the Chazon Ish's response. "You are making a grave mistake," the Chazon Ish told him. "You should not delude yourself that your children will not be affected by this. Anything you do, even in private, seeps into the walls of your home, and it will inevitably have an impact on the children who are raised in that environment" (*Sefer Tocho Ratzuf Ahavah, Parashas Noach*).

We all understand that when a person commits an *aveirah* publicly, it is bound to affect others, decreasing their sensitivity to that sin and even inspiring some to copy his actions. But the *Beis HaLevi* (*Parashas Noach*) teaches that even a sin committed in private can affect others in the same way. Just as the sinner's own lusts are strengthened and his sensitivities dulled by his sin, others around him are affected in the same way. An *aveirah* not only creates a stronger desire within the sinner to commit the act, it also infuses that desire into the atmosphere, like a spiritual "radiation" created by his misdeeds. The *Beis HaLevi* uses this concept to explain why even the animals were corrupted by the sins of the *dor hamabul*: Even though animals are creatures of instinct and do not have freedom of choice, they were affected by the sins of the generation and therefore began to engage in perverse behavior. All the more so, he concludes, an *aveirah* can affect other people, even if they do not witness it being committed.

Takeaway

When a person sins, even in private, it creates a natural pull toward that sin that may cause others to stumble, thus resulting in a chillul Hashem.

Making It Practical

- Think of something that you would never do in front of your children, but that you are not careful to avoid when they are not looking, and train yourself to be consistent in that area.

An Invisible Impact

There is an incredible true story that is told by Rav Elya Lopian. During Rav Elya's time in the Yeshivah of Lomza, a strange phenomenon took place at the local hospital: A series of patients who were admitted with various illnesses began coming down with other, unrelated diseases that caused even greater harm to their bodies. As the scope of the problem became clear, a group of famous doctors from Warsaw were called in to invcs-tigate the situation. The doctors spent weeks studying the issue until they finally announced that they had solved the mystery: The hospital building had been in use for so many decades that its walls had absorbed countless disease-inducing germs, and the viruses and bacteria infesting the hospital walls were now infecting many of the new patients. The only solution, the team of experts announced, was for the hospital building to be demolished and a new, uncontaminated building to be built in its place. Rav Elya explains that this is an apt metaphor for the spiritual world: Every *aveirah* has spiritual effects, just like the impact of physical germs, that spread to other people around the sinner and break down their spiritual defenses.

The *Beis HaLevi* adds that the spiritual fallout of a sin causes certain transgressions to be more common in specific places. In an area where a particular *aveirah* is very common, people will feel an increased desire to engage in that sin, and every country has its own unique desires. Like a nuclear explosion, the con-stant repetition of a sin can poison the atmosphere in the coun-try where it takes place.

But just as an *aveirah* can have such a destructive effect, a good deed can create a pull toward positive change. Once, dur-ing a visit to a certain city in Russia toward the end of his life, the Chofetz Chaim asked to be taken to a specific address. He was pleased to find a *shul* at the location, and as soon as he saw it, he stated that he was ready to return to his host. The Chofetz Chaim explained to the puzzled *talmidim* who had accompanied him, "Forty years ago, I was visiting this city during Elul. Early one morning, as I was walking to *shul* for *Selichos*, I heard the sound of impassioned weeping coming from one of the homes. I knocked on the door of the home, and a woman answered; I explained that I had heard her crying and I wanted to know if she needed help.

"The woman replied through her tears, 'I am Jewish, but I never learned how to read Hebrew and I can't *daven* from a sid-dur. At this time, when everyone else is *davening Selichos*, I am praying to Hashem from the depths of my heart, even though I do not know the words. I hope that Hashem will listen to my cries just as He accepts the prayers of those who can read from a printed text.'

"As soon as I heard that," the Chofetz Chaim said, "I knew that that woman's emotional *tefillos* would have a major impact on that place. Now that many years have gone by, I wanted to see the impact of the *kedushah* she created. Sure enough, it gave rise to a *shul*, where even greater *kedushah* will be present."

Just as there are many invisible forces in the physical world, all of our actions, whether they occur in public or in private, create undetectable spiritual forces that affect not only us but others as well. The day will soon come when we will be able to sense the spiritual forces radiating from our deeds. If we use these forces properly, we will surely be rewarded for the actions of the many others who were inspired by the positive "radiation" of our mitzvos.

Takeaway

All of our positive actions or successes in refraining from sin, even behind closed doors, create an invisible pull that inspires others to conduct themselves similarly.

Making It Practical

- Talk to your children and students about how their actions affect others even when they are done in private.
- Speak to them about the impact of their choices when they look at certain things or use technology in certain ways.
- Use the metaphor of invisible germs or radiation and positive clean air to illustrate the effects of reducing or increasing our *kedushah*.

The Sound of Thunder

The Gemara (*Pesachim* 87b) teaches, "Hashem exiled the Jewish people among the nations only so that converts would be added to them." Rav Gedaliah Schorr, in *Ohr Gedalyahu*, explains that there are many holy *neshamos* among the nations of the world, and the Jewish people were sent into *galus* in order to gather all of these souls and absorb them into their midst. This seems to contradict the idea that the *galus* is a result of our sins. We always assume that Bnei Yisrael would not have gone into exile if they hadn't sinned, but then how would those lost souls have been brought to the Jewish people?

Rav Schorr explains that, if not for Klal Yisrael's sins, they would have exuded such powerful *kedushah* that all the "sparks of holiness" in the outside world would have been drawn to the Jewish nation on their own, as if to a powerful magnet. *Kedushah*, he explains, exerts a pull even from a distance; the more intense the *kedushah*, the farther is its reach. And the *kedushah* that existed when the Torah was given at Har Sinai was so powerful that its magnetism even reached the land of Midian and "pulled" Yisro toward the Jewish people, something that even the miracles in Mitzrayim and at the *Yam Suf* had not been able to accomplish.

Chazal teach us that the thundering sounds that were heard at *Matan Torah*, which drew Yisro to convert and join the Jewish people, continue to be heard throughout the generations. Wherever people learn Torah, they create "sound waves" of *kedushah*, waves of spiritual influence that have the ability to draw in sparks of holiness from far away. And the power of that *kedushah* grows stronger as the Torah learning gains intensity.

Even in *galus*, we can still create this effect: through our Torah study. Rav Gedaliah Schorr explains that the reason that we see so many lost Jews returning to the fold is that a tremendous amount of *kedushah* and Torah learning has blossomed within Klal Yisrael in our days, which subtly influences them to return to Yiddishkeit.

As we have already seen, kiddush Hashem is not dependent

solely on the way we behave in the streets, in our offices, and in our other interactions with non-Jews or irreligious Jews. Our Torah learning and the *kedushah* we create in the privacy of our homes and yeshivos also generates a current of interest in Yiddishkeit and in the Torah. Through the "thunder" of our Torah learning, we dissolve the barriers that block our influence from spreading to others.

The *navi* Yeshayah (2:2-4) teaches us that at the End of Days, all the nations of the world will "stream" to the House of Hashem, "for the Torah will come forth from Tzion, and the Word of Hashem from Yerushalayim." By stating that the people will "stream" to Yerushalayim, the *navi* compares their movement to that of a rushing river; just as the flow of a river is determined by the natural pull of gravity, the nations of the world will be drawn to Yerushalayim by the natural force created by the Torah learning and sanctity of the Jewish people. On a smaller scale, we can also create a natural force that attracts others to everything that is sacred, simply by applying ourselves to study of the Torah.

Takeaway

Torah study creates a special magnetic pull that ignites sparks of kedushah in the hearts of others.

Making It Practical

- Think of ways that you can create an atmosphere in your home that is conducive to Torah study and the Torah lifestyle. Teach your children about the "thunder" of Torah learning, so that they will appreciate what they can accomplish by learning a Mishnah, a Gemara, or a Tosafos.
- Designate a specific time, perhaps once a week, to learn with special intensity, keeping in mind that you may be having an incredible impact on others.

Discussion Points:

❖ We can understand that the things we do in public, that are seen by others, can create a kiddush Hashem. Much of our *avodas Hashem*, however, takes place in private. How does it bring about a kiddush Hashem if no one sees the things we do?

❖ We are taught that a mitzvah that is done in private is sometimes even more valuable than one that is performed publicly, and that we should be modest and unobtrusive in our service of Hashem. How does this fit with our mission to be *mekadesh Shem Shamayim*?

❖ How is the mitzvah of kiddush Hashem meant to be fulfilled by women, who generally remain out of the limelight?

CHAPTER 7

IN THE FACE OF FACE OF HOSTILITY

The company where Yitzchok works is having their annual New Year's celebration, and Yitzchok is beginning to come under pressure. The atmosphere at the party is bound to be inappropriate for a religious Jew; there will be no formal dress code, and alcohol will be served freely. Yitzchok has already heard from his coworkers that he is seen as a "loner," and that his boss, Craig, will be offended if he does not attend the party. Nevertheless, he knows what he has to do.

With a certain amount of trepidation, Yitzchok meets with Craig and informs him that he cannot attend the company event. Craig reacts exactly as he expected: It is not a comfortable conversation, and the boss makes his displeasure clear. Yitzchok tries to explain his reasons, but it is obvious that his boss is not interested in listening to him. Over the next few days, Yitzchok continues hearing from his coworkers that Craig is disappointed and insulted. Some of the other employees try to pressure him to change his mind, but Yitzchok does not give in. Still, he is troubled by the ill will that his decision has caused, and he wonders if he may have caused a chillul Hashem....

Matters of Life and Death

It was Rosh Hashanah in Auschwitz, and for a group of 1400 young boys between the ages of 14 and 18, it was also the very last day of their lives. The previous day, on Erev Rosh Hashanah, a brutal "selection" had been held to weed out the boys under the age of 18 who had managed to evade death when they first arrived. Hundreds of boys were herded beneath a wooden beam raised to a specific height, and those who did not meet the height requirement — 1400 in all — were locked in a separate cellblock.

Their beastly captors' intent was clear: The following night, the boys would be put to death, burned in the infamous crematoria of the annihilation camp.

Rav Tzvi Hirsh Meislish, in his *sefer She'eilos U'Teshuvos Mekadshei Hashem*, describes the heartrending scene that took place on that Rosh Hashanah. Rav Meislish, himself an inmate in Auschwitz, had managed to smuggle a shofar into the camp, and he spent the holy day going from barrack to barrack to sound the entire series of 100 shofar blasts for all of the inmates, despite the risk of immediate death if he were to be caught. When Rav Meislish passed by the block where the boys were being held, they pleaded with him to sound the shofar for them as well, so that they could perform one more precious mitzvah before their deaths.

Rav Meislish knew that if he was found in the barracks together with the doomed boys, he would be sentenced to death along with them. Nevertheless, he could not resist their pleas. He managed to gain access to the block only by paying a hefty bribe to the *kapos* standing guard. The *kapos* also warned him that if the SS men arrived while he was still there, they would do nothing to protect him.

The *rav* began by intoning the words, "*Min hameitzar karasi Kah* — I called out to Hashem from the narrow straits." Tears streamed down every face in the room as he blew the shofar, its high-pitched wails blending with the sobs of the children slated for death. One of the *bachurim* then stood up and declared, "Let us not forget to accept the *ol malchus Shamayim* in our final moments of life," and all the boys cried out the words of *Shema Yisrael* together. That night, the boys went to their deaths.

This captures the very essence of the mitzvah of *v'nikdashti b'soch bnei Yisrael*, the commandment to sanctify Hashem's Name. The message of this mitzvah, and the attitude we convey by observing it, is that nothing in our lives is more valuable than Hashem's honor and Will, and that our lives themselves have value only if they lead to greater *kavod Shamayim*. This was precisely the attitude embodied by those young boys, who wanted nothing more than to observe another mitzvah even as their lives were about to be cut short.[1]

Even when it does not entail actually giving up our lives, we must still make kiddush Hashem the determining factor in *all* of our life decisions. From the most significant life-or-death decision to the most minor choices that we make every day, we must always ask ourselves only one question: What will bring about a greater kiddush Hashem? In the final analysis, the answer to that question is all that really matters.

Takeaway

When a person dies because he has chosen to follow the Will of Hashem, he demonstrates that there is only One Authority in the world, and that Hashem's commandments come before all other considerations. Any sacrifice that one makes for the sake of Hashem is a fulfillment on some level of this great mitzvah.

---

1. Rav Shneur Kotler, in his *sefer Siach Erev* on *Maseches Sanhedrin*, explains that, in truth, a Jew should be required to give up his life to avoid violating *any* of the mitzvos in the Torah. Every mitzvah in the Torah has an element of kiddush Hashem, while every sin has an element of chillul Hashem, and it would make sense for a person to have to surrender his life to avoid that chillul Hashem. The Torah, however, reveals to us in the *pasuk*, "*Vachai bahem* — [One] shall live by them," that it often leads to a greater kiddush Hashem when a person commits an *aveirah* in order to save his life, since the potential kiddush Hashem that one can create over a lifetime generally outweighs the chillul Hashem caused by a single sin. In some scenarios, however, *Chazal* learn from other sources that the greater kiddush Hashem comes from giving up one's life to avoid the sin. These scenarios include cases when a person is publicly coerced to violate any mitzvah, and when one is under duress to violate one of the three cardinal sins. All of these scenarios are encompassed by the mitzvah of *venikdashti b'soch Bnei Yisrael*, which means that one should live in whatever way will bring about the greatest degree of *kevod Shamayim*, whether that comes from preserving one's life or giving it up. In a nutshell, kiddush Hashem is the sole determining factor.

Sanctity Amid Senseless Slaughter

During the Gulf War, Rav Moshe Twersky once asked his
rebbe, Rav Elya Weintraub, how he should react if an
air-raid siren sounded while he was in the middle of *davening
Shemoneh Esrei*: Should he interrupt his *tefillah* to take cover, or
should he remain in his place? Rav Elya replied, "It isn't clear
what is the proper *hishtadlus* to save yourself, so if you are in
the middle of *Shemoneh Esrei*, then if it is not yet your time, you
have no reason to worry. And if your time has come, then what
could be more beautiful than dying *al* kiddush Hashem in the
middle of *Shemoneh Esrei?*"

Over the following years, Rav Twersky often repeated his *rebbe's* words to his family, adding, "If I am to die young, I hope I die
al kiddush Hashem in the middle of *davening*!" As we are all painfully aware, that is exactly how he met his death. In November
2014, two vicious Arab murderers entered Kehillas Bnei Torah
in Har Nof, where they found Rav Twersky wrapped in his *tallis*
and *tefillin* and immersed in *davening Shemoneh Esrei*, and they
brutally took his life. Rav Twersky was one of five members of
the *kehillah* who were cruelly slaughtered on that morning. (This
story was heard in the name of Rav Nissan Kaplan.)

The horrific massacre in a *shul* in the heart of Har Nof was an event that many of us found impossible to absorb. Deep down, many of us struggled with a fundamental question: Were the deaths of the *kedoshim* really a kiddush Hashem, or was the attack actually a terrible chillul Hashem? Isn't it a major affront to Hashem's honor for those murderers to have invaded such a sacred place — a *shul* that is a hub of Torah and *tefillah* — at the height of the *kedushah* of the morning *tefillos*, and to cut down holy people while they stood wrapped in their *tefillin*, the sacred protection gear of the Jewish people?

Let us take a step back and examine the concept of dying *al* kiddush Hashem. We tend to think of it as the heroic act of a person faced with a stark choice: either violating the Torah or being killed. We can understand that a person who chooses death rather than committing a sin is considered a martyr who has died *al* kiddush Hashem. But there have been many times when Jews were killed simply because they were Jews, without being given the option to save their lives by sinning. Why are their deaths considered to be *al* kiddush Hashem? How can this lead the world to a greater recognition of Hashem's existence?

The *Malbim* teaches (*Vayikra* 22:32) that there is a link between a person's act of self-sacrifice and a miracle performed by Hashem. When a person defies his natural instincts and is prepared to surrender his life to do the Will of Hashem, then Hashem responds in kind, by suspending the natural laws that govern the world so that miracles can take place.[2] When we lift ourselves above our natural desires, then Hashem, in turn, raises us above the laws of nature.

Rav Shimon Schwab points out (*Maayan Beis Hashoeivah, Parashas Beshalach*) that throughout our history, all of the major

---

2. The *Sforno* explains that this is why the Torah connects the mitzvah of kiddush Hashem to *Yetzias Mitzrayim*, in the *pesukim* (ibid., 32-33), "I shall be sanctified in the midst of Bnei Yisrael; I am Hashem, Who sanctifies you, Who takes you out of the Land of Egypt to be a G-d for you; I am Hashem." Kiddush Hashem, the *Sforno* explains, comes about through miracles such as those of *Yetzias Mitzrayim*, when Hashem demonstrated His ability to act outside the constraints of the laws of nature.

miracles and explosions of *kedushah* that we experienced came on the heels of major displays of *mesirus nefesh*. False prophets vanished after the heroic acts of self-sacrifice of Chananyah, Mishael, and Azariah, as well as Daniel. The dreadful suffering of the Crusades was followed by the era of the *Baalei HaTosafos*, and the pogroms of *Tach veTat* were followed by the era of the *gedolei Acharonim*. It is also possible that the tremendous growth and flourishing of the yeshivah world in America and Eretz Yisrael over the past few decades was fueled by the *kedushah* created by the murder of many Jews during the Holocaust.

Based on this principle, we can understand that even a person who does not have the opportunity to save himself from death by sinning, and who is killed simply because he is a Jew, can be considered to have died *al* kiddush Hashem. Even if he didn't choose death over betraying Hashem — because he was never given the chance to save himself by sinning — his death can bring tremendous honor to Hashem by virtue of his remaining devoted to Hashem even in the face of death. This, too, is a way of rising above one's natural instincts, and can create a corresponding massive wave of *kedushah*.

However, this does not fully answer the question. Many Jews have died suddenly in terror attacks and the like, without even having the opportunity to think about maintaining their *deveikus* before they were killed. What *kedushah* was generated by their deaths?

In these cases, the *kedushah* emanates not from the inner strength of the victims themselves, but rather from the reactions of the rest of Klal Yisrael to their deaths. When other Jews are affected by those tragic murders, when they are moved to transform themselves in response to such barbaric acts, *that* is the source of *kedushah* from the deaths of these *kedoshim*. Through the deaths of the *kedoshim* in Har Nof, Hashem brought their greatness to the attention of the entire Jewish people. They died *al kiddush Hashem* not in order to become *kedoshim* as individuals, but rather so that the entire Jewish people could become *kedoshim* collectively. Many of us knew the victims or felt some connection to them, and it is our response to their deaths that will turn a senseless, brutal act that might even be a chillul Hashem into an outstanding kiddush Hashem.

In the aftermath of the murders, many people made improvements in various areas of spirituality. There was an increase in respect for the *kedushah* of a *beis medrash* and the *kedushah* of *tefillin*; many people committed to refrain from having mundane conversations in shul or while they were wearing *tefillin*. Others redoubled their efforts to avoid the spiritual pitfalls of modern technology, or to work on their *middos* and *chessed*. Every person has his own struggles, and every person must determine how to add *kedushah* to his own life.

Let us hope that the waves of increased *kedushah* that have begun rippling through our nation will lead us into the era of Mashiach once and for all, and Hashem's Kingship and supreme goodness will finally be revealed to the entire world.

Takeaway

Takeaway: When a person dies al kiddush Hashem, kedushah can be generated either by his own sacrifice or by the response of others who are spurred by his death to increase their own kedushah.

Making It Practical

- If someone you know is sick or suffering, or if you are going through a challenging time, take the opportunity to commit yourself to some form of *avodas Hashem*. This will turn your suffering into a catalyst for kiddush Hashem.

Surrendering to Hashem

On the Shabbos of *Parashas Vayikra* in the year 2015, seven precious *neshamos* were torn from our midst in a horrendous tragedy, when a fire broke out in the Sassoon family's Brooklyn home and claimed the lives of seven of their eight children. Throughout Klal Yisrael, tears flowed freely as we all struggled to assimilate the tragedy.

At the *levayah* of his seven children, Gavriel Sassoon said passionately, "I had everything, and now I have nothing. The only way to deal with this is to completely surrender to the Will of Hashem." Then he announced that he was returning his "angels" to the Almighty. "To You, G-d, my children," he said. "To You, G-d, their dreams. To You, G-d, my grandchildren."

He understood that Hashem's calculations are hidden from us, that the reason for his unspeakable suffering will not be revealed until Mashiach comes, and that the only attitude with which he could face such suffering was the understanding that he is nothing more than a tool in Hashem's Hands.

Throughout the generations, Jews not only have chosen to give up their own lives but have also surrendered the lives of their children to avoid betraying their religion. Rambam states (*Hilchos Yesodei HaTorah* 5:1), "The entire House of Israel is commanded to sanctify His great Name, as the *pasuk* says, 'I will be sanctified in the midst of Bnei Yisrael.'" *Emes L'Yaakov* infers from Rambam's use of the phrase "the entire House of Israel" that even children are subject to this mitzvah.

We can understand how an adult can surrender his own life; after all, the Torah commands us to be *mekadeish Shem Shamayim*. But how can one surrender a child's life? After all, children are not obligated in mitzvos! What makes them required to give up their lives?

The reason for this is that kiddush Hashem is fundamentally different from other mitzvos. The reason children are generally not subject to mitzvos is that they cannot *choose* to perform them, but the mitzvah of kiddush Hashem is not a matter of making a choice. This mitzvah calls for every Jew to be a vehicle through which Hashem's honor is upheld, which is something that even a child can do. In fact, this is implied by the wording of the *pasuk* itself. The Torah does not state, "You shall sanctify Me," which would be the usual form of a command. Instead, it says, "I *will be* sanctified," implying that this sanctification is not something we choose to do, but rather something that is bound to happen, and our role may even be passive.[3]

We can never fully understand Hashem's calculations, nor will we ever completely grasp the purpose of suffering in this world. We do know, however, that sometimes people are chosen to be instruments of kiddush Hashem, for reasons unknown to us, and they may contribute to Hashem's honor even without playing an active role in doing so. Certainly, anyone who plays a role in this process, whether by choice or by force, will receive an eternal reward beyond our comprehension.[4]

---

3. See *Michtav MeEliyahu*, Vol. 2, p. 194.

According to the *sefer Vezos L'Yaakov*, a person can be considered to have performed an act of kiddush Hashem even if his suffering is completely involuntary. He explains that this idea is derived from *Akeidas Yitzchak*.

In *Parashas Vayeira* (22:1), *Rashi* quotes an exchange between Yitzchak Avinu and Yishmael before the *Akeidah*. Yishmael boasted that he was superior to Yitzchak since he had allowed himself to be circumcised at the age of thirteen, whereas Yitzchak was only eight days old at his *milah* and it was therefore not an act of conscious submission. Yitzchak responded, "You are boasting about your superiority regarding one part of the body. If Hashem told me to sacrifice myself before Him, I would not resist."

On the surface, it seems that Yishmael's argument was perfectly logical. Wouldn't it make sense for a child to have his *bris* at an age when he can accept it consciously? That would seem to be a greater display of dedication to Hashem. Moreover, Yitzchak's answer does not seem to resolve this issue.

Vezos L'Yaakov explains that the *Akeidah* itself was the answer to Yishmael's claim. Yishmael maintained that the ideal form of *mesirus nefesh* is when a person consciously submits to suffering or even death for the sake of Hashem's honor. According to his understanding, involuntary suffering does not contribute to kiddush Hashem. But Yitzchak's role in the *Akeidah* was completely passive. The *Akeidah* demonstrated that the ultimate kiddush Hashem is for a Jew to serve as a tool of Hashem, so to speak, a medium through which *kiddush Shem Shamayim* takes place. This is the lesson of *milah*, the mitzvah performed on an infant without his consent: the role of a Jew is not only to actively create kiddush Hashem but also to be a vessel used by the Creator to bring about kiddush Hashem.

4. In *Parashas Shemini* (10:3), the Torah relates that Nadav and Avihu, the sons of

Takeaway: There are times when we are used as a tool to bring about a kiddush Hashem without even being given a choice in the matter. Even children's lives can be used as a means for creating kiddush Hashem, even though they are not even capable of making that choice.

Making It Practical

- When something happens in life that is beyond your control and you cannot change it — whether you are dealing with a difficult boss, a challenging child, or anything else — instead of fighting it, accept it with *bitachon* and surrender to the Will of Hashem.

The Yetzer Hara's Mission

One of the pivotal events of World War II was the surprise Japanese attack on the United States military base at Pearl Harbor, Hawaii, on the morning of Sunday, December 7, 1941. Until that time, America had remained neutral in the war that was raging on the other side of the Atlantic, but the attack on

---

Aharon, died during the inauguration of the Mishkan. After their deaths, Moshe told Aharon that Hashem had said, "*Bikrovai ekadeish* — I will be sanctified through those who are close to Me." *Rashbam* explains that the kiddush Hashem that results from a tragedy is not a product of the tragedy itself, but rather of the reactions of those who live on and must cope with their misfortune.

Pearl Harbor spurred the country to action. After the attack that destroyed three battleships and cost over two thousand lives, the Japanese general who had planned it declared, "We have awakened a sleeping giant and instilled in him a terrible resolve."

Sure enough, in the aftermath of the devastating attack, the entire American nation rallied to join the war effort. Whereas America had previously been content to remain neutral in the war, the American people now understood that they were facing the same enemy as the other embattled nations in Europe. The American army joined the fight, and the outcome of the war was radically altered as a result.

We are all familiar with the concept of loving Hashem "with all your soul," which means that a person must be prepared to surrender his very life for Hashem's honor. The Torah also teaches us that we must love Hashem "with all your hearts." *Chazal* point out that it is actually referring to two "hearts": the *yetzer hatov* and the *yetzer hara*. How can a person serve Hashem with his *yetzer hara*?

When the letters of the word *ra* ("evil") are reversed, they spell the Hebrew word *eir* ("awake"). The purpose of the existence of evil is for us to become "*eir*," to awaken us and cause us to become strong. Fighting and overcoming the *yetzer hara* helps us develop spiritual strength. In that sense, the *yetzer hara* can be likened to a boxing coach, who will fight his own student with all his might in order to train him to overcome the most powerful opponent. For the coach, there is no greater joy than being defeated by his own student, for it means that his training was successful. Similarly, the *yetzer hara*'s ultimate goal is for us to defeat him.

We are living in an era that is filled with *nisyonos* and challenges. As our spiritual "coach," the *yetzer hara* is throwing more numerous and powerful "blows" at us than ever before. Everywhere we turn, there are temptations and opportunities for sin. And if the *yetzer hara* is presenting all these enticements to us, it must mean that he is making a supreme effort to empower us.

The *Rambam* teaches (*Hilchos Yesodei HaTorah* 5:10) that when a person refrains from sinning or performs a mitzvah with no motivation other than serving Hashem, he creates a massive kiddush Hashem. Rav Avrohom Schorr pointed out at an Agudas Yisroel convention that the challenges of modern technology, by their very nature, present us with the most private *nisyonos* possible. A person could easily be ensnared by these temptations without anyone else being aware; therefore, when a person chooses to resist their pull, it is solely out of a sincere desire to serve Hashem. Rav Schorr added that this situation, the likes of which has never existed before, is clearly Divinely ordained for the purpose of creating kiddush Hashem.

During World War II, the United States of America entered the war only when the country recognized that it had an enemy and was facing a severe threat. We, too, must recognize that we are fighting a major war, the war against the *yetzer hara*, and that we are facing an existential threat. If we understand the reality of our situation, then we will wake up the "sleeping giant" within ourselves, and we will be strong enough to create a kiddush Hashem on an unimaginable scale.

Takeaway

When a person overcomes challenges and temptations, he strengthens his yiras Shamayim and becomes a more dedicated servant of Hashem. We must recognize our temptations as what they are: challenges that have been given to us to overcome.

Making It Practical

• To ensure that your kiddush Hashem is completely sincere, make a point of overcoming a temptation that is totally private, purely for the sake of serving Hashem.

A Culture of Discipline

I was once approached by a non-Jewish teacher in the general studies department of the Cincinnati Hebrew Day School, who informed me that her year in the *frum* day school had led her to make a decision about schooling for her own son. "Rabbi," she said, "after seeing how the boys behave in this school, I have decided to enroll my own son in an all boys' school for this coming year, even though it is a Catholic school and I am not Catholic. You see," she explained, "you have no idea how much healthier and cleaner your Jewish boys are, because they are cut off from all the drama and immorality of the outside world. You really should appreciate your lifestyle, with its separation of the genders and all the other things that come along with it. I have learned from your school that when a boy is raised in a cocoon during his teenage years, he can come out of it as beautiful as a butterfly."

One of the most impressive qualities of our community is its culture of discipline, the practice of self-control that stems from the Jewish people's innate *yiras Shamayim* and their ability to overcome their base desires.

The benefits of the disciplined Jewish lifestyle often make a powerful impression on the secular world. Rav Tzvi Steinberg, the *rav* of Kahal Zera Avraham of Denver, Colorado, discovered this during a meeting with the officers of the Denver police force.

Every year, Rav Steinberg is invited by the Denver police department to give a presentation about the culture and values of the Orthodox Jewish community. Rav Steinberg has written a booklet explaining many of the norms and sensitivities of the Orthodox population, which is meant to help the police understand the unique needs and requests of Orthodox Jews. One police officer, for instance, was once called to a residential street where a car alarm was sounding on Friday night. The alarm had prevented the expensive car from being stolen, but the car's window was smashed, and the officer realized that the car's owner was not aware of the attempted theft. He knocked on the door of the owner's home, and the door was answered by an Orthodox Jew. After the officer explained the situation, the homeowner thanked him and then added, "Would you mind covering the window with a plastic sheet for me? It's raining and I don't want my new car to get ruined."

When the officer spoke about this incident at Rav Steinberg's yearly presentation, he said, "At first, I was indignant when he asked me to do that. It isn't my job to cover someone's car, and I felt it wasn't appropriate that he had asked me to do that. But then I remembered your booklet, and what you explain about Shabbos, and I realized that he probably wasn't allowed to do it himself."

Rav Steinberg thanked the officer for his story and then addressed his audience. "Has any of you had any incidents in which a crime was committed by an Orthodox Jew?" he asked. Silence fell throughout the room, and the police officers' expressions reflected their mounting respect for the religious population. Rav Steinberg went on to speak for a half-hour about various Orthodox sensitivities, explaining that most men and women do not even shake hands, and that if an Orthodox woman needs assistance, it would be best to provide a female police officer. Finally, he said, "Does anyone have any questions?"

One police officer raised his hand and said, "Your community is known for its strong family structure. So many Orthodox families stay intact, much more than the norm in today's society. How do you accomplish that? What is the key to your success?"

Rav Steinberg looked around and said, "I would like to hear if anyone else can suggest an answer to that question, after hearing my presentation. What do all of you think is our secret?"

After a moment, another police officer said, "You spoke a lot about the Orthodox rules of modesty and the separation of men and women. That probably creates an atmosphere of discipline and fidelity within marriages, and it probably gives rise to strong family values."

Let us see to it that we maintain the discipline and self-control that are the hallmarks of the Jewish people, so that our behavior will never lead to anything less than a powerful kiddush Hashem.

Takeaway

Our elevated values are seen as a shining light in a world that is constantly falling to greater depths of moral decay.

Making It Practical

- Take care to maintain your *shemiras einayim* even as you make a point of noticing and greeting the people around you.

Discussion Points:

❖ There have been many times when Jews were killed simply because they were Jewish; they did not even have the chance to save their lives by committing a sin. Why are their deaths considered to be *al* kiddush Hashem? How does the murder of innocent Jews lead the world to a greater recognition of Hashem's existence?

❖ *"Mesirus nefesh"* means sacrificing one's life to avoid betraying Hashem, but it also means sacrificing one's own desires and resisting temptation in order to fulfill the Will of Hashem. How does it create a kiddush Hashem when a person overcomes temptations?

CHAPTER 8

PUBLIC RELATIONS

It is a stormy winter day in the 21st century. A peaceful neighborhood is being battered by a massive hail storm, and the roofs of many homes are destroyed by the hail. When the storm is over, the residents come out of their homes and rub their eyes in disbelief. Every single roof in the neighborhood has been destroyed, with the exception of the roofs of the homes owned by Jews. It is an undeniable miracle: Every Jewish-owned home has survived the storm unharmed.

This is a fictional scenario, of course, but imagine what would happen if this actually took place, and the world was forced to admit that they had witnessed a Divinely ordained miracle. News reporters would rush to the neighborhood and would strive to find the common denominator among the specific homes that were spared. They would interview the neighbors of the people whose homes survived the storm, eager for a clue as to what made them worthy of such a miracle. They would ask if the fortunate homeowners are people who are pleasant and kind, and they would scour the Internet for information about them, searching for details about how they live, what moral values they observe, what sort of entertainment they enjoy, and how they conduct business. And if their investigation shows that the Jewish people truly represent Hashem and His values, then a major kiddush Hashem will result. They will understand that G-d loves these people and wishes for the world to take notice of their actions; they will conclude that that is the reason that He allowed their homes to be spared.

Although this is a fictional scenario today, it may well become the reality in the future. The more we make ourselves into a reflection of the Will of Hashem, the more Hashem will shine his *hashgachah* on us and will reveal Himself to the world through us.

Uncovering Providence

It was the end of the winter, and the residents of the town of Dvinsk were facing life-threatening peril. One section of the Dvina river, which flows past the town, had thawed much earlier in the season than usual. The snow and ice melted and began flowing downstream, but much of the river was still frozen, and the water was unable to flow into the bay at the river's mouth. Instead, the rushing waters, along with large pieces of ice, began overflowing onto the banks of the river, wreaking havoc on the river's bridges and in many nearby villages.

On Shabbos morning, the residents of Dvinsk watched anxiously as the snow dam that protected them from the river began to give way. It seemed certain that the river would soon break through the dam, flooding the town and bringing death and destruction in its wake. When a group of men entered the *shul* during Shacharis that morning, announcing that the situation was critical, Rav Meir Simcha HaKohen — the legendary *gadol* and author of classic *sefarim* such as *Meshech Chochmah* and *Ohr Samei'ach* — left the *shul*, still cloaked in his *tallis*, and headed toward the dam. The rest of the *mispallelim* followed him, still wearing their *talleisim* as well.

When the group of men reached the dam, Rav Meir Simcha climbed onto it and began *davening*. His *tefillos* were answered quickly: The frozen river suddenly cracked, and the waters that had threatened to flood the town flowed past it instead. News of the miracle spread quickly, and even the non-Jews of Dvinsk admitted that the *rav* had performed a supernatural feat.

What made Rav Meir Simcha capable of creating such an enormous kiddush Hashem? It was simply the fact that he was a dedicated servant of Hashem. The huge number of mitzvos he performed and the tremendous amount of Torah he learned made him worthy of being able to work wonders with his *tefillos*. That, in turn, brought honor to Hashem by demonstrating the power of a *tzaddik* and *talmid chacham*.[1]

---

1. David HaMelech states in *Tehillim*, "The heavens relate the honor of G-d,

One of the primary ways that the Jewish people create kiddush Hashem is by revealing Hashem's *hashgachah* to the rest of the world. We bring honor to Hashem when we tear away the veil that conceals His Presence, exposing His guiding Hand behind every event. This becomes possible when we follow Hashem's Will and faithfully observe His commandments; when we do that, Hashem reveals himself through us, and that demonstrates His absolute dominion over the world.[2]

In his book *Inside Their Homes*, Rabbi Nachman Seltzer tells the story of a child who was born at Maayanei HaYeshuah Hospital in Bnei Brak and became gravely ill. The child's condition deteriorated to the point that the doctors were certain he would not survive, but fortunately, he did recover. When the grateful parents were finally able to take their baby home, they made sure to thank the hospital staff for their devotion to the child's care. The head of the department, an irreligious woman, had an interesting response.

"There is no medical explanation for the fact that your child survived," she told the parents. "It is clearly a miracle; however, I can explain why it happened. When this hospital was first founded, the Steipler Gaon gave a *berachah* to its founder, the *tzaddik*, Dr. Rothschild, that no baby should ever die in the maternity ward. To this day, thousands of children have been born in this hospital, and the Steipler's blessing has come true:

and the firmament tells of His handiwork." The Gemara (*Kesuvos* 5a), according to *Rashi*, explains that the "handiwork" mentioned in this *pasuk* actually refers to the deeds of *tzaddikim*; the heavens "tell of" the good deeds of *tzaddikim* when rain falls in response to their prayers. Since *tzaddikim* are people who have molded themselves in Hashem's image, so to speak, their actions reflect the "deeds" and "traits" of Hashem Himself. Consequently, when the rains attest to the greatness of *tzaddikim*, they actually increase the honor of Hashem.

2. In *Parashas Yisro* (19:5), the Torah states, "You shall be a treasured nation to Me, for the whole land is Mine." What is the connection between these two thoughts? The *Meshech Chochmah* explains that when the Jewish people observe the Torah and its commandments, they will be a "treasured nation," subject to special *hashgachah pratis* (Divine Providence) that will guide them and save them from all calamities. This special Providence, which will be clearly recognizable to the nations, will cause the entire world to accept Hashem as the King of the universe, essentially making the whole world "belong" to Hashem.

Not a single baby has died in the maternity ward here." Because the Steipler Gaon was a devoted servant of Hashem, he had the power to give a *berachah* that would come true, revealing even to an irreligious doctor that Hashem controls the events of His world.

In a similar vein, Rav Chaim of Volozhin (in *Ruach Chaim*, his commentary on *Pirkei Avos*) explains that an *aveirah* committed in private can create a chillul Hashem because it makes the sinner *unworthy* of being the vehicle for a display of Hashem's *hashgachah*. Therefore, even if a person commits a sin in a place where no one else can witness it, it can still add to the concealment of Hashem's Presence. When a person contaminates himself with sin, he causes Hashem to remove His *hashgachah* from the world and thus make His Presence less apparent. This is the very definition of a chillul Hashem, a term derived from the word *"challal"* (void); a chillul Hashem is the void created by the absence of Hashem's Providence.

This leads to a simple equation: Every mitzvah that we perform leads to a further revelation of Hashem's *hashgachah*, giving rise to a kiddush Hashem. Similarly, every *aveirah* adds to the concealment of the Divine Presence, causing a chillul Hashem. *Tzaddikim* have the power to create change in the world through their *berachos* and *tefillos*, since the power of their *berachos* demonstrates that Hashem controls the world and responds to those who serve Him. Every mitzvah we perform is therefore an act of kiddush Hashem, since it creates a greater opportunity for Hashem to demonstrate *hashgachah* and to drive away the darkness that hides His Presence.

Takeaway

When we serve Hashem properly, we make ourselves worthy of benefiting from His Providence — and when Hashem reveals Himself through His servants, that creates kiddush Hashem.

Making It Practical

- When you feel that you are faced with a choice between fulfilling the Will of Hashem and satisfying the desires of the people around you, make Hashem's Will your priority. Even if you are worried that your actions will displease others, Hashem will see to it that the ultimate result will be a Kiddush Hashem.

- If a relative of the opposite gender wishes to give you a hug and will be insulted even if you explain that it is forbidden by your religion, do not allow that to deter you from following the halachah. Your job is to represent Hashem's Will; He will take care of everything else.

Miracles of Recent History

Chevrah Hatzolah played a pivotal role in the rescue operations at the World Trade Center on September 11, 2001. The very first ambulance to arrive at the Twin Towers following the first plane crash was a Hatzolah ambulance. By the time the second airplane crashed into the second tower, there were two dozen Hatzolah ambulances, including their communications and command center trailer, and 200 EMTs, paramedics, and doctors from Hatzolah on the scene. By the time the buildings collapsed, ambulances and emergency medical personnel from all the branches of Hatzolah throughout the five boroughs of the city of New York and as far away as Rockland County had arrived on the scene. During the first hour of the disaster, over

123 patients were transported to area hospitals by Hatzolah ambulances. At the south end of the Twin Towers, Hatzolah was the dominant ambulance service covering the disaster scene. They transported numerous victims to safety, including police officers and fire fighters.

When the buildings collapsed, about 3,000 people were killed. In addition to the people inside the buildings themselves, everyone in the vicinity was endangered by the huge pieces of metal and glass falling from great heights. People raced for cover. Many were killed by falling debris or died from suffocation by the dust and smoke. The Hatzolah dispatcher was advised by two-way radio that many Hatzolah members had been trapped under the debris, and he began calling each member by name over the radio. For the 850 members and their wives, it was an extremely long hour as they waited to hear responses from their colleagues and husbands. At the end, although there were injuries, every single Hatzolah member was accounted for and confirmed to be alive. It was clear to everyone that hundreds of miracles must have taken place for all of the members of Hatzolah to be saved. They all attributed their miraculous salvation to the *zechus* of being part of an organization that engages in constant lifesaving *chessed*.

Rabbi Mechel Handler, then executive director of Chevrah Hatzolah, was one of the people who came close to death as he struggled to breathe and race for cover in the midst of the falling debris. When Rabbi Handler later met Chief Robert McCracken of FDNY/NYCEMS, the two men immediately hugged each other. After hearing that all of the Hatzolah members had survived, Chief McCracken said with conviction, "It is obvious that your G-d has miraculously saved all of you" (*Even in the Darkest Moments*, by Zeev Breier).

This was not the only large-scale disaster in which countless Jewish lives were saved through overt miracles. During the Gulf War, Iraq fired deadly Scud missiles into heavily populated areas in Israel. These missiles carried powerful warheads that had the power to cause massive damage. Incredibly, over the days that

Israel was bombarded by the Scuds and its people found themselves constantly racing to their bomb shelters, no Jewish people were killed, although some buildings and houses were severely damaged. This frustrated the Arab enemy; in a prominent newspaper, an Arab was quoted as exclaiming, "What can we do? Their G-d is protecting them, He is obviously on their side!"

This is precisely what will transpire when the final *geulah* arrives: Hashem will demonstrate in the clearest possible way that the Jewish people are His chosen people. He will bring us to Eretz Yisrael and shower us with the benefits of His Presence and His *hashgachah*. When the Jewish people emulate Hashem's *middos*, then He considers it appropriate to demonstrate His love for us to the world. The miracles that He performs for us are His way of proclaiming to the world that the Jewish people represent Him and have proven themselves worthy of His favor — and this will ultimately lead the entire world to recognize His timeless values and to accept Him as their King.[3]

Takeaway

We must constantly ask ourselves if we are worthy of Hashem gracing us with special hashgachah. If Hashem performed miracles for us and made His love for us evident to the world, how would the other nations react? Would they feel that we are deserving of His miracles and worthy of being His chosen nation, or would they be mystified by G-d's love for us because they consider us dishonest and unrefined? If we wish

---

3. In the *Shemoneh Esrei* we state, "*V'chol hachayim yoducha selah* — All the living beings will praise You forever ... the G-d Who is our Savior and Protector." The *Meshech Chochmah* explains this to mean that Hashem's protection of the Jewish people *causes* all the nations of the world to praise Him. (See also *Malbim* and *Metzudos Dovid* on *Yeshayah* 12:2.) This concept is also conveyed by a series of *pesukim* in *Melachim I* (beginning with 8:56) in which the *navi* describes the blessings Hashem has bestowed upon the Jewish people and concludes that the purpose of those blessings is to ensure that all the nations will recognize Hashem as the One and Only G-d of the world; see also *Radak* on those *pesukim*.

to benefit from special Divine hashgachah, we must behave
in such a way that a show of that hashgachah would result in
a kiddush Hashem.[4]

Making It Practical

- During the many times that you *daven* in the *Shemoneh Esrei* for our final redemption, have in mind that you are also *davening* for the spreading of kiddush Hashem that is the ultimate purpose of the coming of Mashiach.

- Keep in mind that we must avoid creating a chillul Hashem so that we can hasten the arrival of the *geulah*.

---

4. The *navi* Tzefaniah tells us (3:13), *"She'airis Yisrael lo yaaseh avlah v'lo yidaber kazav* — The remnant of Israel will not commit wrongdoing or speak falsehood." Not all of the Jewish people will have sufficient merits to experience the *geulah*. The only Jews who will merit redemption are those who do not engage in thievery and falsehood. Why do these two sins, specifically, prevent one from experiencing redemption?

Rav Mattisyahu Salomon quotes the *Smag* (*Lo Saaseh* 2 and *Aseh* 74), who explains that the distinguishing feature of these sins is the very public nature of the transgressions. People who engage in blatant deceit, thievery, or dishonesty in business dealings are often scorned and reviled by the nations of the world. Hashem would not allow such people to benefit from the Redemption, for it would be a chillul Hashem for the nations of the world to assume that such evildoers are the objects of Hashem's love. As we have learned, the *geulah* is very much dependent on the Jewish people's image in the eyes of the world.

What can we do to bring the *geulah* closer? In light of the above, it should be very clear. We must act with the utmost integrity in all of our financial transactions and business dealings. We must take care to be beacons of honesty, to eschew any form of falsehood or deceit. Only then will we be a nation worthy of being the instrument of kiddush Hashem.

Core Values

We all know that the mitzvah of kiddush Hashem calls for us to model the values and morals of the Torah. In many cases, we can understand this easily. When a Jew displays refined *middos* and a high ethical standard, it demonstrates to the world the perfection of Hashem's Torah. This contributes to Hashem's honor by leading the rest of the world to admire and love Him.

In many cases, though, it is difficult to understand why the nations of the world should be moved by our *middos* or moral values. After all, the other nations have an entirely different perspective from our own on many issues. They value material advancement, while we attach more importance to spiritual goals. They have their own concepts of equality and justice, while the foundations of Judaism are the timeless values of the Torah. How can our acts of kiddush Hashem truly have an impact on the rest of the world?

In *Pirkei Avos* (3:10), the Mishnah states, "*Kol she'ruach habrios nochah heimenu ruach haMakom nochah heimenu* — Any person who brings satisfaction to [other] human beings brings satisfaction to Hashem." *Rabbeinu Bechaye* explains that when the Torah describes the creation of man by stating that Hashem "blew a spirit of life into his nostrils," it indicates that the spirit of every human being is drawn from the Divine. As a result, every person has certain innate sensitivities and values that mirror the values of Hashem, so to speak. It is natural for any human being to feel fulfilled when he gives to others, or to admire another person's evident honesty and integrity. These are qualities that come naturally to most of the human race. Therefore, when we evince the virtues we learn from the Torah, it will make a positive impression on other people by stirring the recognition of right and wrong that lies deep within their souls.[5] When other

---

5. In *Kovetz Maamarim*, Rav Elchonon Wasserman cites this concept to explain

people find our actions pleasing, it generally means that we have touched that G-dly spark within them, which means that Hashem is pleased with us as well.

Nevertheless, the Mishnah does not state that a person's actions must be pleasing to *all* human beings. Although the foundations of morality are woven into the human psyche, it is possible for a person to lose that basic sense of humanity. People who have been raised under highly adverse conditions, such as in abusive or dysfunctional homes, may be so traumatized that they will lose their sense of moral values. They may become wicked, and therefore they may fail to respect those who mirror the qualities of Hashem.

To take this concept to an extreme, consider the case of John Ssebunya, an orphaned child from a remote village in Uganda who wandered into a forest after his parents were killed during a civil war in 1988. The small child was found by a family of African vervet monkeys, who adopted him as one of their own and from whom he learned to climb trees and forage for food. Ssebunya lived that way for months, until he was found and adopted by a British couple. When he was discovered, he was hardly recognizable as human; he walked on his knees, his hair and nails were long and unkempt, and he behaved wildly. Even after he had returned to civilization, he retained many of the habits he had picked up while living with primates. It took time for him to learn how to speak, and when he did, it was only with a severe stutter. In addition, he never made eye contact with other people, staring straight ahead even when he spoke with

---

why the nations of the world are responsible to observe the seven mitzvos of *bnei Noach*, even though they were never explicitly commanded to do so. Since the values embodied by those mitzvos — such as refraining from theft, appointing judges, and the like — are inherent components of the human condition, every human being is automatically responsible to abide by them. Likewise, even before the Torah was given, people were punished for acts of immorality or cruelty. The generation of the *mabul*, for instance, was destroyed because of their sins and corruption, and Avimelech was punished for abducting Sarah Imeinu. Although those people had never received a commandment from Hashem to refrain from those acts, they were expected, like any other human being, to innately understand the basic tenets of morality.

someone. The trauma of being raised by animals was so great that he was never able to make a full recovery.

Thus, there certainly may be some people in the world who have lost all feeling for human virtues. However, the vast majority of people possess an instinctive sense of morality and will be affected by a show of virtue. As unlikely as it may seem, and as daunting as we may find a world filled with corruption and immorality, we must recognize that when we expose other people to the spirit of Hashem, it can have a profound impact on them. Our job is to tap into the hidden qualities and values that lie deep within the human soul, reconnecting others to the Divinity within them by demonstrating the positive attributes we possess. If we do that, we will certainly contribute to the growth of *kavod Shem Shamayim* throughout the world.

Takeaway

There are certain basic values that are built into the human psyche. When we reflect the attributes of Hashem, we can be assured that almost any human being will sense the truth of those values and will be duly affected by what they have witnessed.

Making It Practical

- Show appreciation for any service you receive, and voice your thanks to the people who serve the public: police, army personnel, mailmen, crossing guards, and the like. The value of appreciation is something that all human beings appreciate.

The Leader Within You

Melissa Poe was worried.

She had been reading about the dangers of pollution and its devastating effects on the environment, and she feared for the future. She felt certain that something had to be done about the problem, and she decided to contact the person she felt would be most able to bring about a positive change: the president of the United States.

After sending an impassioned letter to the president, Melissa waited expectantly for change. But as the weeks went by and there was no response to her letter, she became disheartened. Finally, she decided that if she wanted change to take place, she would have to work for it herself.

Melissa began her work within her own home, encouraging her family to recycle, to avoid wasting electricity, and to plant trees. Her next step was to contact her mayor, as well as the local congressmen and senators, and then the media. Before long, she founded a club dedicated to preserving the environment, whose members worked to clean up litter, plant trees, and advocate for environmental protection. The club, which began with only six members, soon grew into a major organization known as Kids F.A.C.E. (Kids For A Clean Environment), which maintained over 2000 chapters spanning 22 countries. When Melissa stepped down from serving as the organization's president, it had 350,000 members; today, its membership has grown even further.

The most impressive aspect of this story is the fact that when Melissa founded Kids F.A.C.E. she was only in fourth grade. She headed the organization until she was 17 years old, at which time she handed the reins to a pair of 15-year-olds.

At a reception honoring her for her accomplishments, Melissa shared some sagacious insights. "Change does not begin with someone else," she said. "Change begins in your own backyard, no matter your age or size. I had no idea that one simple step could change my life so much.... The difference about being a leader is that you take the step; you take the journey. The greatest obstacle you will ever encounter is yourself.... You can't look for the man behind the curtain to solve your concerns. Everything you need, you already have. It's all about taking the first step."

Many people think that the quality of leadership is the exclusive domain of a select few individuals. There are many people who are passionate about various causes or issues, but who are reluctant to begin initiatives to deal with those causes. The general sentiment is that if the prominent *askanim* are not tackling an issue, if the "big guns" are not pouring their energy and resources into a subject, then there is no point in the average person making an effort to address it. Those who do decide to take some initiative often spend years trying to connect with large organizations or to interest prominent *rabbanim* in their issues, and when they are rejected, they give in to despair. In reality, though, the best thing to do would be to launch an initiative program of their own. There are many endeavors dedicated to worthy causes that have been started by ordinary people who did not shy away from assuming a leadership role.

There is no need for us to wait for the most prominent people in our society to take action. There are many things that the average person can do to promote *kavod Shem Shamayim*, and Klal Yisrael needs demonstrations of leadership on a small scale just as much as it needs its more well-known leaders. Any of us, any ordinary individual, can take a small step toward creating greater kiddush Hashem. It can begin in our own backyards, with the simplest and most unassuming endeavor; yet the results we achieve can be incredible.

Take, for instance, the family in Boro Park who became concerned about the chillul Hashem caused by inconsiderate driving habits within the *frum* community. On their own, this family began distributing letters and bumper stickers that would remind people to drive with greater sensitivity for others, keeping in mind the importance of kiddush Hashem. Then there is the young man who decided to raise awareness of the value of kiddush Hashem by designing colorful cards that would remind people of the mitzvah. Acting completely on his own, without the backing of any organization, this man distributed tens of thousands of those cards at the Siyum HaShas and in other strategic locations.

If you have thought of an issue that needs to be addressed or a way to generate greater kiddush Hashem, there is no reason to wait for *askanim* or organizations to take the lead; on the contrary, you can do it on your own. And even the smallest efforts can be of extraordinary value. On your own street or in your own apartment complex, you can be the one who will shovel snow in the winter or clear away leaves in the fall; you can take the initiative of putting away the children's riding toys every night, seeing to it that the garbage is organized and contained, and making sure, in general, that you live in a place that is fit for royalty. If there are tensions on your block between the religious residents and their irreligious or non-Jewish neighbors, you can be the one to communicate with those neighbors by placing letters or flyers in their mailboxes, offering some explanation of *frum* culture to foster understanding and mutual respect. These are a few examples of the small steps anyone can take toward creating a kiddush Hashem, and the impact can be unimaginable.

If we do not take the small steps, then we can be certain that our goals will not be achieved. But if we recognize that we all have the capacity for leadership, and that all we must do is take a tiny bit of initiative on our own, we may find that we will achieve far more than we could ever have dreamed.

Takeaway

All of us, in our own backyards and our own communities, can make a difference and take the lead in making a kiddush Hashem.

⟹◈⟸

Children Are Watching

I once received a letter from an older man named Ralph, who had been interested in converting to Judaism for a number of years and wanted to share his story with me. Ralph related that he first became interested in Judaism as a young child, when he was inspired by a kindhearted Jewish neighbor. That childhood experience ignited an attraction to Judaism that persisted throughout the years that followed.

The letter writer recalled asking his mother about Mr. Snyder, their Jewish neighbor, who spoke with a European accent and regularly treated him to Twinkies, his favorite snack. Ralph's mother explained that their kind neighbor came from "a place far, far away, where they don't talk like us." When Ralph questioned her about why he had come to America, she said simply, "There were evil people there who wanted to hurt Mr. Snyder."

"But who would want to hurt him?" the bewildered boy exclaimed. "He's nice and he gives me Twinkies."

"Ralph, you're too young to understand yet, but Mr. Snyder is a Jew," she replied.

Later that year, Ralph came down with advanced chronic pneumonia and was admitted to the hospital, where he hovered on the brink of death. His parents and other relatives visited him while he recovered, as did the benevolent Mr. Snyder, who came equipped with a large bag full of Twinkies. The nurse dutifully confiscated the goodies and allowed the boy to have only one each day.

Years later, Ralph's mother revealed to him that the doctors had believed that he would not survive for long after his admission to the hospital. His illness had already reached an advanced stage, and there seemed to be little hope that he would recover. Nevertheless, she said, he had recovered as a result of the many prayers that were said on his behalf.

"Did Mr. Snyder also pray for me?" Ralph asked.

"Yes, he did," his mother replied. "He prayed every day, all day long, for you to live. Jews never stop praying."

It was then that Ralph learned the full truth about Mr. Snyder's tragic past. His mother revealed that their former neighbor had once had a wife, a daughter, and two sons, but they were brutally murdered during World War II. Out of his entire family, only his mother-in-law had survived. Ralph was filled with rage. "Who could hate that much?" he demanded.

"They called themselves the Aryan master race, the Nazis, and they wanted to kill all the Jews because they are the chosen people of G-d," his mother said.

"Then we should kill all those Aryans!" Ralph shouted in response.

"Then begin with yourself, Ralph," his mother said, "because you are an Aryan too." She explained that their family's Anglo-Saxon heritage made them part of the Aryan race. Ralph admitted that he had no desire to harm anyone, and his mother agreed. "You can honor Mr. Snyder, who was always kind to you, by mirroring his love and kindness to others," she added. "He was very good to you, an Aryan boy. Treasure his memory and keep it in your heart."

Ralph concluded his letter by revealing that he had never forgotten Mr. Snyder; even years later, he could still see the man's kind smile and joyous expression in his mind's eye. And along with the warmth of those recollections, he remains haunted by the same question he posed to his mother all those years ago: "Who would want to hurt Mr. Snyder?"

We are all conscious of the danger of chillul Hashem when we are in the presence of non-Jewish adults. We recognize that our actions are being observed and will influence their perception of our nation, the chosen people of Hashem. What we sometimes do not realize, though, is that the same is true when we are observed by non-Jewish children. This is especially the case when the children are young, as their impressions of the world haven't yet been fully formed and their prejudices have not yet taken root. During those formative years, the impressions that enter a child's developing mind may mold his views and feelings for years to come.

Rav Yaakov Kamenetsky was once sitting in the waiting room of a doctor's office, along with a five-year-old non-Jewish boy. While the revered *gadol* certainly could have spent his time learning, he chose to take a ball and play catch with the little boy instead. After the encounter had ended, he explained to a *talmid* who was accompanying him, "I wanted that little boy to have positive memories of an elderly bearded Jew."[6]

If we see a child who needs help crossing a street, or who is lost and crying, or who is struggling with a heavy package, we

---

6. This story appeared in an article in the *Jewish Observer* by Rabbi Yonason Rosenblum, in January 2001.

can make a tremendous impact simply by bending down and demonstrating compassion, asking the child how we can help or reassuring him that everything will be all right. Certainly, a child will be affected if a Jew helps him at a time of crisis, but even under ordinary circumstances, a small display of kindness or compassion can have far-reaching effects.

As we pursue our mission of kiddush Hashem, let us always remember: The children of the world may be watching.

Takeaway

Our actions have the potential to leave lasting impressions on impressionable non-Jewish children. It is easy to ignore them, but they are at an age when we have an excellent opportunity to create a Kiddush Hashem. There can be tremendous benefit to teaching them to associate a man with a beard or a yarmulka with kindness and compassion.

Making It Practical

- If you see a child looking for his parents or trying to reach something on a high shelf in a store, take a minute to help him. Your act of kindness may go a long way.

Discussion Points:

❖ If our ultimate mission in life is to create kiddush Hashem, then the Torah and mitzvos must be tools for achieving that purpose. How do all of the mitzvos in the Torah contribute to kiddush Hashem?

❖ There are many mitzvos in the Torah that we do not understand, and that strike others as strange. The society around us also has its own set of values that are different from our own, and the nations of the world are often not impressed by our version of ethics and morality. How can we bring honor to Hashem by observing mitzvos that others do not understand, and by displaying values that they do not appreciate?

❖ We are a tiny fraction of the world's population; is it really possible for us to make a difference on a global scale?

CHAPTER 9

IN SANCTUARIES AND CELEBRATIONS

A few of Chaim's non-religious coworkers have often expressed interest in learning more about his community, which they call "the ultra-Orthodox world." Finally, Chaim decides to take them on a tour of a yeshivah, where they can get a firsthand look at the world that intrigues them so greatly. In the corridors of the yeshivah building, they take an interest in the pictures of gedolim that decorate the walls; they question Chaim about the identities of these great rabbanim and the reason that they are held in such high esteem. Chaim then leads his companions into the ezras nashim, where they look down at the beis medrash and take in the astounding sight of hundreds of bachurim davening with great intensity. They have arrived in the middle of a Monday morning Shacharis, and the guests take special notice of the way the sefer Torah is handled with reverence and the beauty of the aron kodesh. As they leave the yeshivah, they comment that it is clearly a place of great sanctity, and they have been deeply moved by the respect shown by the yeshivah students.

The Power of Celebration

Seventeen is the *gematria* of the word *"tov,"* and when the participants in Rabbi Zev Cohen's learning program completed 17 percent of *Shas*, he arranged a festive *siyum*. This may seem to be an odd point at which to celebrate, but Reb Zev had an excellent reason for it. The learning program that he oversees moves at a pace of one *blatt* every week. At that pace, it would take 52 years to complete the entire *Shas*. When Reb Zev first heard about this type of program, he approached Rav Aharon Leib Shteinman and asked if it was worthwhile to undertake it. "Yes," the illustrious *rosh yeshivah* replied, "but you should make elaborate *siyumim* with good food very often, in order to be *mechazek* the participants." In keeping with that advice, Reb

Zev uses every appropriate opportunity to schedule a *siyum*.

This piece of advice is even more astonishing when we consider what is known about Rav Shteinman himself. An attendee at a *shiur* in halachah once asked Rav Shteinman when he had last eaten a meal with bread on an ordinary weekday. "Over fifty years ago," Rav Shteinman replied.

"And when was the last time the *rosh yeshivah* made the *berachah* of *mezonos* on a weekday?" the man asked.

"I haven't done that in seventy years," Rav Shteinman revealed. Yet this *gadol*, who had not eaten a piece of cake on a regular day in almost three quarters of a century, understood the power of a celebratory meal.

Rav Dessler (*Michtav MeEliyahu*, Vol. 5) likens the human heart to a field that has not been plowed. Until a field is plowed, its earth is hard; no seeds can penetrate its surface to take root, and the earth cannot absorb water to nourish developing plants. In order for the earth to produce crops, the field must be plowed so that it will be softened. Similarly, the human heart is naturally apathetic, resisting any external source of inspiration. In order for an emotionally moving or inspiring experience to affect the heart, it must be "softened" and made receptive to those influences.

There are two ways to "soften" the resistance of the heart. One is through suffering or tragedy; these things naturally make a person more emotional and more open to establishing bonds with others, including Hashem Himself. But that is not the only way to affect the heart; physical enjoyment can have the same effect. When a person enjoys good food or other types of material pleasure, it is natural for him to become more impressionable and more receptive to inspiration or influence.

This is the reason that we celebrate Shabbos and Yom Tov with lavish meals. Good food opens our hearts, making us more receptive to an emotional connection with Hashem. However, this is true only when the food is used as a means to an end. When physical enjoyment is an end in itself, without a strong connection to a higher ideal, then it inspires a person only to increase his pursuit of *gashmiyus*. This, too, is reflected by the analogy to a field: In order for crops to grow, one must sow the seeds immediately after the earth has been plowed.

The Yeshiva of West Bloomfield once celebrated a *hachnassas sefer Torah* with a festive *seudah* and spirited music and dancing. After the festivities, the *menahel* received an e-mail from a veteran general studies teacher, who had been deeply moved by the event. "Never have I experienced such warmth and joy connected with a religion," the man wrote.

Years ago, a story circulated about a *baal teshuvah* in Eretz Yisrael who had once been a staunch supporter of the Meretz party, a group known for its fierce opposition to Torah and *chareidi* society. The man was asked what had prompted him to make the radical turnaround of becoming religious, and he explained that his return to Yiddishkeit had been sparked by a powerful experience.

"There was a *hachnassas sefer Torah* in Tel Aviv, which was rare for a mostly secular city," he related. "It was a festive event; a decorative stage was brought out to the street, and children dressed in their finest held torches as they marched along. Joyful music blared from speakers, and many of the celebrants were dancing. As the procession made its way along the street, it was met by a group of protestors from Meretz, myself included. We were waving banners bearing the words '*lihiyos am chofshi*,' expressing our desire to be a 'free' nation, liberated from the Torah. Our group blocked the street and did not allow the procession to pass. The police were called, and they discovered that a permit had not been issued for the street to be used for the celebration. The procession was stopped and all the torches were extinguished, and everyone waited while the appropriate phone calls were made. After an hour had passed, the permit was issued and the police ordered us to move to the side as they allowed the festivities to continue. We watched as the music blasted and the *frum* participants danced with joy and enthusiasm. As I watched this scene, I was shocked by their excitement and happiness. I had always viewed the Torah as a book of rules that did nothing but restrict and inconvenience people. Once I saw that there was another side to the Torah lifestyle, that it could be a source of extraordinary enjoyment and satisfaction, I knew that I had to investigate it further. Ultimately, I discovered its true beauty."

Sometimes, a simple celebration can be the source of a tremendous kiddush Hashem, and if the festivities are unmistakably connected to a mitzvah, they can soften even the most impervious hearts.

Takeaway

Celebrating spiritual accomplishments is a powerful way to increase the honor of Hashem. Those festivities can be a source of inspiration and can highlight the importance of the spiritual in our lives.

Making It Practical

- Make a lavish *siyum* when you or your children finish a *masechta*. Invite your children's friends in order to foster a healthy atmosphere of *kinas sofrim*.
- Celebrate spiritual accomplishments with your family, such as by dancing spontaneously when one of your family members performs a significant *chessed*.

—————◆◆◆—————

Respect in the King's Palace

Imagine the following scene: Two defendants are brought into a courtroom and charged with publicly insulting the king of the country. To the surprise of the spectators, the judge lets one of the defendants go with a slap on the wrist, while the other is sentenced to a lengthy prison term. A murmur of surprise runs through the courtroom at the imbalance in the verdicts. No one can understand the reason for the blatant inconsistency between the two sentences.

The judge soon becomes aware of the wild speculation sweeping through the courtroom. He announces, "Ladies and gentlemen, you have all missed a crucial difference between the two cases. The first defendant was accused of speaking against the king on a public street. The second defendant, though, insulted the king in the royal palace itself. You can all understand that a visitor to the palace is expected to act with much greater respect and deference toward the king. An insult to the king is magnified exponentially when it takes place in his own home, or in his presence. With that in mind, I am sure you can understand the difference between the sentences handed down by this court."

This concept has great relevance to us, as servants of the King of kings. While we must see to it that our actions promote *kevod Shamayim* everywhere we go, that responsibility is even greater when we are in the places that are considered the "royal palaces" of Hashem — the *shuls* and *batei medrash* where we learn and *daven*.

The *Mishnah Berurah* (151:1) warns us to take particular care to avoid *lashon hara*, quarreling, and other forms of forbidden speech when we are in a *shul* or *beis medrash*. "Aside from the fact that these are very severe sins," he explains, "the sin is magnified even more in a holy place, because it is an affront to the honor of the Shechinah. There is no comparing a person who sins in private and one who sins in the palace of the King and in the King's presence." The *Mishnah Berurah* also warns that if one person fails to maintain the proper decorum in a *shul*, his conduct is very likely to spark a chain reaction, quickly leading the entire *shul* to be engulfed in strife. "These quarrels are like a flood," he explains. "The sin begins with a few people, but eventually they form separate factions to fight with each other, to the point that the entire *shul* becomes like a huge inferno …

causing violence and slander, and the desecration of Hashem's Name among the nations will be great. Therefore," the *Mishnah Berurah* concludes, "a person who fears and trembles at the Word of Hashem should ... never engage in idle talk in a *shul* or *beis medrash*, and those places should be, for him, designated solely for Torah and *tefillah*."

The potential for chillul Hashem identified by the *Mishnah Berurah* is a major concern. When a visitor at a royal palace shows a lack of respect for the king, his crime lies not only in his attitude toward the king himself, but also in the fact that he has lowered the king's honor in the eyes of others. In a place that is the personal domain of a king, people expect the king's subjects to be on their best behavior, showing the utmost deference toward their ruler. When one of the king's subjects fails to live up to those expectations, he is guilty of tarnishing the image of the royal palace.

It is logical to assume that even actions that are not inherently wrong, but simply are not considered in keeping with proper decorum, should be avoided in any *shul* or *beis medrash*. For instance, a number of *poskim* prohibit smoking in a *shul*, on the grounds that non-Jews refrain from smoking in their own houses or worship and courthouses (see *Shu"T Melamed L'Ho'il, Orach Chaim*, sec. 15 and *Shu"T Yaskil Avdi*, Vol. 6, *Even HaEzer*, sec. 1). The same is probably true of using cell phones in a *shul*: Even if it is not halachically prohibited, a person should refrain from using those devices within a *shul*, out of respect for the *shul*'s special status.[1]

---

1. Historically, the concern over chillul Hashem in *shuls* has been so great that it even led the *Rambam* to radically alter the procedure for an ordinary *tefillah*, calling for the *chazzan* to recite *Shemoneh Esrei* aloud while the congregants recite their own individual *tefillos*. This replaced the practice with which we are familiar, in which the *chazzan* repeats the *Shemoneh Esrei* aloud *after* the entire congregation has completed it in silence. The reason, as the *Rambam* explains in a *teshuvah*, was that it had become common for people to have conversations or engage in other activities during the *chazaras hashatz*, and the *Rambam* felt that their attitude of indifference toward the *tefillah* was liable to result in a major chillul Hashem. That concern, the *Rambam* felt, was enough to justify making an extraordinary change in the way *tefillos* are conducted.

Our behavior in our *shuls* and *batei medrash* may be noticed by others much more than we realize. A couple of years ago, Rabbi Avi Shafran received a video recording of a *shul* custodian speaking in broken English about proper decorum in *shul*. "Me no understand," said the obviously non-Jewish gentleman, who was wearing a worn T-shirt and was clearly an immigrant. "When they come to the synagogue — fifteen minutes, twenty minutes, thirty minutes, one hour, whatever — it's for the G-d, not for the phone. Somebody call? 'Oh, wait G-d! Somebody call me,'" he exclaimed, mimicking the attitude of the *mispallelim* he had seen in action. This non-Jewish janitor urged his listeners to turn their phones off in *shul*, or at least to refrain from answering them during the *tefillos*.

It was advice that we would all do well to follow.

Takeaway

We all spend large parts of every day in a shul or beis medrash. We must remember that these places are akin to "palaces" of the Master of the Universe here on earth, and we must be careful to create only kavod Shem Shamayim during the hours we spend there.

Making It Practical

- Treat a *shul* and *beis medrash* with the utmost respect. Make sure that your cell phone is turned off while you are in *shul*, and refrain from talking during *davening*.
- Dress appropriately to enter a *shul* and make sure that your appearance is orderly and your shirt is tucked in. This will convey the sense that you are standing in the presence of Hashem.

Embassies on Foreign Soil

When the United States Embassy was moved from Tel Aviv to Yerushalayim, the entire world was abuzz. The pros and cons of the move were heatedly debated, with many people analyzing its significance in the context of the Israeli-Palestinian conflict. As I was contemplating the concept of an embassy, I came to realize that all of us, as *frum* Jews, spend a large portion of our time in other "embassies." Let us examine what an embassy is, and then we will understand how the concept plays a major role in our lives.

An embassy is the headquarters of a country's diplomatic mission in a different country. The embassy's responsibility is to represent its home country on foreign soil and to preserve the rights of its country's citizens while they are abroad. The Vienna Convention on Diplomatic Relations sets forth the rights and immunities granted to foreign embassies and their staffs in every country. Among the stipulations of the treaty, which contains 53 articles, is that the host country must allow the diplomats to communicate freely with their home country. In addition, visiting diplomats are granted diplomatic immunity, and their families receive most of the same protections that they enjoy.

Now, when do we find ourselves in an "embassy" of any sort? The Gemara relates (*Berachos* 8a) that Rabbi Yochanan was surprised to find out that there were Jews in Bavel who had lived to an old age. He pointed out that the Torah states, "So that your days and the days of your sons will be increased *on the land that Hashem your G-d swore to give you*," implying that longevity is accessible to the Jewish people only in Eretz Yisrael. Rabbi Yochanan was then told that the elderly Jews of Bavel entered their *batei medrash* early every morning and left late at night, and he was satisfied with that explanation.

The *Kli Yakar* questions how this answered Rabbi Yochanan's question. Regardless of the virtuous practices of the Jews of Bavel, Rabbi Yochanan had inferred from the *pasuk* that it is possible to attain longevity only in Eretz Yisrael. How did the Jews of Bavel circumvent that?

The *Kli Yakar* answers this question with the teaching of *Chazal* that in the times of Mashiach, all the *shuls* and *batei medrash* of *chutz la'aretz* will be transported to Eretz Yisrael. As a result, he states that even now, when these institutions are still in *chutz la'aretz*, they have the status of Eretz Yisrael itself; in effect, like embassies on foreign soil. That is why the Jews of Bavel were able to enjoy long lives when they spent time in their *shuls*; since it was considered as if they were in Eretz Yisrael itself, they were able to benefit from the unique effects of the Land.[2]

Whenever we enter a *shul* or a *beis medrash*, we are effectively in an "embassy" of Eretz Yisrael, a piece of the most sacred country on earth that has been transplanted to wherever we may be. One would imagine that the interior of an embassy reflects the atmosphere and feel of the diplomats' home country, that the décor is designed to give the diplomats a taste of home, and that the language of their country is spoken on the embassy's premises. Likewise, our *shuls* give us a taste of the atmosphere of Yerushalayim and the *Beis HaMikdash*, places that are dedicated to the pursuit of *ruchniyus* and the service of Hashem.

There is another similarity between a *shul* and an embassy, as well. The diplomats and staff at an embassy are granted special immunity that protects them from prosecution in the host country. Inside an embassy, even visitors are considered to be on territory belonging to the diplomats' home country, and the host nation may not exercise any authority over them. Similarly, just as the *Beis HaMikdash* was once the conduit through which all of Hashem's blessings, protections, and special *hashgachah* flowed to the Jewish people, our *shuls* now serve that purpose.

---

2. In fact, the *Maharsha* (*Megillah* 29) takes this one step further, stating that every *shul* is considered not only like part of Eretz Yisrael in a foreign land, but actually like a piece of the *Beis HaMikdash* itself. In the future, he explains, the *shuls* and *batei medrash* from throughout the world will be brought to Eretz Yisrael and fused with the *Beis HaMikdash*, forming one immense structure; therefore, these buildings have the status of components of the *Beis HaMikdash* even today.

The Midrash likens the Jewish people to sheep, and their *shuls* to the huts where shepherds station themselves to watch their flocks. Similarly, our *shuls* are the places where the *Shechinah* rests in order to serve as our protection in *galus*, shielding us from harm and protecting our rights and interests.

In order for our *shuls* to afford us the full protection of an "embassy" of holiness, though, we must see to it that they are places where the Shechinah will be "comfortable." In order to achieve this, we must treat our *shuls* with the respect they are due, demonstrating our recognition of what a *shul* represents. Furthermore, we ourselves must act as true "ambassadors," demonstrating our connection to the values and ideals that our *shuls* represent. And that means that we must remain constantly committed to the ideals of *kiddush Shem Shamayim*.

If we do that, then we will always have an embassy close at hand, where we can take refuge from a hostile world.

Takeaway

Treating our shuls and batei medrash properly will ensure that we are blessed with Divine hashgachah even outside of Eretz Yisrael. If we act as "ambassadors" of Hashem and treat these holy places as "embassies" of His land, we will be protected and blessed, and Hashem's hashgachah will be revealed through us even in galus.

Making It Practical

- Do your part to maintain a respectful environment in your *shul*, yeshivah, or *beis medrash*. Keep it clean, put *sefarim* in their place, and make a special effort to treat others with respect while you are there.
- Act in a dignified way while you are in shul, and make it a place where the Shechinah will be comfortable.

Discussion Points

❖ How do festive celebrations serve to demonstrate our values and influence others?

❖ How do we bring honor to Hashem by showing respect for our yeshivos and *shuls*?

CHAPTER 10

MAKING IT PERSONAL

Yechiel is a bachur in a mainstream yeshivah. He has always struggled to keep up with the pace of learning. He does not feel that he is up to the task; there are many boys who are naturally better at learning, and who are superior to him in their hasmadah as well. Feeling more like a "number" than a person, Yechiel finds his motivation slipping away, as he cannot envision having a successful future in learning. He does not feel special or unique in any way, and he begins to search for other ways to derive a sense of importance.

Imitation Leads to Ruin

An interesting story is told about a farmer in Florida who owned a large plot of land. The farmer made every effort to raise useful crops or livestock on his property, but the quality of the land was so poor that none of his ventures succeeded. All that the land would produce was scrub oaks and rattlesnakes. After many failed attempts, the farmer was on the verge of giving up. But then he had an idea: He realized that he could turn his liability into an asset. The unproductive, seemingly useless plot of land was turned into a rattlesnake farm, where the deadly reptiles were bred for a variety of purposes. Their meat was canned, their venom was sold to laboratories, and their skins were sold to be used in the manufacture of shoes and handbags. Eventually, the farm became a major tourist attraction, and the farmer raked in a large profit. His hometown even changed its name to Rattlesnake, Florida, due to his great success (*How to Stop Worrying and Start Living*, Dale Carnegie).

This farmer did not allow his decisions to be shaped by what was normal or standard. Had he been determined to use his land the way other farmers used theirs, he would never have tried to earn a living through the unusual and innovative products that led him to success. It was only because he discovered the true usefulness of his own unique piece of real estate that he was able to prosper.

This concept is relevant to our spiritual lives as well. The story is told of the great *baal mussar* Rav Naftoli Amsterdam, who once said to his *rebbe*, Rav Yisroel Salanter, "If only I had the mind of the Shaagas Aryeh, the heart of the Yesod V'Shoresh HaAvodah, and the *middos* of Rebbe, I could truly serve Hashem." Rav Yisroel disagreed: "No, Naftoli! You must serve Hashem with your own mind, your own heart, and your own character traits. That is what Hashem truly desires!"[1]

Similarly, every human being has his own unique role to play in the service of Hashem. Many people are unsuccessful because they strive to succeed simply by imitating others; they choose tactics that other people use in their own *avodas Hashem* and try

---

1. The Torah states that Bnei Yisrael were commanded to use *shittim* (acacia) wood in the construction of the *Mishkan*. The Midrash (*Midrash Rabbah, Shemos* 35:2) derives an interesting lesson from this: Even though the entire world belongs to Hashem to do with as He pleases, he chose specifically to have the *Mishkan* — His "House" — built from the wood of a tree that does not bear fruit. So too, the Midrash continues, every human being should take a lesson from this to build his own home only from the wood of non-fruit-bearing trees, and not to needlessly destroy a tree that could produce fruit.

What is puzzling about this Midrash is that the Torah's mitzvah of *bal tashchis* expressly forbids cutting down a fruit-bearing tree. Why does the Midrash imply that the prohibition must be learned from the example of the *Mishkan*, when it is stated outright in the Torah?

In his *sefer Matnas Chaim* (on Purim), Rav Mattisyahu Salomon explains that the rationale of the mitzvah of *bal tashchis* is that nothing in the world exists without a purpose, as the Gemara teaches (*Shabbos* 77b), and, as *Chazal* state elsewhere (*Pirkei Avos* 6:11), the purpose of everything in the world is to bring honor to Hashem. The prohibition to wantonly destroy any item is meant to lead us to recognize that everything that exists was created for *kevod Shamayim*.

The *Mishkan* itself, however, was also meant to enhance Hashem's honor in the world. In fact, it was the greatest source of *kevod Shamayim* that existed. One might have thought, then, that any object in the world could be taken for use in the *Mishkan*, since it would then fulfill its purpose in the greatest possible way. But the Torah clearly shows us that this was not the case. It was forbidden to use the wood of a fruit-bearing tree, since those trees were already bringing honor to Hashem in a different way — by producing fruit — and it is forbidden even to change the manner in which an object is used for *kavod shamayim*, even if one does not completely deprive it of the ability to bring honor to Hashem.

to adopt them for themselves, not realizing that they are investing effort in areas where their own strengths do not lie.[2]

Sefer Koheles states that a person should "go in the ways of your heart." The Netziv (*Ha'amek Davar, Parashas Shelach*) comments on these words, "Whatever a person's heart is drawn to, it is clear that his *mazal* sees that it is something good according to the strengths of his soul." Every individual has his own unique strengths and talents. Let us *daven* for the wisdom to discover our own, so that we will be capable of serving Hashem in the best possible way for ourselves.

Takeaway

Each of us is unique; we were created in that way so that we will be able to add to Hashem's honor in our own individual ways. In order to discover our roles, we must avoid imitating others and concentrate on our own abilities.

Making It Practical

• Develop a spiritual "hobby": Have an allotted time weekly or daily to build on a specialized area of *avodas Hashem* that is uniquely suited to you.

2. We are all familiar with the story of Kayin and Hevel, but while we understand that Kayin was punished for murdering Hevel, it is not entirely clear why Hevel himself deserved to be killed. Certainly, Kayin would not have been able to take his life if it hadn't been Divinely decreed for Hevel to die, but what did Hevel do wrong? The answer to that question can be found in the Torah itself. The Torah states, "And Hevel *also* brought from the firstborn of his sheep." The word "also" implies that there was nothing innovative about the *korbanos* that Hevel brought; rather than introduce his own form of *avodas Hashem*, he simply followed the example set by Kayin. But since he was not adding to *kevod Shamayim* independently in any way, there was no purpose to his continued existence (*Kli Yakar* 4:3).

Choose Your Specialty

Imagine the following scenario: A person is told that he is suffering from a heart condition that can be corrected only by cardiac surgery, and is asked to choose between two doctors who are willing to perform the operation. One is an expert cardiologist with extensive surgical experience, while the other is a physician with broad knowledge of the field of medicine in general. Is there any doubt as to which of the two the patient will select?

This hypothetical case illustrates an important principle. Of the two doctors in question, the one who is more qualified, by far, for the job at hand is the one who has poured all of his energies into mastering a specific specialty. The other doctor lacks the needed qualifications precisely because he did not focus his studies on one specific area. This doctor would make only a mediocre cardiologist, at best. And while a general doctor also has a role to play in the medical field, if we use this as an analogy for our spiritual goals, the cardiac surgeon is much closer to our ideal.

The *Netziv* (*Ha'amek Davar, Parashas Balak*) explains that every Jew should try to fulfill as many mitzvos as he can, but every individual should also make it his business to choose one mitzvah in which he will *excel*. Every person has been given the ability to achieve perfection in one specific mitzvah, and each of us has a mission to identify our own unique mitzvah and to observe it in the ultimate way.

"It is the slavery to a single idea or objective," a famous author once wrote, "that has given to many a person of seemingly mediocre talent the ability of a genius." Many of the greatest accomplishments in history were achieved by people who were willing to put aside all other considerations and focus solely on a single goal, and that principle holds no less true when it comes to our spiritual pursuits.

There is a quote attributed to Angelo Patri: "Nobody is so miserable as he who longs to be somebody and something other than the person he is, in body and in mind." The Torah calls on every Jew not to shape himself into an imitation of other people, but rather to become "the person he is." While *kinas sofrim* is an excellent motivating force, it should not drive us to mimic others; instead, it should motivate us to bring out the best within ourselves.

The *Chiddushei HaRim* teaches us that every individual has both the ability and the obligation to become a *"gadol hador"* in his own particular way. But in order to do that, he must follow his own unique path and focus on the areas in which his greatest strengths lie.

Takeaway

By excelling in one specific pursuit, a person can bring out his full potential. A person who becomes an "expert" in a single area can bring more honor to Hashem than one who is mediocre in a broad range of areas.

Making It Practical

- Choose one *masechta* or area of halachah that you are passionate about, and study it with the greatest intensity, until you have become an expert in that field.
- Find one form of *chessed* that stirs passion within you, and make it your own personal cause, to which you are supremely devoted.

Connecting to the Tree of Life

In the previous section, we discussed the need for a person to choose one specific area of Yiddishkeit as his "specialty." It is important to note that this can have an impact on a person's *avodas Hashem* in other areas as well.

Returning to our analogy, a cardiac surgeon certainly needs to be aware of how the rest of the body functions, not just the heart. All of the body's organs and systems are interconnected, and it is impossible to treat one part of the human body without being aware of how it will affect and be affected by all of the other organs. At the same time, a cardiac surgeon is motivated by his interest in his specialty; that motivating force is what fuels his study of medicine.

Like the parts of the body, all of the mitzvos of the Torah are interconnected. When a person pursues the one mitzvah that is closest to his heart, he will find that it will motivate him to learn and observe many other areas of the Torah, as well. The desire to excel in a single mitzvah can be the key to one's entire *avodas Hashem*. The *Sefer Chareidim* (61) explains that this is indicated by the *pasuk* that states, "It [the Torah] is a tree of life for those who hold on to it." When a person takes hold of one branch of a tree, he can keep a solid grasp on that branch, and he will thus be considered to be holding the entire tree. However, if a person tries to hold all of the branches of a tree at once, he will find it impossible to keep a grasp on the tree. Similarly, the way to "take hold" of the entire Torah is to dedicate oneself to a single mitzvah and to pursue it with all of one's strength.

When a person discovers the mitzvah on which he was meant to focus, there is no limit to the degree of greatness he can achieve. The Gemara (*Taanis* 21b) tells the story of Abba Umna, a physician who was greeted every day by a Heavenly *bas kol*; this was something that even the great *Amoraim* Abaye and Rava experienced on a much less frequent basis. Abaye was troubled by the fact that the doctor seemed to have surpassed him in greatness, but he learned that the reason was the doctor's outstanding generosity and absolute dedication to the modesty of his patients, areas in which he excelled. It wasn't that he had mastered the performance of hundreds of mitzvos; he reached a tremendous level of greatness simply through an intense focus on one specific area.

There was once a *bachur* in a yeshivah who felt that he was not succeeding in learning. Eventually, with a heavy heart, he decided that his natural abilities were not suited to Torah learning, and he decided to go to work. But he also made an inner resolution that he would not allow himself to feel like a failure; instead, he would figure out one area in which he could excel, something that would keep him perpetually connected to Yiddishkeit. The area he chose was *davening* with a *minyan*; he made an ironclad commitment to daven every *tefillah* with a *minyan*, refusing to forgo for any reason. And so it was; every day, no matter how difficult it was, he made sure to *daven* with a *minyan*. He went to *shul* even when he was sick, and when he traveled, he scheduled his flights in such a way that he would never miss a *minyan*. He managed to go for years without missing a *minyan*, to the point that he was able to report that he had *davened* 4000 consecutive prayers with a *minyan*. That accomplishment provided him with a sense of connection to Yiddishkeit that proved to be crucial throughout those long, difficult years.

The Jewish nation is made up of millions of different individuals, each with his own unique talents and abilities. Some people were created to spend their lives in the *beis medrash*, while others were given different roles to fill. As long as a person identifies his own unique mission and fulfills it completely and properly, he is guaranteed to receive the ultimate reward, and to be part of the massive tapestry of kiddush Hashem created by the entire Jewish people together.

Takeaway

When a person discovers the "specialty" that is suited to him, he will be filled with motivation, meaning and purpose, which will give rise to a powerful sense of connection to Yiddishkeit.

Making It Practical

- Look out for mitzvos that touch your heart and inspire you. When you discover a mitzvah that has that effect on you, work on developing a strong connection to the mitzvah, to the point that you excel in it and it can be considered your "specialty." This can help you develop a strong connection to the entire Torah.
- Find a mitzvah that you can observe completely *l'Shem Shamayim*, without hope for personal gain.

Discussion Points

- ❖ There are many religious Jews in the world; how can each of us make a unique contribution to kiddush Hashem?
- ❖ How does every person add to the kiddush Hashem in the world as an individual?
- ❖ How can a person identify his own unique strengths and his own personal mission to bring honor to Hashem?

CHAPTER 11

FINDING MEANING IN SUFFERING

Chani has a child who has serious intellectual disabilities. She has spent an inordinate amount of time, energy, and money providing for her child, whom she loves dearly. She knows that her situation is the Will of Hashem, and she tries her best to accept it with love. But there are many questions that trouble her: Why did this happen to her child? What did she do wrong? What did the child do wrong? What does Hashem want from such a child? What can he add to the world, and what will be his contribution to Hashem and to the Jewish people?

When Our True Colors Show

In 2014, the beginning of the summer turned into a time of mourning and fear for the Jewish people. The abduction and brutal murder of three innocent young boys in Israel plunged all of Klal Yisrael into mourning. While the country was still reeling from the tragedy, the piercing wails of air-raid sirens began to fill the air, leading to a military conflict and much loss of life. Is there any way we can find meaning in the suffering of millions of Jews?

The *Kli Yakar* in *Parashas Eikev* (*Devarim* 8:1) provides us with an incredible insight: One of the reasons that Hashem inflicts painful suffering on the Jewish people is to bring to light the true greatness that lies within them, to show the world the level of greatness that Klal Yisrael is capable of attaining. Thus, the Torah (ibid.) states that Hashem led us into the *midbar* and brought hardships on us "in order to afflict you and to test you, to know what is in your heart, whether you will observe His mitzvos or not." This *pasuk* tells us that the purpose of those trials was "*lenasos'cha* — to test you," a term that is derived from the word *neis*, "a banner," which would cause the entire world "to know" what lies within a Jewish heart. (When the Torah says that the purpose of the challenges was "to know what is in your heart," it does not mean that the intent was for Hashem to know, but rather for the entire world to know.) Thus, Hashem's goal was to demonstrate Klal Yisrael's true essence to the entire world, like a banner that is raised for everyone to see. And in order to trigger a demonstration of the Jewish people's true colors, He subjected them to many challenging and extremely trying situations.

The families of the three kidnapped boys in Eretz Yisrael were subjected to one of the most unimaginable torments known to man: the loss of their sons, who were found brutally murdered after days of anguished searching. The bereaved parents' reactions to their ordeal may well have been the epitome of kiddush Hashem, an idea that was expressed by Prime Minister Netanyahu in his eulogy for the boys: "The nation understood immediately the depth of the roots and your strength of spirit. You taught us all a full lesson that we will not forget. A lesson in faith and determination, in unity and sensitivity, in Judaism and humanity."

These families heroically used their personal tragedy to teach the entire nation the meaning of *emunah peshutah*. In a clip shown on Israeli television before the bitter truth of the three boys' deaths became known, Mrs. Fraenkel, one of the three mothers, asked a group of girls at the Kosel to promise her that they would never lose faith, no matter what was the outcome of the situation. "Hashem is not our employee," she told them. "He doesn't always do what we want."

And then came the invasion of Gaza, and with it all the anguish and pain and difficulties that are part and parcel of living in a country at war. And yet, in the midst of the darkness of wartime, so many unexpected points of light began to shine. Reports poured in from soldiers stationed in the south about the unexpected acts of kindness of complete strangers, about care packages laden with every possible item those soldiers might need being shipped down to the battlefront, about letters filled with good will pouring in from all over the country.

During this conflict, even the commander of the IDF's Givati Brigade, who is known as Israel's foremost tactical expert in this type of ground assault, sent a written order to his soldiers before they went into battle, calling on them to pray to Hashem.

This *eis tzarah*, this time of danger and sorrow, brought to light so much of the goodness and compassion latent within the Jewish people. It showed the true essence of Klal Yisrael, the depths of kindness and nobility of spirit of which the Jewish people are capable. But most of all, it lifted all of us to a new level, which will be an everlasting *zechus* for those who gave their lives *al* kiddush Hashem.

Takeaway

Suffering brings out our true colors. Much more than any speech or declaration of faith, a person's reaction to suffering demonstrates his genuine, unshakable emunah.

Making It Practical

- If a tragedy occurs, *lo aleinu*, or you find yourself facing a challenge, try to find ways to turn it into a kiddush Hashem. View the difficulty as a way to be *mekadesh Shem Shamayim*, to strengthen yourself and to show the depth of your *emunah* and love for Hashem.

Kiddush Hashem in Any Kind of Life

A family once came to Rav Elazar Menachem Mann Shach with a heartrending *she'eilah*: Their mother was severely ill, and the doctors had told them that the only way she could survive her sickness was to undergo a complex operation. At the same time, the surgery would not bring about a complete recovery, and she would still suffer from debilitating symptoms. "What should we do?" they asked the *rosh yeshivah*. "Should she have the operation, even though she will continue to suffer afterward?"

"Do you mean to say that her life after the surgery won't be worth living?" Rav Shach responded. "The only factor to consider is whether she will live longer; it is not up to us to gauge whether her life will have enough quality to be worth living."

Rav Shach then quoted a midrash: At the end of Moshe Rabbeinu's life, Hashem told him that the time had come for him to leave this world, and that an extraordinary reward awaited him in the World to Come. But despite the Divine promise of a blissful afterlife, Moshe was unwilling to accept death and begged Hashem to let him go on living, even "like an animal roaming the earth and searching for food, or at least like a bird...."

"You see?" the *rosh yeshivah* explained. "Moshe preferred to live on in such a miserable state, rather than being taken to *Olam Haba* to enjoy his vast, eternal reward, because every living thing in this world, and even every inanimate object, adds to Hashem's *kavod* with every moment of its continued existence. For that reason, life is precious regardless of what form it takes, even if a person lives with minimal *bechirah* or none at all."

Rav Shach shared the same thought when he went to visit the family of Rav Shmaryahu Greineman during the *shivah* after his passing. Rav Greineman had been severely ill and unaware of his surroundings for a while before his passing, but Rav Shach assured the family that even the years he had lived in that state did not go to waste. As long as a person is alive, the *rosh yeshivah* stressed, he continues to enhance the *kevod Shamayim* in the world, even if it is not clear how he does so. In fact, Moshe Rabbeinu himself would have preferred to live in the same state as Rav Greineman rather than leaving this world to reap the reward that awaited him in *Olam Haba*. Life, no matter what form it takes, is always worth living (*Lulei Sorascha, Parashas Va'eschanan*).

Sadly, there are people who live for years, or even for their entire lives, with conditions that severely limit them physically, mentally, or in both ways. Often, watching these people struggle and suffer leaves others with a single painful question: Why are their lives worth living? But as the Midrash indicates, while we may not know exactly how a specific person's life contributes to *kevod Shamayim*, we can be certain that every human being, regardless of his limitations, adds to the kiddush Hashem in the world with every moment he lives. And that is certainly ample reason for a life to be worthwhile.

Aharon Margalit, the author of the autobiographical work *As Long as I Live*, relates how he made kiddush Hashem the basis of his existence while he struggled with a huge burden of medical problems. Aharon was shaken when he learned that he had contacted a rapidly progressing form of cancer for which the survival rate was a mere 15 percent in the first year and dropped to zero over three years. After beginning 18 months of treatment that included 17 operations, Aharon begged Hashem to reveal to him what he was expected to achieve while facing that challenge. At that point, he continues, he felt as if a voice from Above spoke to him and filled him with a sense of purpose: Instead of bringing solace and a spiritual boost to the sick in their homes and hospital wards as he had once done, he was now to accompany them to the "darkest places," the treatment rooms themselves, and show his fellow patients, their families and friends, as well as the medical staff, how a believing Jew copes with the challenge of a grueling illness. In order to connect with other sufferers, Aharon realized, he needed to share their experiences: the pain, the distress, the fear, and the constant uncertainty. Only then would he be able to transmit *emunah* and *bitachon* effectively to those around him. From that point on, Aharon related, he took it upon himself "to remember the objective: to publicly sanctify Hashem's Name in the darkest, deepest places."

All of us have the same mission in life, in our own unique circumstances: to sanctify Hashem's Name. If we remain always focused on that objective, then we will discover, as Aharon did, how to properly carry out that mission. And when we do so, our lives will be filled with meaning.

Takeaway

Even without free choice, every person's life adds to kevod Shamayim, and the value of any life defies estimation. Even Moshe Rabbeinu would have preferred to live even as an animal rather than to be taken from this world.

Making It Practical

- When something happens in your life that is out of your control, imagine that Hashem is lovingly leading you along a path filled with obstacles to a destination that will be well worth the journey.

Discussion Points

❖ In *galus*, when Klal Yisrael suffers, it is generally a chillul Hashem for the people of Hashem to be in difficult straits. However, there are many individual cases of suffering in which it is the mission of an individual to be *mekadesh Shem Shamayim* through his troubles. How does this add to Hashem's honor?

❖ There are many people who seem to be living lives that are filled with pain that prevents them from functioning normally. Some people even live with severe physical or mental impairments. Is it worth living such a life?

CHAPTER 12

PRIDE IN BEING A JEW

Rabbi Feinberg is a fourth-grade rebbi in a yeshivah in New York. One of his goals is to imbue his talmidim with pride in being Jewish. He fills them with excitement for mitzvos and for the Torah, and he impresses on them that the Jewish people are fortunate to have a book of instructions for living a life of connection to Hashem. He sings the song "Ashreinu mah tov chelkeinu" and dances with his students after giving a moving explanation of the words. Whenever he hears or sees a story in the news about something special that a Jewish person did, he shares it with his class in order to add to their appreciation of the special nation to which they belong. Rabbi Feinberg feels that this is a kiddush Hashem, since the boys will be drawn to more Torah and mitzvos and will have greater strength to overcome adversity if they have a sense of pride in who they are.

Feeling Proud

Rabbi Yechiel Spero once told a remarkable story about one of our generation's most well-known philanthropists, Reb Shlomo Yehuda Rechnitz. On a trip from Eretz Yisrael to the United States, Reb Shlomo took a flight with a stopover in Shannon, Ireland. In the airport, he found a group of hundreds of American soldiers waiting for their own flights. It was mealtime, and upon striking up a conversation with the soldiers, Reb Shlomo discovered that they were displeased with the poor quality of the rations they had been served. The philanthropist approached the soldiers' commanding officer and asked him, "Sir, how many soldiers are in your battalion?"

"About four hundred," the man replied.

Reb Shlomo produced a credit card. "Tell your soldiers to go into town, and let each of them buy a fifty-dollar meal; I will sponsor it," he told the astounded commander.

Stunned by the stranger's generosity, the soldiers invited Reb Shlomo to say a few words. He spoke about the Jewish concept of *hakaras hatov*, explaining that Jews attach great importance to showing appreciation to those who benefit them. "People like you are the reason my family and I can be safe," he declared, eliciting a round of applause from the soldiers.

After his speech had ended, Reb Shlomo was approached by a soldier who revealed that he was a fellow Jew. "I come from Kentucky," he related. "All of us are from that area of the United States, and there aren't many Jews there at all. I wear *tefillin* every day, and the other soldiers always mock me, not because they are anti-Semitic, but simply because they think I'm strange. I have always been the laughingstock of the group, but thanks to you, I am now going to be the hero, because they have seen what Orthodox Jews are about."

One of the ways a kiddush Hashem affects others is by enabling other Jews to feel a sense of pride in their Yiddishkeit. When a Jewish person acts in a way that brings honor to Hashem, others who witness it feel empowered to follow his example, and their own commitment to Yiddishkeit is enhanced. This can be a crucial component of *avodas Hashem*. As Rabbeinu Yonah teaches in *Shaarei Teshuvah*, when a person appreciates his own innate worth and recognizes the greatness of his roots as a Jew, he will find it much easier to resist the pull of the *yetzer hara*.

Takeaway

When other Jews do positive things, we feel a stronger sense of pride and hold our heads a little higher. Their actions make it possible for us to be proud of who we are and not to be ashamed, strengthening our resolve and our commitment to a life of Torah.

—⟫◈⟪—

The Treasure Within

In *Pirkei Avos* (3:14), the Mishnah states that *nedarim*, vows,
serve as a "fence" that "protects" the trait of *perishus*. The
very next mishnah goes on to state, "Beloved is man, for he was
created in the image [of Hashem]." Since this mishnah follows
the previous one, it is clear that there must be some sort of connection between these two statements. How are these two ideas
connected?

The *Maharal* explains that when a person builds a fence to
protect something, he will determine the quality of the fence
based on the item he wishes to safeguard. Fort Knox, the noted
United States stronghold that houses much of the country's
gold reserves and is estimated to contain 2.3 percent of all the
gold ever refined in history, is protected by a dizzying array of
security measures. Multiple doors of astonishing weight and
thickness block the entrance to the vault, and those doors can
be opened only by staff members entering separate combina-
tions that are known to no one else. The facility is surrounded
by many fences, including barbed wire and electric fences, and

protected by security cameras, alarms, and mine fields. No less than 30,000 soldiers are assigned to various units involved in guarding the fort, many of them equipped with advanced weaponry and military vehicles. All of these measures are driven by a simple recognition: the contents of the fort are so incredibly valuable that they warrant the most remarkable forms of protection known to man.

Thus, understanding the value of the *tzelem Elokim*, the Divine image within every person, is very much linked with the Mishnah's teaching about how we safeguard that Divine image. If a person is not aware of the value of the *tzelem Elokim*, he will not be motivated to use the protective measures available to him, such as the use of *nedarim*. But if he realizes that his *tzelem Elokim* is priceless — that it makes him worthy of being called "beloved" — then he will do everything in his power to protect it.

Imagine the difference between two people carrying huge sums of cash in their pockets, one of whom is aware of that fact while the other is not. The person who knows about the fortune in his pocket will be extremely cautious, doing nothing that might cause him to risk losing the money he is carrying. He certainly will not walk through a crime-ridden neighborhood or partake in a game of tackle football, lest the precious cash be lost. The person who is unaware of the money in his possession, meanwhile, will take no such precautions. He will go about his regular routine, and he will see nothing wrong even with giving in to silly temptations or acting in a frivolous way.

Every one of us possesses a priceless treasure whose value many people do not recognize: the *Yiddishe neshamah* (Jewish soul). A person who appreciates the value of his *neshamah* will make every effort to protect it, shielding it from influences that might mar its beauty and constantly evaluating his own actions to make certain that he is protecting it properly.

This is what makes the impact of a kiddush Hashem so incredibly valuable and important. When other Jews witness a kiddush Hashem, they are moved to appreciate the enormous value of their own *neshamos*, and to make even greater efforts to preserve the beauty of their souls. Even those who already observe the mitzvos can be moved by a kiddush Hashem performed by others to increase their commitment and resolve. Any Jew can turn himself into a shining example of what a Jewish soul can accomplish, and thus can ignite a desire in countless other people to live up to the ideals he has demonstrated.

Takeaway

When we recognize the true value of our souls, we will be more careful to protect them from being harmed or tarnished in any way.

Making It Practical

- Set high expectations for your children, your students, or other people in your circle of influence, using love and compassion to guide them toward higher ideals. This will send the message that you believe in the incredible capacity of their *neshamos* for greatness.

- If you are a parent or teacher, make it your business to read stories of human greatness to your children or your students, whether about the greatness of *gedolim* or of simple people. There are even stories about children in our own times who have accomplished great things, such as the many children from nonreligious homes who attended religious schools, made great sacrifices, and grew to incredible levels of Jewish devotion.

A Nation Like No Other

In general, there is a tendency to focus on the negative. In our constant quest for self-improvement and perfection, it is only natural for us to focus on our flaws, as part of an effort to rid ourselves of them. But as important as it is to work on ourselves, it is also important for us not to forget the other side of the coin: We must not allow ourselves to lose sight of the greatness of our nation, the Jewish people.

The *Mesillas Yesharim* teaches us that Hashem loves only those who love Bnei Yisrael. "The more a person loves Yisrael," *Ramchal* asserts, "the more Hashem loves him.... This can be compared to a [mortal] father, who loves no person more than someone whom he sees genuinely loving his children." Of course, Hashem does not have an emotional need for others to love His children. But Hashem does want His Name to be sanctified in the physical world, and His honor is closely connected to that of the Jewish people. The more respect is accorded to the Jews, the more Hashem Himself is honored.

When Eliyahu HaNavi spoke negatively about the Jewish people, accusing them of abandoning their *bris* (covenant) with Hashem (*I Melachim* 19), his position of leadership was taken from him and transferred to his successor, Elisha. Hashem also required him to see the positive in Klal Yisrael by attending every *bris milah* that would take place throughout the generations, so that he could see with his own eyes how the nation maintains its *bris* with Hashem.

It is crucial for us to counter the trend of negativity by reminding ourselves of our nation's true greatness. We must never allow ourselves to take for granted the fact that we are part of such a noble people. We must never forget the message of *"mi k'amcha Yisrael."*

On a summer visit to Eretz Yisrael, Chaim Berkowitz (name changed) was driving from the Galil to Rosh Hanikra with his family and a group of friends. The hot summer sun beat down on their two cars as the vehicles drove along the rough dirt roads. Suddenly, a loud boom startled Chaim, and he quickly braked. Emerging from his car, he was dismayed to discover that two of its tires had blown out. The Berkowitzes waited wearily at the side of the deserted road, while their friends in the other car drove further down the road to look for help.

Just a few miles away, the passengers in the other car found a small, rundown gas station. The owner of the gas station was friendly, and when he heard about the Berkowitzes' plight, he leapt into action. With the help of a friend, the station owner spent several hours finding replacement tires of the right size and installing them on the car. When the process was over, the Berkowitzes were amazed when the man named a very reasonable price for his efforts. But the truly astonishing part of this story was yet to come.

"You probably wonder why I spent so much time helping you," the gas station proprietor said, accepting his payment and the family's profuse thanks. "The truth is that whenever I see Jews, I do my best to help them. You see, we are Druze. My cousin was Zidan Seif, the policeman who was killed in the terror attack in Har Nof this past fall. He was the first police officer to arrive on the scene, and he shot at the terrorists, almost certainly curtailing their attack, but he paid for it with his own life. Hundreds of Jews came to the funeral and then to the house of mourning to offer us their consolation. I will never forget the outpouring of compassion, love, and caring from the Jewish community in response to Zidan's death."

The warmth and kindness that impressed that man are echoed by countless caring, selfless people in our nation in many other circumstances. We do not have to look far to find wonderful, altruistic, and noble Jews. Let us make sure that these qualities always define our own outlook on our people; let us look at the wonderful things about our nation, rather than focusing on the negative.

We must take care to not spread negativity about Klal Yisrael; Hashem's honor is closely connected to the honor of the Jewish people, and when we honor our nation, we bring honor to Hashem. By focusing on the kindness and altruism of many Jews, we can help create a positive image of our nation that brings honor to Hashem as well.

Making It Practical

- Whenever you have a chance, speak about the positive qualities of Klal Yisrael, such as their penchant for *chessed*, their moral values, the lack of crime and violence among observant Jews, the incredible array of *gemachim* in religious communities, the *achdus*, the Torah learning, and the *kedushah* of the Jewish people. This will train you and others to feel fortunate to be members of such a nation.

In a Positive Light

Mrs. Bornstein's son suffered from a medical condition that required him to spend one full week every year in a hospital in Boston, where he received special treatments. On one of her visits to the hospital, Mrs. Bornstein struck up a conversation with a non-Jewish woman in the waiting room, whose child was receiving the same treatments. The other woman revealed that she had moved to Boston from a distant location because of her child's condition. Mrs. Bornstein was surprised. "Why would you move to a different city just because you have to spend one week here every year?" she asked.

"You are Jewish; you wouldn't understand," the other woman replied. "When you come here, your community takes care of everything for you: food, accommodations, companionship, and anything else you may need. When I come, I am all alone. I found that to be an impossible situation. You should appreciate your good fortune."

When Moshe Rabbeinu traveled to Mitzrayim with his wife and sons, after having been told by Hashem that he was to liberate the Jewish people from slavery, he met up with Aharon on the way. *Rashi* states in his commentary on *Parashas Yisro* (*Shemos* 18:2) that Aharon advised Moshe to send his family back to Midian, rather than bringing them to Mitzrayim to suffer along with the rest of the Jewish people.

At first glance, this is very difficult to understand. Moshe was a member of *Shevet Levi*, who were not enslaved in Mitzrayim, and his family would not have experienced the burden of slave labor. In fact, had they come with him, they would have witnessed the ten *makkos* and all the other miracles of *Yetzias Mitzrayim*. According to some *mefarshim*, Moshe's wife and sons weren't even present at Har Sinai when the Torah was given. What reason was there for them to be deprived of all these incredible experiences?

Rav Elya Svei explains that it would have been so detrimental for Tzipporah and her sons to see the Jewish people in their downtrodden, oppressed state that it was not worthwhile for them to come to Mitzrayim, even if it meant that they would miss all the historic miracles of *Yetzias Mitzrayim* and the profound impact of those events. The hardships of *galus*, Rav Elya explained, can cause a person to lose sight of the true greatness of a Jew. It was more important for them to maintain their understanding of a Jew's greatness than to be inspired by the liberation from Mitzrayim.

One of Rav Elya's *talmidim* recalls his *rebbi* adding that this idea should be kept in mind when children are taught about the Holocaust. The issue must be approached with tremendous caution, so that the stories of horrific suffering do not eclipse the children's sense of pride in being Jewish.

As we noted in the previous section, we must never lose sight of our nation's greatness and capacity for noble deeds. If Moshe Rabbeinu's wife and children were sent away so that they would not see the Jewish nation in a wretched state, one can imagine how important and valuable it is to focus on things that demonstrate the greatness and exalted status of Klal Yisrael.

Takeaway

In galus, it is very easy to become caught up in the negative aspects of our experiences. We must learn to focus on the tremendous benefits of being part of such an incredible nation, and the fact that as members of the Jewish people, we are never alone, even in the bleakest of times.

Making It Practical

• When you discuss the Holocaust or other times when Klal Yisrael suffered from persecution, use it as a springboard to point out the *emunah*, fortitude, resilience, and strength of character that the Jewish people showed during those trying times. Speak about the way that Jews rose above their plight to show incredible qualities.

Discussion Points

❖ Should we take pride in being Jewish and in the greatness of our nation, or is that an arrogant, elitist mentality? When we show pride, does it make us seem arrogant or holier-than-thou?

❖ Why is it so important to take pride in being Jewish? Why is it so important to find the positives in Klal Yisrael and to be proud of our nation?

❖ When there are shortcomings within the Jewish people, should those deficiencies be publicized so that they can be corrected, or should they be hidden so as not to cause a greater chillul Hashem?

CHAPTER 13

RESPECT AND DIGNITY

A group of Bais Yaakov girls are vacationing together in the Pocono mountains. On the first day of their getaway, the group goes for a hike. It is a hot, sunny summer day, and all the girls are dressed modestly, wearing long skirts and long-sleeved blouses. They pass many other vacationers who are not dressed in even a remotely similar fashion; some of the other people look at them askance, and others even comment on their attire with ridicule. A few people, however, express respect for their modesty.

Later that night, back at their cottage, the girls discuss their experiences and how they felt. They decide that they are proud of their standards of dress, they are not embarrassed to be different, and they will continue to wear the attire that is appropriate for religious Jews. They agree that their way of life is special and they are supposed to be different from others. Having fortified themselves with that discussion, they continue their vacation with even more confidence that they can make a kiddush Hashem specifically by being different from the people around them.

Winning Respect by Respecting Ourselves

One year, shortly before Pesach, Rabbi Chaim Miller (name changed) of Denver, Colorado, placed a call to the city's sanitation department. With the large volume of *chametz* being thrown away right before the festival, it was necessary for the city to schedule an extra day of garbage collection in the neighborhood. After he was connected to the head of the department, Rabbi Miller politely explained about the upcoming Yom Tov and the unusual volume of trash that would be generated before it began. He received an even more effusive response than he could have hoped for. "You're Jewish?" the city official exclaimed. "Of course I will help you! I'll do anything you like! I have a lot of respect for Jews!"

Rabbi Miller was understandably curious about what had made such an impression on the government employee. Apparently, the man was eager to share that information as well. "There is a high school with Jewish boys who live in a dormitory on the corner of Colfax and Perry Streets, isn't there?" he asked.

"There is," Rabbi Miller confirmed. "It's Yeshivas Toras Chaim."

"Let me tell you," the official continued excitedly, "I am very impressed with those boys. I see them all the time, walking to school in their white shirts and black pants and looking very dignified. And it isn't just the way they look. One day, I saw a group of boys walking down the street when a car drove past them and the people inside shouted insults at them. I wondered at first how the boys would react, and I was impressed with what they did: They ignored it totally. They simply kept on walking with their heads held high, maintaining their pride and dignity, as if they knew that they were superior to the people in that car. Yes, Rabbi," he concluded his monologue, "we will certainly make accommodations for your community anytime."

What was it that made such a powerful impression on that non-Jewish official? It wasn't merely the boys' *derech eretz* and good manners; it was their sense of pride in their Yiddishkeit, their confidence, and their dignity. The reason the boys did not react when a carful of hooligans hurled insults at them was that they were firmly rooted in their beliefs and staunch in their convictions. They radiated pride and self-assurance, which touched the heart of the stranger who witnessed the episode.

Takeaway

When we exhibit a sense of pride in who and what we are, it can make a powerful impression on others.

- Don't be embarrassed when you observe a halachah or mitzvah. Be proud of who you are and what you are doing. Show confidence, and you may have a powerful impact on others.

A Show of Respect

It was a beautiful summer day at Niagara Falls. Against the backdrop of the constant, majestic cascade of water, another magnificent scene was taking place. The *bachurim* of Camp Agudah Mesivta were visiting the falls, and they stood listening to their revered *rebbi*, Rav Chaim Yisroel Belsky, drinking in his words of wisdom. The *rosh yeshivah* leaned on two boys for support, while the rest of the group listened intently as he spoke, mesmerized by the *rosh yeshivah*'s boundless knowledge and insight. The boys' awe for their *rebbi* was nearly tangible; the group exuded both deference and reverence for Rav Belsky.

Unbeknownst to the boys, they had attracted the attention of some other tourists. Before long, a man approached a small cluster of boys to make a heartwarming comment. "I've seen many beautiful sights at Niagara today," he told them, "but this truly tops it all. The way you boys treat your elders is like nothing I have ever seen before. This is even more inspiring than all the natural wonders I have witnessed here."

When we show respect to others — whether to our parents, our elders, or even strangers on the street — it can play a major role in bringing about a kiddush Hashem.[1]

---

1 The Gemara states (*Kiddushin* 30b), "When a person honors his father and his

Often, we fail to realize when we have unintentionally been guilty of disrespect, or to recognize how much of an impact we can make by correcting the oversight. Pinchas (name changed), a yeshivah *bachur*, was about to purchase a drink at a 7-Eleven convenience store when he noticed that a disgruntled-looking man was standing off to the side, holding three large cups, while a group of yeshivah *bachurim* waited to pay for their purchases. Pinchas instantly realized that his friends had unintentionally cut in front of the man in line, and he motioned for the other customer to go ahead of him. "You just go ahead with all your friends," the man said in an irritated tone.

"Please," Pinchas said, "you were here first; you should go ahead of me."

With that, the man's demeanor changed. After the cashier had rung up his purchases, she asked, "Will there be anything else?"

"Yes," the other customer said loudly. "Please charge me for this boy's drink as well. I want to treat him; he deserves it."

The Gemara relates that after the plague that claimed the lives of Rabbi Akiva's thousands of *talmidim*, he rebuilt the Torah world by teaching a new group of just five Torah sages, and these five *talmidim* succeeded in recreating the Torah that had been lost because they demonstrated respect for each other. Rav Yitzchok Hutner is quoted as explaining that this was not a *reward* for their conduct toward each other, but rather the *natural result* of the respect they showed each other. *Kavod* can have a rejuvenating effect; it fills a person with life-giving energy. When

---

mother, Hashem says, 'I will view this as if I lived among them and they honored Me.'" Why does the Master of the Universe value the mitzvah of honoring parents so greatly? The *Iyun Yaakov* explains that the Gemara goes on to relate (ibid. 31a) that when Hashem taught Bnei Yisrael the first commandments in the *Aseres Hadibros*, the obligation to believe in Him and the prohibition of worshiping *avodah zarah*, the nations of the world scoffed at them. It was only when they heard the fifth commandment, "Honor your father and your mother," that they acknowledged the earlier commandments as well. Similarly, it is only when the Jewish people display respect for others and keep the laws of *bein adam lachaveiro* that the world will recognize the value and primacy of the *mitzvos bein adam laMakom* as well.

a person is treated with respect, it empowers him to accomplish great things. When Rabbi Akiva's *talmidim* displayed respect toward each other, it enabled them to rebuild the entire spiritual world that had been devastated by the plague.

Takeaway

Showing respect to other people is an incredibly powerful way of making an impression on others. Being respected also makes it possible for people to live up to their potential to fill the world with kevod Shamayim.

Making It Practical

• Focus on the positive aspects of every person's character.
• Make someone else feel very important by holding a door open for them, or allowing someone to go ahead of you in line.

Taking a Stand

Many of our *berachos* state that Hashem "sanctified us with His mitzvos." Rav Yerucham Levovitz explains (*Daas Torah, Parashas Emor*) that the definition of *kedushah*, sanctity, is recognizing the value and importance of something. *Chillul*, the opposite of *kedushah*, likewise refers to belittling something of importance or failing to recognize its value. Thus, Rav Yerucham states that *bnei Torah* should avoid misplaced modesty, conducting themselves with pride and in a way that indicates their exalted status. He adds that when *bnei Torah* demonstrate "love for other people and respect for other people, and speak gently to everyone, until everyone says about them, 'Fortunate is his father who taught him Torah' … that is an expression of sanctity that is revealed and recognizable to all." At the same time, he adds, a *ben Torah* who acts like an ordinary person is guilty of making himself "profane."

Just as a student of Torah must take pride in his involvement in Torah learning, every Jew should exhibit pride in his Jewishness. This was the lesson learned by Mrs. Fine (name changed), a saleswoman who works in an upscale furniture store in Cleveland. A couple once came to the store in search of a dining-room set for their home. After they had spent some time discussing the options with the saleswoman, the husband, a man who spoke in a coarse and unrefined way, announced, "Now let's talk business. I want you to jew down the price for me."

Mrs. Fine was shocked at the man's words. "Did I hear you correctly?" she asked. "What did you say?" The man repeated his offensive comment, and Mrs. Fine began to tremble. "I'm sorry, but I am appalled at the language you are using, and I will have to get a different saleslady to work with you. I am Jewish and I take pride in my Jewishness," she said.

The customer was nonplussed. "What's the matter with what I said?" he demanded. "I'm Jewish too, and I see nothing wrong with the phrase."

The saleswoman grew even more indignant. Although she knew that taking a stand might cost her a customer who was about to make a major purchase — and that she might even lose her job — she felt that she had no choice but to express her convictions. "My father was a Holocaust survivor, and after everything that he experienced, he was always proud to be a Jew. He taught me to be proud of who I am as well," she said in an impassioned tone. "I can't understand how you can possibly use such an offensive and demeaning phrase."

At this point, the man's wife took Mrs. Fine to the side and said quietly, "My husband didn't mean any offense; he is simply not careful about how he speaks, and he doesn't realize what he is saying. Please tell us the best price you can offer." Mrs. Fine named a figure and the couple left the store, promising to return the following week with their decision.

The next week, the couple returned to the store with their entire family in tow. "Where is the lady who helped us last week?" the man boomed as he stepped through the door.

Mrs. Fine approached them hesitantly, fearing that a confrontation was in store for her. But a young man stepped forward with a smile and said, "Are you the one who put my father in his place last week? We all wanted to come meet you! No one has ever rebuked my father in that way before, and he has been speaking about you all week long with the greatest respect. He has decided that he wants to buy the furniture here in order to give your store the business, *and* he will pay the full price that you are asking for it."

The father then approached Mrs. Fine himself. "Thank you for teaching me about this sensitivity and about being proud of who we are," he said. "I promise that I will never use that term again."

Somewhere deep within the heart of this estranged Jew, a chord had been struck. A Jewish woman's pride in her religion had pierced the thick layers of apathy that surrounded his heart, touching something deep within his soul. The lesson is clear: A display of pride can have an enormous impact on others.

Takeaway

When we express strong convictions, it radiates confidence in our way of life and indicates our certainty that the Torah is the ultimate truth.

Revealing Greatness

It was one of the last days of summer camp at Camp Kol Torah of Cleveland, and the boys were enjoying an end-of-summer trip to "Fun and Stuff," an entertainment center featuring bumper boats, an arcade, a roller-skating rink, and many other enjoyable activities. As lively Jewish music blasted from the sound system, a large group of boys spun about merrily on their skates, joining hands as they performed a dance, and exuding joy and camaraderie. Eventually, the evening drew to a close and several boys made their way to the counter to return their borrowed roller skates. The woman behind the counter took the skates and let out a deep sigh. "I was watching you boys tonight," she confessed, "and I realized that I made a major mistake in life. I should have chosen to become Jewish." Noting the boys' quizzical looks, she explained, "I was given a choice when I was younger, since my father was Christian and my mother was Jewish. I chose my father's religion, but now that I have seen the beautiful way you boys interact and get along with each other, and the joy that you feel, I realize that I should have chosen Judaism."

In *Sefer Devarim* (4:6), the Torah tells us, "You shall observe and perform [the mitzvos of the Torah], for it is your wisdom and insight in the eyes of the nations." Rav Shamshon Raphael Hirsch comments on these words, "Whatever arts and sciences may form the characteristic inheritance of the culture of other nations ... the Jewish science and art is the science and art of building up the whole of personal and national life on the fundamental basis of the consciousness of G-d and the duties to one's fellowmen... [T]he arts of beauty appealing to the senses one must seek at other nations, but the art of building huts, cities, states in which G-d shows His bliss-bringing Presence will only be found at the sons of Shem...and if you will live knowing and practicing the Divine Torah before the eyes of the world, your whole existence will be a motivation for the establishment of the kingdom of G-d on earth." As Jews, we should not aspire to blend in to the society in which we live. Instead, we should take pride in being recognizable and in modeling the type of conduct that befits the people of G-d.

A group of Jewish boys were once practicing *parkour* (a unique type of exercise based on military training) in a public park. Several non-Jewish children were watching and asked their mother if they could play with the boys. The mother responded, "Sure; they are Jewish and are nice boys, so we can trust them." She then turned to the Jewish boys and added, "I know that you are doing *parkour*, but since you boys are Jewish, you won't be doing this for long. You're going to grow up and do something really good for the world; you're going to make contributions and help change the world for the better, right? After all, that's what Jews do."

That mother in the park understood that the Jewish people were placed in the world with a special mission, one that should be the source of much pride to us. And those Jewish boys learned a powerful lesson: When a person stands out as a Jew, he will have an enormous ability to make an impression on others.

When we go out into the world, we should not be afraid to stand out. On the contrary, being noticeably different from others is actually the key to making a difference.

Making It Practical

- Be aware when you are entering an environment where you may feel a need to fit in or to lower your standards, such as when you are visiting relatives in a different city, or you are on vacation. Remind yourself to be proud of your differences and not to compromise on your standards. It is not a mistake that you are unlike people in the outside world; rather, it is a way for you to make an impact.

Discussion Points

❖ Sometimes, religious Jews are especially visible because of the way they dress. To some people, the Orthodox mode of dress might even seem outlandish. Why do we set ourselves apart from others? Won't this make it even more difficult for others to relate to us or to feel a connection to us?

❖ Is it a chillul Hashem if we create tension or strife by standing up for our principles?

CHAPTER 14

UNIVERSAL HONOR

Rabbi Hefter, the principal of Yeshivas Kevod Shamayim's elementary school, is struggling with a dilemma. He has observed that while the students show respect and deference toward the rebbeim who teach them in the mornings, their attitude toward their secular teachers leave much to be desired. He is greatly disturbed by the chillul Hashem caused by this situation, but he does not know how to teach his talmidim to respect the teachers who do not live a Torah lifestyle. The yeshivah places much emphasis on living up to the ideals of the Torah, and the rebbeim often talk about the severity of disobeying its laws. How can he teach his students to respect people who do not lead religious lives, without compromising that message?

A Nation of Teachers

K lal Yisrael is a *nation of teachers*.
    If we analyze what makes a teacher successful, we may be able to understand how *we* can succeed in our task as "teachers" of the world. Naturally, a teacher must be knowledgeable in the subject matter he or she is teaching, and be confident in that knowledge. A teacher must fully believe in what is being taught, and a teacher should be passionate about the material. A teacher who is ill equipped to instruct others or has little interest in the subject matter will be exposed before long as an inadequate educator. But even this is not enough; there are several other factors that may prevent a teacher from properly transmitting his material or outlook to his students. Let us examine those factors.

First, it is crucial for a teacher to take pride in his or her ability to influence and effectively educate students. If a teacher prides himself only on his own knowledge and education, he may come to look down on his students, possibly even disparaging them or showing disrespect for them. This attitude would create a rift between teacher and students that may make it impossible for them to be influenced by their teacher.

Second, a teacher must view every student as a person with a bright future in store for him. Some teachers do not believe in their own students and do not expect them to be successful or capable. This can greatly hinder the teaching process.

Third, a teacher must recognize the scope of his own responsibility. He must be aware that he has the ability to make a difference; in fact, he must feel that his influence could be the determining factor in his students' futures. Some teachers do not feel this sense of responsibility simply because they believe that their influence is negligible.

As the "teachers" of the world, we must keep in mind all of these vital factors. We certainly have the knowledge, the faith, and the confidence in the Torah way of life that are the initial foundations of every educator's work. We live and breathe the Torah, and we are passionate about it. But in order to succeed in being true *mekadshei Shamayim*, we must master the other three factors, as well.

First, we must take pride specifically in the fact that we were chosen to increase Hashem's honor in the world. If we take pride only in our own knowledge and the fact that we ourselves lead a Torah lifestyle, we might easily end up disparaging anyone who differs from us in that way. This can harm our ability to influence others.

Second, we must recognize the potential in every human being. We must internalize the fact that there is a bright future ahead for all of mankind, and that every person we meet has the potential to recognize the truth of Hashem's existence and sovereignty. When we believe that the entire world will one day recognize Hashem and serve Him, and we recognize that it is our mission to bring that to pass, then we will succeed in creating kiddush Hashem. But in order for us to do that, we must recognize that all other human beings also have a purpose in life, and that Hashem created everyone and everything in the world for a reason: to bring honor to Him.

Finally, we must internalize the fact that we do have the power to make a difference and that, in fact, it is up to us to create kiddush Hashem. If we know that it is we who are responsible for generating kiddush Hashem, then we will not look down on others who fail to recognize the truth, for we will realize that it is our failing more than it is theirs. We should continue exposing the futilities and falsehoods of modern society , but we should also make note of the fact that we have the capacity to make a difference, and that we can bring about a change in that situation.

If we ingrain these ideas in our children, they will recognize that there is no reason for them to feel contempt toward irreligious Jews. On the contrary, they will be aware that it is their responsibility to set an example that may influence people who do not live in accordance with the Torah. A teacher does not look down on his students for the things they do not know; instead, he sees the potential within them that he can inspire them to develop. By the same token, when we see people who are far removed from Yiddishkeit, we should consider it a reminder of our own responsibilities.

Takeaway

A focus on kiddush Hashem brings a tremendous sense of balance into our lives. When we have that orientation, our pride in our way of life will not cause us to denigrate others. On the contrary, we will have respect for all human beings, and we will develop a sense of responsibility to make a difference.

- When you find it necessary, as a parent or teacher, to point out the ills of modern society to your children or students, make sure to add that it is our responsibility to be models of *kedushah* and morality and thereby to elevate society out of these lowly places.

- When you speak about the implacable hatred Eisav feels toward Yaakov, point out that if we acted the way we should, the kiddush Hashem would overwhelm the nations of the world and they would develop love for the Jewish people.[1]

Finding the Good Everywhere

A certain *gadol* once observed two boys who were involved in a heated debate, with each boy insisting that he was bigger than the other. Finally, one of the boys pushed the other one

---

1 The *Netziv* (*Sefer She'air Yisrael*) explains that the relationship between the Jews and the other nations is similar to the relationship between fire and water. Fire and water work together very effectively as long as they are separated; when the water is in a pot and the fire is beneath it, the fire heats the water and enables it to cook food. If the pot were to be removed, however, the water would extinguish the fire, ruining it. Similarly, as long as we do not mix with the non-Jews, we can have an incredible impact upon them, but when the barriers crumble, the resultant assimilation robs us of our ability to have any impact at all on the world. For this reason, Hashem instills anti-Semitism in the nations of the world; if the Jews fail to maintain their uniqueness, the separation is restored and preserved by the natural hatred for Jews that denies the Jewish people access to non-Jewish society. It is important to recognize that the non-Jews' hatred is not inevitable; it simply cannot be cured by shedding the distinctions between us. On the contrary, their hatred increases when the Jews try to socialize and be influenced by them. When we maintain our *kedushah* and distinction, on the other hand, we benefit from their respect and love.

down to the floor and crowed triumphantly, "You see? I *am* taller than you!"

Turning to his companions, the *gadol* remarked, "There is something very unhealthy about that child. You can see that he was standing right next to a large boulder; he could simply have stood on it in order to raise himself above his friend. Why did he have to knock the other boy down?"

Every human being needs to feel a sense of pride, but there are different ways to go about cultivating that feeling. One way is to deride others or to find reasons to disparage them, all for the sake of building one's own sense of superiority. This, however, is an approach that is both unhealthy and improper. Rather than searching for the negative in others, it would be best for a person to identify all the things that are positive and praiseworthy within himself, to boost himself without demeaning others. There is no reason for one person's sense of pride to be developed at the expense of the self-image of others.

Unfortunately, this lesson was learned in a certain girls' school only after a difficult and painful experience. It began when a group of girls decided that they were superior to their classmates, who were not on the same level of *frumkeit* as they. The "*frummer*" girls formed a clique and openly expressed disdain for their classmates. The rest of the girls in the class were pained by the demeaning exclusion, and the situation evolved into an epidemic of bullying. When the girls' parents discovered how polarized the class had become, they were equally devastated by the situation. As the parents began working on rectifying the problem, a painful question surfaced: Why was it that the girls' pride in their level of *frumkeit* had led them to look down on their peers? Couldn't there be a way for children to be taught to feel good about themselves without belittling others?

In our society, there are many different groups and subgroups within the *frum* world. There are some communities whose members do not dress exactly as we do, and who *daven* somewhat differently. It is important for us to be aware of the messages we convey to our children regarding these people. If we, as parents, speak positively about *frum* Jews who are different from us, if we praise them for their strengths and the good things about them, then our children will absorb the message that all people are worthy of respect. A *Litvak*, for instance, can praise *chassidim* for certain aspects of their *avodas Hashem*, while a *chassid* can marvel at certain qualities of his *Litvish* counterparts. Even Jews who are on an objectively lower level of *frumkeit* may still have certain positive qualities, certain traits or habits that we can respect and learn from.

Often, it is fear that prevents us from doing this. We are afraid that if we speak positively about Jews from other circles, our children may be tempted to abandon our own communities to look for fulfillment elsewhere. That is something we might find undesirable, and in some cases, it might even mean a decrease in their level of observance. But if we fear that we may lose our children in that way, it may mean that we lack the confidence that we ourselves have something of value to offer. At the same time that we must cultivate a healthy sense of respect for others, we must also teach our children to appreciate the values with which they have been brought up.

Let us take this idea a step further: How should we react if a child makes a remark or a joke that shows prejudice against certain types of non-Jews? Obviously, we do not want our children gravitating toward the nations of the world, but there is nothing wrong with commenting on a positive quality that that group possesses, in order to offset the child's views. We can make comments such as, "You know, people in that circle always have such *simchas hachaim*; we could learn even from them."[2] If we take this approach, our children will learn that there is good in all people; there is something to respect in everyone.

We know that we can learn *middos* even from animals: We can learn *tznius* from a cat, diligence from an ant, and so forth. It stands to reason, then, that we can also derive positive lessons

---

2 Although the Torah prohibition of *lo sechaneim* prohibits praising the members of other nations, some *poskim* maintain that it is permitted to praise them for manifesting the *middos* espoused by the Torah.

from other human beings. We can never completely write off the non-Jewish world or the less observant circles within our nation, for there is always some positive lesson that we can derive from them.[3]

Takeaway

Takeaway: In order to raise our children to be respectful, we must exercise caution in the way we speak about other Jews, even those elements within our people with whom we do not agree. Likewise, we must take care to speak about non-Jews in a way that will cause our children to respect them as Hashem's creations.

Making It Practical

- When conversation mentions other groups or types of people, find something positive to say about them.
- Discourage your children from using demeaning nicknames or making stereotypical comments about people who are different from them.

---

3. The *korbanos* of *Succos* teach us that we are not meant to feel complete antipathy toward the nations of the world. On *Succos*, we are commanded to bring a series of seventy bulls to atone for the seventy nations of the world; in effect, these *korbanos* insure their survival. Rav Yechezkel Levenstein (quoted in *Kuntres Mevakshei Torah*) points out that a *korban* that is brought without a genuine desire or interest is not considered a valid *korban*. Consequently, when the Jewish people brought these *korbanos* on *Succos*, it had to be with the wholehearted desire for the *korbanos* to achieve their purpose and to protect their beneficiaries.

Rav Yechezkel points out that these *korbanos* were brought on behalf of the entire non-Jewish world, including our most ardent enemies. Could a Jewish person really desire to benefit the most despotic, bloodthirsty enemies of Klal Yisrael? Yet that was precisely the purpose of these *korbanos*. From this, Rav Yechezkel infers that we are meant to develop *ahavas habriyos* — love for other human beings — even for our enemies.

Conquering New Territory

In order to have an impact on others, we must treat them as equals. We must show that we do not judge them or consider ourselves superior to them. At the same time, in order to be *mekareiv* others, we must give them the impression that the Yiddishkeit we possess is something crucial that is lacking from their lives. How can we do that without seeming to hold ourselves above them?

The Gemara states (*Sanhedrin* 74a) that it is forbidden to sacrifice another life in order to save one's own. The Gemara explains this with a simple rhetorical question: "Why would you consider your blood redder than [the other person's] blood?" This is a blanket rule, meaning that even the *gadol hador* would not be permitted to save himself by taking the life of any other person. The message is clear: Although it may seem to us that some lives should be more precious than others, the Torah does not agree. There is no way that we can assess any person's life as more valuable than another's.

Chazal teach us, "*Hevei shfal ruach bifnei kol adam* — Be humble before every man." This statement is quoted by *Tanya* (Ch. 30), which points out that the Mishnah makes no distinction between different types of people; it instructs any person, however great he may be, to feel humbled and unimportant in the presence of others, regardless of their levels of observance. How can this be possible?

There is a famous parable in *Michtav MeEliyahu* that explains the nature of our struggles in life. In any war, Rav Dessler explains, the opposing armies meet on a battlefield in the disputed territory. Each country has a specific piece of land that is considered its home turf, areas behind the lines that are safe from the enemy. It is the battleground itself, the place where the front lines are located and the armies combat each other, that will be conquered by one of the two sides. When the war is over, the winner will be the country that expanded its territory through battle. Even if the winning country remains smaller than its opponent, it can still claim victory by virtue of having seized territory that it did not possess before the battle.

Rav Dessler explains that this analogy reflects our situation in this world. Every person is at war with the *yetzer hara*, but every individual's war takes place on a different "battlefield." Every person comes to this war with a specific quantity of "home turf"; this represents the virtues and practices that come naturally to him and that he does not have to fight to master. But a person is not judged based on the things that are inherently ingrained in him; rather, he is judged on the actual battles that he fights.

Many of the actions we do are simply actions that come naturally to us. Many of our mitzvos, our good deeds and virtuous practices, are the result of our upbringing or our desire to fit into our society. But if we go through our lives without winning a battle, without achieving something beyond the norms we have learned from society, then we may never actually have accomplished anything. Our mission in life is to fight to grow beyond our starting point, to add to the "territory" that comes to us automatically. For every person, that has a different meaning.

An irreligious Jew typically spends his life fighting different battles than a *frum* Jew. But while it is true that he enters the fray with far less spiritual "territory" of his own, that makes no difference in terms of how he is judged. A person who is not *frum* may be battling his natural inclinations and winning the war, while some of us may spend our lives far removed from the "front lines" of our own personal wars, never even trying to overcome the *yetzer hara*.

The struggle of an irreligious Jew, for instance, may be in the realm of *sur mera*: avoiding serious sins. A person who was not raised in an observant environment may be far more susceptible to temptations that the typical *frum* Jew is used to resisting, and those temptations may be the focus of his battle in life. A *frum* Jew, on the other hand, might have to struggle with the concept of *aseh tov*: increasing his positive actions by giving more *tzedakah*, learning more hours even when it is difficult for him, adding to the *chessed* he performs, and so forth. If he fails to conquer this new "territory," then he may be considered less successful than the irreligious Jew who seems to be on a much lower spiritual level.

In addition, a *frum* Jew who has been trained to go through the motions of Jewish observance — *davening*, performing mitzvos, reciting *berachos* and so forth — may still be challenged by the need to fill those actions with meaning and emotion. His task may be to infuse his *davening* and *berachos* with *kavannah* and to develop an emotional attachment to mitzvos; his battle may lie in the "*avodas haleiv*" of Yiddishkeit, while another person may struggle to master the actions themselves. And there are other possibilities as well: Sometimes, a religious Jew may be accustomed to living an observant lifestyle, but he may still succumb to sins that are taken lightly even in *frum* circles, such as *lashon hara*, *onaas devarim* (causing others emotional pain), or *bittul Torah*. If a person was raised religious, he should feel a greater sense of responsibility and accountability; rather than looking down on those who were not as fortunate, he should recognize that his upbringing makes him subject to much loftier expectations.

We are all familiar with the tendency to group people into the categories of BT (*baal teshuvah*) and FFB (*frum* from birth). I once heard of a new acronym, FFH, which stands for "*frum* from habit." That is hardly a category in which we would want to find ourselves; I can only wonder what would happen if the standard *shidduch* research began to include the question, "Is he (or she) an FFH?"

How much of our *avodas Hashem* is actually a product of habit, rather than the result of our own hard work? Such habits are good, of course, but we can credit only our parents or grandparents for them; we ourselves do not earn a deeper relationship with Hashem or a loftier place in *Olam Haba* through the things we do by rote. Our task is to continue pushing the front lines of battle further into "enemy" territory, to constantly improve ourselves and our deeds. We are defined not by our level of observance, but by the journey we took to arrive at it.

With this mindset, we can seek to influence others without viewing ourselves as a spiritual elite. If we understand what

Hashem values in our behavior, then we will recognize that anyone who is growing, regardless of where they come from and how they were raised, is truly precious in His eyes. And since no person can ever assess the value of another person's growth, we can never consider ourselves superior to any other human being. If we master this mentality, then we can achieve the respect for all people that is crucial for us to be *mekadeish Shem Shamayim*.

Takeaway

The only way to impact others is through having true respect for others. We must recognize that we cannot judge others by their level of religiosity; the true measure of a person is the extent to which he is growing, and we can never really know the extent of another person's growth. If we understand these points, we will be able to show respect for all human beings.

Making It Practical

- Learn to praise growth rather than status. Don't speak highly of people only because of their brilliance or knowledge; express your admiration for anyone who works hard, who tries hard, or who has grown in his or her own way.
- Praise your children and students for their effort and growth, even if the results are not apparent.

Discussion Points

❖ In what way can I respect people who live their lives in a way that is not in line with Torah values?

❖ In what way can I respect people if I do not agree with their views and attitudes?

CHAPTER 15

THE PURSUIT OF HAPPINESS

One of Nosson's co-workers is a man named Joe, who he knows is Jewish but not religious. One week, Nosson decides to invite Joe to his home for a Shabbos meal, and his co-worker hesitantly agrees.

The atmosphere at the Shabbos meal is lively; Nosson's children are excitedly talking about everything they learned in school, and the conversation and zemiros flow like water. But after the meal, Nosson is unsure if his family made a positive impression on his guest. Will Joe want to come back? Was he overwhelmed by the experience of having a meal with such a large family?

The next week, Nosson is surprised when Joe tells him that he enjoyed the meal and would like to experience more Shabbos meals in the future. He becomes a regular Shabbos guest at Nosson's house and begins visiting other families as well. This turns out to be the start of his journey to religious Judaism.

Years later, Joe is asked what he experienced during those early meals that kindled his interest in Yiddishkeit. He replies that he was inspired by the joyous atmosphere in his host's home and the way that his children's faces glowed with happiness and contentment. That sort of happiness, Joe feels, is something that every human being is on a quest to find, whether or not he realizes it. He feels fortunate to have discovered a source of happiness to fill the void in his own life.

The Elusive Quality of Happiness

One of the most effective ways to influence others to adopt a Torah lifestyle is showing them that a life of Torah observance leads to happiness. When people who observe the mitzvos are seen as being happy and fulfilled, others will be more likely to be inspired to follow their example. When people see that the religious lifestyle breeds happiness, they will naturally be drawn to take an interest in it for themselves. Likewise, when we succeed in filling our homes with *simchah*, our children will be more likely to remain firmly attached to their Yiddishkeit.

Happiness is the one thing everyone in the world seeks. Every human being is on a quest for happiness; it is a crucial ingredient for our mental and physical health alike, and no person can survive or thrive without some degree of happiness. At the same time, it is a highly elusive goal. While every person in the world is searching for happiness, many people attempt to find it in places where it does not actually exist. People often make the mistake of thinking that they have found happiness, when they have really attained nothing but a fleeting sense of excitement or fun. Once that excitement fades away, they are left with nothing.

In order to achieve true happiness, we must have a clear understanding of what it means. If we wish to fill our own lives with happiness, we must develop an understanding of how and where it can be found, and that means being able to distinguish between true happiness and the transient rush of excitement that many people mistake for it.

In broad terms, happiness can be described as a state of contentment and satisfaction. A person who has achieved true happiness will have a sense of serenity, stability, and general well-being. False happiness, on the other hand, often takes the form of a temporary feeling of excitement. It may create intense stimulation or exhilaration, causing the person to feel that he is on a "high," but it is no substitute for genuine happiness.

How can one tell the difference between true happiness and a false thrill? Rav Pam taught that the litmus test is to determine whether the feeling is permanent: Genuine happiness is a lasting feeling, while excitement usually fades after the experience has ended.

This is a lesson that I once shared with a *talmid* who was an avid football fan. One day, he came to school in a state of exhilaration. His team had won the Superbowl, and he was filled with excitement over their victory. To him, it was a miraculous occasion, a cause for ecstatic celebration. On the day after that game, he spent the entire day practically jumping up and down with excitement. The next day, though, he was unusually dejected. "*Rebbi*, it's all over," he lamented to me, as the glow of his team's victory faded into the past. "What do I do now? They won, and that was it; what a waste of time!" I gently explained to the young man that he had discovered the difference between happiness and excitement. Excitement is a shallow experience, a fleeting high that dissipates as quickly as it came. That was why his pleasure over his team's victory had not afforded him a lasting sense of satisfaction.

Another *talmid* once confided in me that he struggled with a lack of interest in learning. We discussed his situation at length, and we came up with a strategy: He chose a *sefer* that he would study during his free time, and he spent an entire year making his way through the *sefer*, diligently studying page after page every day. Finally, after an entire year, he celebrated his completion of the *sefer* with a gala banquet. The next day, he approached me and admitted that he was feeling morose once again. "This whole year was a great year," he said wistfully. "I learned a lot from the *sefer*, and the project really kept me going. But now that it's over, I feel lost and unaccomplished again."

The explanation for his feelings, I told him, was also rooted in understanding the nature of happiness: Happiness comes from the journey toward a goal, not the destination itself. When a person is involved in a process and working toward a goal, he feels fulfilled; once he has achieved the goal, a gnawing feeling of emptiness may set in again. Celebrating an achievement is exciting, but it does not make a person happy; it is the process of working *toward* an achievement that generates true happiness. That is why the Torah way of life creates happiness: It keeps us focused on the fact that our entire lives are a journey toward a goal, and the fact that we are involved in that journey can be our greatest source of satisfaction. For my *talmid*, this meant that it was time to begin a new learning project.

A life spent seeking excitement may be thrilling at times, but it will ultimately lead a person to feel empty and unfulfilled. Very often, he will not have an opportunity for excitement, and his ordinary routine will leave him lacking a sense of joy or accomplishment. A person who understands how to achieve true happiness, though, will appreciate how to tap into that experience even within the context of the most mundane activities. In the end, he will lead a much more satisfying life than a person who is constantly waiting for the next thrill.

For ourselves and our children as well, this is an important outlook to master. Life often presents opportunities for fun and excitement — a vacation, a wedding, a birthday party, and the like — but these experiences are not a recipe for happiness. True happiness comes from hard work and accomplishment, and if we set our sights on those goals, rather than giving in to the allure of passing thrills, we will learn how to access the power of joy.

Takeaway

The first step toward attaining happiness is understanding and differentiating between happiness and excitement. One should not expect excitement from the Torah lifestyle; rather, it is a life that leads to fulfillment and contentment. As long as our goal is true happiness rather than a fleeting substitute, then the Torah lifestyle is the perfect prescription to attain it.

The Power to Say No

Now that we have learned about the importance of differentiating between enduring happiness and the fleeting experience of excitement, we will discuss how to resist the temptation to seek shallow gratification in place of true happiness.

The key to resisting temptation is to develop discipline and self-control. A person must train himself to be the master of his own impulses, to overpower his physical drives rather than allowing them to dictate his actions. In today's generation, this is a rare ability; it is far more common for a person to surrender to every temptation that crosses his path. In fact, the world today offers a seemingly endless array of pleasures and enticements, many of which are readily within the reach of the average person. At an early age, children absorb the idea that none of their whims or desires can be denied to them, as parents fear turning down the slightest request — or, to be more accurate, the slightest demand — that their child makes. Even in *frum* society, perhaps out of fear of the "at risk" phenomenon, many parents lack the confidence to say no to their children, or to impose consequences for bad behavior. But even secular society recognizes the pitfalls of this reality, with child psychologists bemoaning the phenomenon of "Discipline Deficit Disorder" that has resulted from overindulgent parenting.

Science has shown that children are much more likely to accept discipline and self-control if it is introduced at an early age. If a child reaches his teenage years without ever hearing the word "no" from his parents, their efforts to teach him discipline at a later age are much more likely to fail. In order for our children to be able to resist temptation when they are older, we must begin training them at an early age, and that means that when it is appropriate, we must not hesitate to say "no."

According to science, this has a good deal to do with the way the human brain works and develops. The brain contains billions of neurons, each of which transmits electrical impulses to neighboring neurons through thousands of branches at the end of a cablelike structure protruding from the neuron. A baby is born with approximately one hundred billion neurons, each with about ten thousand branches of its own. At birth, only 17 percent of the neurons in the brain are linked, but as the neurons pass electrical impulses to each other, connections are created and strengthened between them. These connections influence the configuration or "wiring" of the brain, which affects a person's thought patterns, inclinations, and behaviors. Some of the branches of the neurons do not transmit electrical impulses; those branches wither and eventually disappear, in a process known as "pruning."

The connections made between neurons, as well as the process of "pruning" and sculpting that occurs within the brain, is a function of the person's experiences. Every experience shapes the configurations that are formed within the brain; thus, it makes sense that at an early age, when the brain is first beginning to configure and organize itself, a child's experiences can be much more powerful and influential. It is the parent's responsibility to provide a child with experiences that will foster the appropriate growth and connections within the brain; thus, when a parent trains his child at an early age to accept a negative response to a demand, he will create connections within the child's brain that will affect his behavior for years to come.

At the same time, this does not mean that we should despair of teaching our children discipline after they reach their teenage years. Scientists have discovered that the mass of the brain does not increase after the age of ten; nevertheless, recent studies have shown that a significant change still takes place within the brain even until the early twenties. And although the plasticity of the brain diminishes as we grow older, making us less receptive to change and more firmly rooted in our ways, that plasticity is never fully lost, even in the adult years. Therefore, change is always possible; it may grow harder as we grow older, but the power to grow and improve ourselves will always be within us.

Takeaway

The second step toward attaining happiness is developing discipline and avoiding indulgence in excitement and fun. The Torah itself encourages this with the mitzvah of "kedoshim tihiyu." If we begin to teach children at a young age that they will not always get everything that they want, if we help them grow accustomed to the idea of saying no, they will be able to resist their own desires when they become older.

- At a young age, begin setting limits on your children's indulgence. Learn how to say no in a way that will enable your children to listen
- Use good parenting techniques to help your "no" have meaning and power: Say "yes" when you can, so that your children will respect the limits you set for them. When you do deny something to a child, stick to your guns and don't give in to tantrums. Don't say no with frustration or emotion; keep it calm and matter-of-fact.
- Set limits for older children, as well, by giving them curfews and making rules about the use of devices. Remember that even if they are upset by your rules, they still need your help to learn limits.

Finding Contentment

As we have seen, understanding the definition of happiness and learning to resist temptation are two of the key components of the process of attaining a life of joy. But these two things are not enough; there is one more crucial ingredient in this process, which is perhaps the most important element of all.

Let us take a look at *Megillas Rus*. Rus was a princess in the land of Moav, a woman who grew up in the lap of luxury. Due to her position, she certainly possessed fabulous wealth and every creature comfort imaginable at the time. Yet Rus was willing to exchange a life of pure pleasure for a life of poverty, which doomed her to begging for charity and spending her days gathering forgotten stalks of wheat from others' fields. What could possibly have led a privileged princess to make such a choice? What motivated her to stay with Naami in spite of the tremendous personal sacrifice it would entail? In short, what was the force that drew her away from her world of excitement and pleasure?

This is a question with tremendous relevance to all of us. We live in a society where the most incredible forms of excitement, the most tantalizing opportunities for pleasure or fun, are available everywhere we turn. Any excitement that we can incorporate into a life of Torah will never be able to compete with the allure of the outside world. Parents, *mechanchim*, and *kiruv* professionals today can all attest that no amount of prizes or other exciting incentives alone can inspire children to retain their interest in Torah; the competing attraction of the outside world is simply too strong. In order to create the motivation to maintain a life of Torah, we must identify a different appeal within it: the appeal that drew Rus away from her royal upbringing and inspired her to join the Jewish people.

Rav Elya Svei (in *Ruach Eliyahu*) explains that the source of Naami's power to influence Rus can be seen in her very name; as *Chazal* teach us (*Rus Rabbah* 2:5), she was known as "Naami" because her actions were pleasing (*"ne'imim"*). Pleasantness and sweetness were the hallmarks of Naami's personality, and those traits somehow were more attractive to Rus than all the riches and thrills available to her as the princess of Moav.

There is no need for us to make the Torah attractive by "augmenting" it with thrills and excitement. The Torah way of life already has something extraordinary to offer, something that will always be far more appealing than simple fun. The Torah is pleasant; it creates a sense of contentment that contributes to authentic happiness. True, it does not generate heart-pounding excitement or thrills, but those are shallow feelings that tend to fade away very quickly. Excitement lasts for a few moments and then dissipates until another temporary thrill can be found;

the Torah way of life, meanwhile, creates a long-lasting sense of satisfaction and contentment that is much more fulfilling. The Torah and its *mitzvos* give us the prescription for attaining this contentment, which is reflected in the behavior and demeanors of those who live the Torah way of life.

This is the key to having a positive influence on our children, our students, and everyone else around us. The way to make Hashem and His Torah beloved to others is to demonstrate that the Torah can be a source of contentment. When people are repeatedly exposed to true happiness, they will learn not to be fooled by the empty opportunities for excitement that serve as cheap substitutes. The pleasure of a Shabbos, the subtle beauty of the Torah's truth, the loving atmosphere of a strong family, the inner sense of satisfaction that stems from living with moral values and discipline, the sense of belonging and security that is fostered by *emunah* — all of these things can create true contentment, which will enable people to be strong enough to withstand the allure of the world's empty thrills.

A *yungerman* in Eretz Yisrael was once making the rounds of the homes in a secular moshav, knocking on every door to ask the residents of each home if they were interested in learning Torah. At one house, the man who answered the door had been enraged by a recent incident in which several *chareidim* burned an Israeli flag, causing an uproar among the general populace. "I don't want to have anything to do with people who burn our flag!" he thundered at his visitor.

The *yungerman* responded in a sweet, gentle tone. "Before we speak about that, let's sit down and learn a little," he suggested. "I will discuss it with you later."

The man complied, and after they had finished learning, he had only one question: "Will you come back again?" He did not bring up the issue of the flag-burning again.

When Rav Elya Svei was told about this incident, he remarked, "The man's change of heart certainly had to do with experiencing the beauty of the Torah, but I am certain that was not the only reason. The encounter with that *yungerman*, and the exposure to his pleasant and sweet personality, must have had a good deal to do with that change."

In order to appeal to our youth, I would suggest that we should not fight the proverbial fire with fire; we should not try to meet the outside world on its own terms and compete with it by offering fun and excitement of our own. Rather, we should expose our children to an entirely different experience: the wonderful feeling of contentment and satisfaction that the Torah can offer. If they perceive how sweet and pleasant a life of Torah can be, they will certainly never wish to exchange it for anything else in the world.

Takeaway

The third step in the process of creating happiness is filling the void with experiences that create true satisfaction. Our children will learn how to attain happiness by experiencing the contentment that is created by the Torah way of life. If we give them multiple tastes of true satisfaction, they will not be fooled by the glamour and glitz of the outside world.

Making It Practical

- Make your home a happy and pleasant place to be by keeping the atmosphere serene and cheerful.
- Turn Shabbos into a special experience for the family. Make the Shabbos table a fun and entertaining place for your children by holding their attention with stories and songs.
- Prepare for Yamim Tovim together with your daughters in an atmosphere of laughter and sweetness. Let them participate in the preparations in ways that they will enjoy.

Discussion Points

❖ To a non-religious person, the Torah way of life seems to be filled with restrictions and burdensome laws. How can we help other Jews recognize the pleasantness of the Torah lifestyle?

❖ Our own happiness is a crucial ingredient for creating a kiddush Hashem; Yiddishkeit will not be attractive to anyone if the people living a Jewish life are not satisfied and don't exude happiness. But how do we ensure that we will have internal reserves of happiness?

❖ What is it about the Torah lifestyle that creates true happiness?

CHAPTER 16

THE KIDDUSH HASHEM IMPERATIVE

Zev Goodman is always careful to make the best possible impression on others. He is always meticulous about tipping workers, whether it is a painter working in his home, a porter at the airport taking his bags for check-in at the curb, or anyone else who provides a service. In his business dealings, he is extremely cautious to avoid seeming aggressive or ruthless. He knows that as a visibly Orthodox Jew, he has a responsibility to cause others to love Hashem, and he works hard to achieve that goal.

Recently, though, Zev has been feeling somewhat conflicted. He invests so much time and energy in kiddush Hashem, but he wonders if he is really being insincere. Does he really love Hashem so much that he can claim to feel passionate about causing Him to be loved by others? Is it really appropriate for him to be working so hard to spread kevod Shamayim, when his own feelings of ahavas Hashem leave much to be desired? Should he shift his focus to working on himself, instead of being concerned about the impression he makes on the rest of the world?

Loving Hashem — Cause or Effect?

The mitzvah of *ahavas Hashem*, loving Hashem, is one of the primary sources of the mitzvah of kiddush Hashem. The *pasuk* that is the source of this mitzvah, *"V'ahavta es Hashem Elokecha* — You shall love Hashem your G-d," is expounded by the Gemara (*Yoma* 86a) to teach that one should *cause* Hashem's Name to be beloved by others: "A person should learn *mikra* and mishnah and serve *talmidei chachamim*, and should deal with other people in a gentle way. And what will people say about him? 'Fortunate is his father, who taught him Torah;

fortunate is his *rebbi*, who taught him Torah.'"[1]

This seems to indicate that we are required to love Hashem to such an extent that we will desire to cause the rest of the world to experience the same love. This concept presents a dilemma for many people. Many of us have not yet attained the level of love demanded by the mitzvah of *ahavas Hashem*. Our love for Hashem, in essence, is a work in progress. How can we be expected to have this degree of concern for kiddush Hashem when we haven't yet perfected our own feelings of love for Hashem?

According to Rav Dessler (*Michtav MeEliyahu*, Vol. 3, p. 123), this question is based on a fundamental misunderstanding of the Gemara. Rav Dessler quotes the Alter of Kelm, who explains that the Gemara's intent is not to teach us the *outcome* of the mitzvah of *ahavas Hashem*, but rather to identify a means of *attaining* that love. Many mitzvos have both *chitzoniyus* and *pnimiyus* — an outward manifestation and an internal effect on the person's heart and emotions.[2] With regard to *ahavas Hashem*, the Gemara introduces the idea that, although it is a mitzvah of the heart, it also has a dimension of *chitzoniyus*; there are actions associated with the mitzvah, and by performing those actions, a person can develop the feeling of *ahavas Hashem* in his own heart. The acts that develop one's love of Hashem are the acts of being *mekadeish Shem Shamayim*. Hence, a person should pursue kiddush Hashem even before he has developed true *ahavas Hashem*, for his efforts will help him cultivate his love for the Master of the Universe.

Rav Dessler himself once instructed several of his *talmidim* to actively search for opportunities for kiddush Hashem. One

---

1. Rav Yosef Shalom Elyashiv used to say that the mitzvah that is the mission of our generation is "that the Name of Heaven should become beloved through you."

2. The *Chinuch* (mitzvah 16) teaches us that many mitzvos in the Torah are based on the principle that "the hearts are drawn after the actions." Hashem commanded us to engage in certain acts precisely because those actions will shape our feelings and personalities.

talmid was told to board a double-decker bus and sit in a spot where the conductor would likely not reach him before he arrived at his stop; before getting off the bus, he was to make a point of asking another passenger to hand his fare to the conductor when he arrived. Another *talmid* was told to walk down a certain street frequented by beggars and to give a coin to each one.[3] In all likelihood, Rav Dessler's intent was not only to promote *kevod Shamayim* in the eyes of those observers, but also to inculcate in his *talmidim* the crucial sensitivity to Hashem's honor.

A *frum* father was sitting in a parked car with a number of his children when one of the smaller children chose to have a temper tantrum. As the child ranted and screamed, the man's eight-year-old son suddenly began shouting as well: "Close the windows! Close the windows!" Turning to the older child, the father asked, "Why do you want the windows closed? It's warm in the car!"

"I don't want his crying to make a chillul Hashem," the child said innocently, pointing to his hysterical brother. "There are people passing by."

Everywhere we go and in everything we do, we are walking advertisements either in favor of Hashem and His Torah or, *chas v'shalom*, against Him. If we train ourselves and our children to keep this in mind, it can lead to many benefits: It can help us develop empathy, consideration, and respect for all human beings. It reminds us that we are not living in a bubble, and that our words and actions can have many repercussions, affecting others as well as ourselves. It can also provide us with a sense of pride and the knowledge that we are living with a mission, that we are charged with transforming the world and that we have the power to do so. It infuses our lives with meaning, with the recognition that we are living for a purpose that transcends ourselves. And as we have seen, it is a vital step on our journey toward the all-important ideal of true *ahavas Hashem*.

---

3. "The Kiddush Hashem Imperative," Rabbi Yonason Rosenblum, *Jewish Observer*, January 2001. See also Rav Avigdor Miller (*Shaarei Orah*, Vol. 2, p. 228) in regard to actively pursuing opportunities to create a kiddush Hashem.

Being cautious about kiddush Hashem and chillul Hashem will not only help us inculcate love for Hashem in others but will help build our own love for Him as well.

Making It Practical

- Take some actions to promote kiddush Hashem, having in mind to develop love for Hashem within yourself. For example if you see some wrappers on the floor, make a point of picking them up. If someone needs help carrying shopping bags, go out of your way to lend them a hand.

⟫•◇•⟪

Starting with the End in Mind

All of us, at times, struggle with the temptation to do things that are improper for the sake of achieving a desirable goal. Some people are overly aggressive in their business dealings, but they justify their practices with their need to support their children in kollel. Others might drive aggressively or recklessly, rationalizing that they must get to *davening* or learning on time. Schools and yeshivos may at times be tempted to twist tax laws or misuse student aid money for the greater benefit of their students. As Jews who are committed to the ideal of kiddush Hashem, we must come up with a way to combat such temptations, which are clearly not in the spirit of our mission in this world.

One of the commonly taught tools for success is a concept called "starting with the end in mind." This means that in order to succeed in any endeavor, one must always begin it with a clear understanding of its ultimate goal. Keeping the final goal in mind will ensure that every step that is taken leads in the appropriate direction, and every decision or judgment call is informed by that goal.

According to a popular self-help book,[4] there are three basic elements of any endeavor: leadership, management, and production or problem solving. As an example, the author presents the case of a group of people cutting their way through a jungle with machetes. The problem solvers are those who wield the blades and actually clear the path. Behind them are the managers, who provide the machetes, set up work schedules and policies, and arrange exercise programs so that the problem solvers will be capable of performing their work. And then there is the leader, who climbs the tallest tree in the jungle, examines the situation, and then shouts to the group, "You're in the wrong jungle!" The leader is the person who always keeps in mind the ultimate goal of the work and ensures that everyone is headed in the right direction.

In the words of Peter Drucker, "Management is doing things right; leadership is doing the right things." In business, leadership — defining and keeping the focus on the goal of a project — must always precede management. And the same concept applies to our personal lives.

Besides managing all the details of our *avodas Hashem,* it is important for us to maintain a constant vision of the goal of our *avodah.* In *Shaarei Teshuvah* (3:158), *Rabbeinu Yonah* presents a fundamental principle: The reason that Hashem chose the Jewish nation, elevated them above the rest of the nations of the world, and sanctified them with His Torah and mitzvos, is *entirely so that they would fear Him and sanctify His Name.*[5] In other words, kiddush Hashem is the *raison d'etre* of the Jewish

---

4. The 7 Habits of Highly Effective People, by Stephen Covey.
5. *Rabbeinu Yonah* cites the *pasuk, "V'nikdashti b'soch Bnei Yisrael ani Hashem*

people. Not only is it a mitzvah of great significance; it is the sum total of our mission on this world.

This is the goal that we must keep in mind as we apply the principle of leadership to our lives. We must make sure that all of our actions are informed by a vision of our destination, making sure that we are climbing the right "ladder" or cutting a path through the right "jungle." If that is our goal, then even when we are involved in worthy activities such as learning Torah, *davening*, or performing other mitzvos, we will see to it that we do not violate the ideals of the Torah in our efforts to attain those objectives. Furthermore, even when we leave our shuls and *batei medrash*, we will remain always conscious that all of our actions must be geared to promoting kiddush Hashem.

The following beautiful letter was written by a non-Jewish secular teacher at Mesivta of West Bloomfield (in Detroit) to the school administration after one of the school's annual dinners:

> *Thank you very much for including us in last night's festivities. We had a wonderful time. It was so good to see the students all scrubbed and dressed up, and to talk with their families. The food was delicious, the setting was elegant, and I was inspired by the speeches and by the beautiful warmth of the Mesivta community. I have gained a great admiration and affection for the Mesivta community and, by extension, for all Orthodox Jews.*
>
> *My life was enriched last night, as it is each day at the yeshivah.*
>
> *Sincerely,*
>
> *Pete*

Upon contacting the yeshivah to congratulate them for this, I received the following response: "It's the boys who truly deserve credit. We also had a nonreligious Jewish teacher who became *frum* as a result of teaching here and still keeps up with us today.

---

mikadishchem — *I will be sanctified in the midst of Bnei Yisrael; I am Hashem Who sanctifies you*," as proof that the purpose of the Jewish people's sanctity is to bring about kiddush Hashem.

He began keeping Shabbos and learning every day as a direct result of the impression the *bachurim* made on him."

It can be a great challenge for *bachurim* in a *mesivta* setting to conduct themselves in a way that evokes the admiration of the teachers in their secular classes. The boys are taught — and rightly so — that their Torah study is of paramount importance, and their secular classes play a secondary role. If these boys were able to make such an impression on their secular teachers, it can mean only one thing: They had absorbed the message of the centrality of kiddush Hashem in their lives, and they recognized that all of their actions, at any time of day, must be calculated to enhance the honor of Hashem.

In other words, they had learned to "start with the end in mind."

Takeaway

When we keep the objective of kiddush Hashem in mind at all times, all of our actions will contribute toward this goal.

Making It Practical

- Start every day with your ultimate goal in mind. Pick a *tefillah* that reminds you of the ultimate purpose of *avodas Hashem* — perhaps the *berachah* of *mekadeish es shimcha b'rabim* at the beginning of *davening*, or Aleinu at the end of *davening*, or perhaps *Shema Yisrael,* and focus intently on the meaning of that *tefillah*.
- If you are late for *shul* or a learning *seder* and you are tempted to cut someone off in traffic or on line, stop and say to yourself, *Why am I trying to be on time, anyway? There is only one reason: to serve and bring honor to Hashem. And in this case, I am serving Him by being late!*

The Spirit of the Law

If you are a parent, you may be able to relate to the following scenario: A child is instructed to clean his room. The parent checks the room later in the day and finds that everything in the room has been stuffed haphazardly into the closet, and the child defends himself by reasoning, "You said only that I had to clean the *room*, not the closet." As you can imagine, the parent will not appreciate that particular feat of logic.

Every parent expects his children to fulfill the intent of his requests, rather than looking for ways to deliberately misinterpret his meaning and do as they please. The same is true, *l'havdil*, in our relationship with Hashem. The Torah is filled with mitzvos and rules for us to follow, but observing the Torah means more than simply following the rules in the most literal sense; it also means understanding the spirit of the law and striving to fulfill that, as well. We have been placed in this world with a mission to develop our *kedushah*, our *middos*, our *deveikus*, our *emunah*, and our integrity. Every person is charged with becoming a pure *tzelem Elokim* and a true ambassador of Hashem. At times, that means following the Divine Will even in ways that are not governed by explicit rules in the Torah.[6]

The Torah itself, in a number of places, alludes to this idea. For instance, the *Ramban* (*Vayikra* 19:2) teaches that the Torah's commandment "*Kedoshim tihiyu* — You shall be holy" means that a person should not become "a degenerate with the Torah's

---

6. The epitome of the approach of the wayward child, who seeks every excuse to do as he pleases while pretending to adhere to his parents' will, is the behavior of Bilam *Harasha*. Rav Elchonon Wasserman (*Kovetz Shiurim, Kuntres Divrei Sofrim*, 1:23-24) points out that Bilam insisted to Balak's messengers, "Even if Balak gives me his house full of gold and silver, I cannot transgress the Word of Hashem," yet he is still considered a *rasha*. Bilam's wickedness, Rav Elchonon explains, lay in his utter disregard for Hashem's actual Will; as long as he did not violate an explicit Divine command by accompanying Balak's men, he was willing to do so, even though he knew that his actions were against Hashem's wishes.

permission," i.e., a person should not indulge in too much worldly pleasure, even in ways that are technically permitted by the Torah. Similarly, the mitzvah of *"V'asisa hayashar v'hatov* — You shall do that which is upright and good," according to the *Ramban*, is a general commandment to act properly in all of our interpersonal dealings. The *Ramban* (*Devarim* 6;18) explains that the Torah could not possibly have given us rules for every issue that might arise in our dealings with other people; there are far too many possible scenarios for any rulebook to deal with them all individually. Therefore, after presenting us with a number of mitzvos governing the laws of *bein adam lachaveiro*, the Torah added a final, general admonition to conduct ourselves properly in every situation.[7] Thus, both of these precepts indicate that in addition to following the letter of the law, we must understand and abide by the spirit behind it.

We often make an effort to fulfill all of the details of the Torah's laws and to uphold every possibly stringency involved in every mitzvah. This is admirable, but our *avodah* would be even more meaningful if we took it a step further, and instead of relating to the Torah as a set of rules, we made sure to live in keeping with the spirit of the law as well.

This is one of the reasons that there is great benefit to focusing on kiddush Hashem. When we make kiddush Hashem our goal, we will not focus merely on the observance of each individual mitzvah on its own. Rather, we will pursue the general goal of increasing *kevod Shamayim*, which is a fundamental underpinning of all of the mitzvos. We will understand how all of the mitzvos come together to form a beautiful tapestry that represents the

---

7. Rav Elchonon Wasserman (*Kovetz Shiurim, Kuntres Divrei Sofrim*, 1:23-24) adds that this principle is a fundamental underpinning of the very concept of *dinim derabbanan* (rabbinic laws). All of the halachos enacted by the *rabbanan* are meant to uphold the spirit of the law, so that we will follow not only the literal meaning of Hashem's commandments, but also their underlying spirit and intent. In a sense, this is also true of the rulings of *rabbanim* today. Rabbinic guidance can help us remain focused on Hashem's true Will even in the many ambiguous areas of contemporary life, from dealing with the challenges of modern technology to determining whether to engage in questionable business practices.

Will of Hashem in its purest form. As Rav Eliyahu Dessler states (*Michtav MeEliyahu,* Vol. 1, p. 22), kiddush Hashem is the most significant mitzvah in the Torah because it encompasses all of the Torah's other precepts. When we achieve this understanding, then we will observe not only the literal meaning of the Torah's laws, but the spirit of the laws as well.

Takeaway

Concentrating on kiddush Hashem helps us tap into the spirit of the Torah's laws. With this attitude, we will not be drawn to take advantage of halachic loopholes; instead, we will lead our lives in accordance with the values of the Torah, rather than becoming "degenerates with the Torah's permission."

Making It Practical

- Come up with one area of your life in which you can take an extra step, performing an act of virtue that is not strictly required by the Torah. You will find that it will fill your life with more meaning and that you will increase your potential for creating a kiddush Hashem.

- Before eating a specific food or going to a particular place for recreation, ask yourself not only whether it is permitted or forbidden, but also whether Hashem would want you to do what you are about to do.

- Once in a while, abstain from something that is technically permitted — simply for the sake of becoming closer to Hashem.

- Get used to asking *she'eilos* even about matters that are not purely halachic issues. Your *rebbeim* can help you determine the Will of Hashem in many situations.

Every Man Has His Hour

There once was a Roman shepherd named Duklat Chazira, whom the Jews treated with great contempt. To their surprise, Duklat Chazira gradually became a powerful figure in the Roman empire, until he ascended to the throne itself. The former shepherd did not forget the insults he had endured from Jews, and he resolved to use his newfound power to take revenge. When he informed the Jewish sages that he planned to avenge his honor, though, the *chachamim* persuaded him to relent.

This story, which appears in the *Talmud Yerushalmi* (*Terumos* 8:4), is cited by many *mefarshim* as an illustration of the Mishnah's teaching in *Pirkei Avos*, "*Ein lecha adam she'ein lo shaah* — There is no man who does not have his hour." Any human being, no matter how powerless or insignificant he may seem, may one day rise to a position of great power or influence. This is yet another reason to be extremely cautious in our dealings with others: There is no telling when an insult or slight may come back to haunt us.

This is especially true in the modern world, when technological advances have made it possible for any individual to acquire his own "kingdom" of followers. Anyone who has had a few bad experiences can begin a blog and attract a wide audience for his tirades against our society. Any individual can wreak havoc for years, using the power of the Internet to spread his poisonous messages to a huge number of readers.

Very often, we have found that when there is friction between Jews and non-Jews in a particular community or town, one or two troublemakers take the situation to the next level and spread slanderous messages to a huge online audience. In one case, someone took a segment of a video of an Orthodox convention and misinterpreted just a few words that were spoken there, taking the comment entirely out of context and publicizing it for the entire online community to see. The result was a tremendous uproar and a major heartache for the organization in question, which was even forced to defend itself in court. Ultimately, huge amounts of time and effort had to be expended in order to repair the damage.

In another city, a certain blogger spent every waking moment searching for the tiniest violations of the neighborhood's bylaws by the *chassidic* groups who lived in that town. This person worked tirelessly to alert local politicians and other people in high places to every infraction, exerting tremendous pressure on them to oppose the *chassidim* in every way they could.

I believe that the non-Jews in our society were not born with anti-Semitic leanings that make them eager to join forces against the Jews whenever a controversy or tension erupts. When we witness hostility, it probably can be traced back to some chillul Hashem that someone experienced years earlier, and that left them, and those they influence, predisposed to become antagonistic to us when a pretext arises. We must be extremely cautious in our interactions with the outside world, keeping in mind that if we offend others or give them grounds to resent us, our actions may lead to immense harm.

But the inverse is also true: When a person creates a kiddush Hashem, the positive impact can be beyond anything he can imagine. A case in point is the story of Raoul Wallenberg, the legendary Swedish diplomat who saved thousands of Jews from death at the hands of the Nazis during World War II. Wallenberg risked his life for the sake of his efforts. After the war, the Russians took him captive and he died in their custody. What led him to his extraordinary heroism?

It was discovered after the war that Wallenberg had spent a few months in Israel (then known as Palestine) several years before the war had begun. He had been sent to the country, which was then under British control, by his parents, in order to learn about the British banking system. While in Israel, Wallenberg shared a room in a boarding house with a Jewish young man who had fled to Israel from Germany to escape Nazi persecution. The two roommates developed a close friendship, and Wallenberg was invited to participate in many Shabbos meals and other

Jewish activities, which led him to develop a deep appreciation for Yiddishkeit and the Jewish people. The two friends parted on good terms, and while Wallenberg's roommate never saw him again after those days, he was certain that their warm relationship had inspired the diplomat's rescue efforts.[8]

That young Jewish refugee had no inkling at the time that his friend would one day save thousands of Jews from annihilation. He could never have imagined that his kindness toward the young Raoul Wallenberg would bear remarkable fruits many times over. But this should be a lesson to all of us: Just as a negative word can have the most devastating effects, a positive gesture can one day lead to enormous good.

Takeaway

Nowadays more than ever, any person can amass a platform of followers to whom he can spread his ideas and experiences. It is incredibly easy for anyone to enlarge their circle of influence and readership virtually without limit. This makes it even more vital for us to take care to act honorably in all of our interactions.

Making It Practical

- Treat every individual you meet as someone who may have a blog or thousands of online followers, and who will report interactions with you to every member of their following.

- If you find yourself irritated at someone on the street, in a store, or anywhere else, pause for a minute before you make the comment that is on the tip of your tongue, and ask yourself, *Do I want these words to be recorded and published for millions of people to see?*

---

8 *For Goodness' Sake*, Rabbi Boruch Brull.

> • If you appreciate the service of a receptionist, waiter, cashier, or any other person with whom you come in contact, take a few seconds to voice your appreciation. Never let yourself believe that a passing compliment or word of thanks will not make a difference.

⟫•◇•⟪

Defining Kiddush Hashem — An All-Encompassing Mitzvah

The mitzvah of kiddush Hashem is far more than a simple imperative to behave nicely in public; it is a precept with many facets and with far-reaching implications. It is the mission of the Jewish people and the purpose of all of our mitzvos.[9] It has bearing on our *middos*, and on our conduct in private and in public alike. It can require a person to give up his life to avoid a sin, but it can have almost innumerable applications in the course of life itself as well. What is the unifying theme that connects all the aspects of this mitzvah? How can we understand the basic definition of kiddush Hashem?

Rav Chaim Friedlander (*Sifsei Chaim al HaTorah, Parashas Emor*) explains that the concept of "*kedushah*," or the act of being

---

9 In *Shaarei Teshuvah* (3:158), *Rabbeinu Yonah* sets forth a fundamental principle: The reason that Hashem selected the Jewish nation, elevated them above the rest of the nations of the world, and sanctified them with His Torah and mitzvos, is *entirely so that they would fear Him and sanctify His Name.* Rav Dessler writes (*Michtav MeEliyahu*, Vol. 1, p. 22) that kiddush Hashem is the essence of every mitzvah.

"*mekadesh*" an item, means attributing great value to that item. For example, there is a mitzvah to be "*mekadesh*" the Kohanim, which we observe by inviting them to lead a *zimun*, giving them the first *aliyah* when the Torah is read, and so forth. Through these actions, we demonstrate that the Kohanim possess an exalted position in our society; we treat them as people of great value because they are the servants of Hashem.

In a similar vein, kiddush Hashem means attaching superlative importance to Hashem and His Will. Being *mekadesh Shem Shamayim* means expressing through our words or deeds the fact that Hashem's Will supersedes everything else, that it is of more importance and value than anything else in our lives. When a person demonstrates this, whether it is through an action performed in private or a public act, he fulfills the mitzvah of kiddush Hashem.

An act performed in private can create a kiddush Hashem by expressing the pure desire to do Hashem's Will. When a person performs a mitzvah solely because Hashem has commanded it — rather than for the sake of personal gain of any sort — he demonstrates that the Divine Will takes precedence over any other considerations. When a person resists the temptation to sin because of the Will of Hashem, he demonstrates that the *ratzon Hashem* is of greater importance than his own desires. And when a person gives up his very life for the sake of Hashem's Will, he demonstrates that he values the Divine Will even more than his own existence. Even if these actions are not witnessed by other human beings, a kiddush Hashem is effected because of this demonstration of priorities.[10]

At the same time, when a person's actions *are* witnessed by others, he can create a kiddush Hashem even if his personal motivations are not pure. When a religious Jew speaks pleasantly or demonstrates some other form of refinement, he may cause others to have greater regard for Jews who observe the Torah, even if his behavior was not driven by the purest intentions. Likewise,

10. *Hilchos Yesodei HaTorah* (5:10).

a person who speaks highly of *talmidei chachamim* or of others who exhibit *yiras Shamayim* may increase his listeners' respect for such people. A person may also increase others' appreciation for Hashem Himself by speaking about Divine *hashgachah*, and giving thanks to Hashem, or through various other means. Even if he did not have the specific intent to demonstrate the importance of Hashem and His Will, the impact of his words and actions on others will nonetheless constitute a kiddush Hashem.

As a corollary to this definition of kiddush Hashem, a chillul Hashem is the exact opposite: Whenever a person's words or actions appear to detract from the value or importance of Hashem's Will, a chillul Hashem has been created. For this reason, whenever a person performs an *aveirah*, his actions contain an element of chillul Hashem. Even if the sin is committed in private, the chillul Hashem stems from the mere fact that the transgressor has given in to his own desires in violation of Hashem's Will.[11] In public, the danger is even greater: If a person commits an act in public that merely *appears* to be an *aveirah*, even if it is not technically sinful, it will still constitute a chillul Hashem, since it will cause others to lose their respect for the Divine Will. This applies to behaviors that others consider loathsome or repulsive, or even to a simple lack of etiquette. If a person who is visibly religious does not adhere to the higher

---

11 This can answer a question regarding the *pasuk* that is the source of the mitzvah of kiddush Hashem. The Torah states, "I shall be sanctified in the midst of Bnei Yisrael ... and you shall not desecrate My holy Name." This seems to imply that there is no middle ground between these two extremes; if we fail to make a kiddush Hashem, then a chillul Hashem will be the automatic result. But why should this be the case? Couldn't there be a neutral area between the two extremes, in which a person's actions represent neither a kiddush Hashem nor a chillul Hashem?

In light of our definition of kiddush Hashem, the answer is clear. We know that the entire world was created in order to fulfill the Will of Hashem; everything in creation exists solely for that purpose. Hence, if a person uses any part of the world for a purpose other than honoring Hashem, he will thereby disconnect that thing from the true objective of its existence. Instead of treating it as a vehicle for serving Hashem and promoting *kevod Shamayim*, he will be assigning an independent value to it, as something that has value simply because of the benefit or enjoyment that it offers him.

standard that is expected of him, it will lessen his observers' respect for Hashem and the Torah.[12]

According to the *Nefesh Hachaim* (*shaar* 1 Ch. 11), this is the message of the custom of lifting ourselves up on our toes at the words *"kadosh kadosh kadosh"* in *Kedushah*; this practice alludes to the idea that our mission is to elevate ourselves, along with everything else in the world, to attain a state of *kedushah*. The definition of true kiddush Hashem is precisely that: attributing great value to Hashem by elevating everything in the world to serve the Divine Will. The failure to do that, by definition, means that a person has placed his own desires above the dictates of the *ratzon Hashem* — and that, as we have seen, is precisely the meaning of chillul Hashem. That is why our mandate of kiddush Hashem is so incredibly vast and all-encompassing.

Takeaway

Kiddush Hashem means using our words or deeds to express the idea that Hashem's Will is of greater importance and value than anything else in the world. This is an idea that we can convey through our actions both in public and in private.

Making It Practical

When you make a show of kevod Shamayim in public, have in mind that you are demonstrating the supreme importance of Hashem's Will.

Even when you are serving Hashem in private, be conscious of the fact that you are putting His Will ahead of your own.

---

12. *Shu"T Chasam Sofer, Choshen Mishpat, Likutim, #59; Smak,* mitzvah 85.

Discussion Points

❖ Why do we need to focus on kiddush Hashem? If we simply concentrate on keeping the Torah and mitzvos, won't we automatically create a kiddush Hashem even without giving thought to the matter?

❖ How can I inspire others to develop their love for Hashem, if I haven't yet developed such sentiments within myself?

❖ Do you need to be on a certain level yourself in order to be involved in kiddush Hashem?

CHAPTER 17

LESSONS FROM OUR GEDOLIM

"Rabbi Gross," Yechiel says hesitantly, "I am having trouble with something."

Rabbi Gross turns to look at Yechiel, a talmid who has captured a special place in his heart. Yechiel is an incredibly sincere young man, who is always striving to grow to higher levels of avodas Hashem. His expression always radiates purity and an earnest desire to grow, but now his forehead is creased with worry. "What is bothering you?" the rebbi asks kindly.

"I have been reading the biographies of gedolim and hearing stories about their lives, and I have begun to feel depressed," Yechiel confesses. "They were all born with superhuman qualities and abilities; I know that I will never be able to come close to their levels of greatness. How can I expect to achieve anything meaningful in life, when everything I do will pale in comparison to the gedolei Torah?"

Rabbi Gross acknowledges the wisdom of his young talmid's question. "The Chiddushei HaRim states that every Jew should be a gadol in one specific area," he says. "When you learn about the gedolim, you should identify one specific area in which you can excel. There are many simple sensitivities that our gedolim displayed from which we can learn. Every gadol in Klal Yisrael was unique, and every one of them had his own individual focus on kiddush Hashem. We can learn from them in those specific areas, and we can adopt them as our role models in certain specific ways.

"You don't have to become the next Rav Pam or the next Chofetz Chaim," Rabbi Gross concluded encouragingly. "Just try to emulate one of their traits. You will find that goal to be within your reach!"

Rav Pam — A Life of Sweetness

One of the ritual garments of the Kohen Gadol described in the Torah is the *ephod*, a robe that was adorned with approximately 90 small bells attached to its hem. Rav Mordechai Gifter explains that the bells of the Kohen Gadol allude to the proper conduct of a servant of Hashem: With every step the Kohen Gadol took, he would be surrounded by the soft, sweet sounds of the bells ringing. Similarly, Rav Gifter explains, an *eved Hashem* should leave an impression of sweetness and pleasantness on anyone with whom he comes in contact. His every move should be music to the ears, so to speak, of the people who observe him.

In the recent past, we were blessed with a spiritual leader, a Kohen and a *gadol b'Torah* who embodied this ideal: Rav Avrohom Yaakov Pam, the *rosh yeshivah* of Torah Vodaas. Rav Pam was a model of the sweetness of a true *eved Hashem*, a man who exuded caring and compassion and whose charm never failed to touch the hearts of those who encountered him.

✎ Kiddush Hashem with Every Move

Rav Pam always taught his *talmidim* that their exclusive goal in life should be to foster kiddush Hashem. "Wherever he goes and whatever he does," he would remind them, "a Jew must always ask himself if what he is about to do will create a kiddush Hashem, or if it will have the opposite effect." Before every *bein haz'manim,* he would remind his *talmidim* of various actions that they might view as trivial, but that he considered important. He would urge them to help their parents at home, to be available for errands, and to have *divrei Torah* prepared for the *seudos* on Shabbos and Yom Tov. Before they left for summer camp, he would also remind them to thank the cook in the camp and never to poke fun at the food if it would cause the cook pain. He would also admonish the *masmidim* among them, "If learning for an extra 15 minutes will cause you to come late to lunch and make the waiters work harder, it isn't worth it."

An Eved Hashem's Speech Patterns

Rav Pam often quoted the *Rambam*'s teaching in *Hilchos Dei'os* (5:7), "A *talmid chacham* does not scream or shout ... he does not raise his voice ... but rather speaks pleasantly to all people ... and extends greetings to everyone so that they are pleased with him." At that point, he would interject his own comment: "This means greeting even non-Jews, such as neighbors or the maintenance workers in the yeshivah." He would then read the next lines in the *Rambam*: "He never reneges on his words; in general, he speaks only words of wisdom and kindness." At that point, Rav Pam would interject again, "This is because words are not *hefker* or cheap. They are a gift that we must use wisely; we must choose our words carefully and make certain that they are constructive, and not destructive."

In his younger years, Rav Pam worked hard to perfect his pronunciation and vocabulary in English and to rid himself of his European accent. He once explained that he had invested this effort because he felt that it creates a kiddush Hashem when a *ben Torah* expresses himself properly.

Exquisite Sensitivity

A *yungerman* posed a question to Rav Pam: Every morning, he *davened* Shacharis at a local *minyan* that *davened* at a slow pace. One day, on his way to *shul*, he passed another man who was standing outside another *shul* and calling out, "A *tzenter*! A *tzenter*!" The man asked the *yungerman* to help complete the *minyan* in his own *shul*. The *yungerman* agreed, but he found the pace of the *tefillos* distressingly fast, and he asked Rav Pam if he would be required to help complete the *minyan* again if he were asked to do so.

"You are not obligated to sacrifice your own *davening*," Rav Pam replied. "Nevertheless," he added, "the members of that *minyan* would never understand how a *ben Torah* could refuse another Jew's request to help form a *minyan*. Therefore, I suggest that you take a different route to *shul* so that you will not encounter this problem at all."

On another occasion, a *talmid* asked Rav Pam how he should respond when a nonreligious aunt attempted to greet him with a handshake. Rav Pam replied, "For a long time, I have lived by the rule that if a person behaves in a pleasant and refined manner, people will respect him even if he is different from them. You should tell your aunt respectfully that as a yeshivah student, you do not shake hands with women."

࠹ *The Talmidim of Rav Pam*

Rav Yisroel Reisman, a close *talmid* of Rav Pam, once pointed out that the famed *rosh yeshivah* taught a broad range of *talmidim*. Some went on to become *rabbanim* or *roshei yeshivah*, while others became businessmen or professionals, yet they all share the same inner values and traits. They cannot tolerate the thought of taking something that is not theirs, and they are invariably polite and pleasant to others, including their own family members. They are calm even at trying times, and they exude love for other Jews. He recalled that Rav Pam himself once commented, "Our *talmidim* have such pleasantness."

After Rav Pam's *petirah*, a non-Jew who had been acquainted with him wrote that "Rabbi Pam's passing is a loss not only for the Jewish people, but for the entire world."

Let us absorb the example of Rav Pam, the Kohen Gadol of our times, and emulate the sweetness that accompanied him throughout his life.[1]

Takeaway

*Make it a priority to be pleasant
in all of your dealings with other people.*

---

1 Much of the material in this segment was culled from the book *Beloved by All* by Rabbi Shimon Finkelman, on the subject of Rav Pam's life of kiddush Hashem.

- Try to emulate Rav Pam's example by speaking with a pleasant voice, using kind words, and always smiling to everyone you pass.
- Be the first to say "good morning" to people in the neighborhood
- Say "good Shabbos" to Jews of all "flavors."

Rav Shlomo Zalman Auerbach — Oxygen for the Soul

One of the names for the *neshamah*, the human soul, is "*kavod*." This is because the *neshamah* is taken from the *Kisei Hakavod* — Hashem's Throne of Glory — itself. Due to its origins, the *neshamah* craves honor; therefore, it is natural for a human being to spend his life in search of *kavod*. In effect, honor is oxygen for the soul, a form of nourishment that satisfies one of the deepest desires of every human being.

Why is the desire for honor so deeply ingrained within the human condition? Rav Yerucham Levovitz explains that this stems from the *neshamah's* recognition of the purpose of a human being's existence: to promote *kevod Shamayim*, using both himself and others as vehicles for bringing honor to Hashem. Rav Yerucham adds that the greatness of a human being, and the extent to which he is in touch with his *neshamah*, can be measured by the degree to which he shows respect to others. When a person treats others with *kavod*, it is a sign that he has remained cognizant of his purpose as an instrument for bringing honor to Hashem. When a person is disrespectful to others, though, it indicates that he has lost touch with his soul.

The ideal of demonstrating respect to everyone, regardless of their identity or station in life, is exemplified by Rav Shlomo

Zalman Auerbach, a *gadol* who lived in our midst as recently as three decades ago. Throughout his life, Rav Shlomo Zalman epitomized this trait, and while we may not be capable of reaching the same lofty heights he attained, we can certainly try to emulate his example at least within the limits of our abilities.

✌§ *Respect for Family*

Rav Shlomo Zalman was once asked to visit a prominent surgeon who was scheduled to operate on a noted *talmid chacham*; the *askan* who contacted him believed that a visit from the *gadol hador* would motivate the surgeon to take his responsibility even more seriously. When Rav Shlomo Zalman arrived at the doctor's home, the man was shocked. "Rebbe, what brings you here?" he exclaimed.

"Doctor," Rav Shlomo Zalman said gravely, "you have saved many lives in the course of your work, and a person who saves even one Jewish life is viewed as if he had saved an entire world. You are certainly deserving of a visit." He went on to speak at length about the weighty responsibility borne by every doctor, and spent a few moments discussing the impending operation.

Perhaps the most noteworthy part of Rav Shlomo Zalman's visit, though, was his brief exchange with the surgeon's wife just before he left. Rav Shlomo Zalman noticed that the lady of the house had been listening with great interest from an adjacent room while he spoke with her husband, and as he was about to leave, he made a point of approaching her. "I know that life in the home of a doctor can be very difficult," Rav Shlomo Zalman said, "and I am sure that your husband's busy schedule is often a burden to you as well. As the wife of a doctor, though, you have an equal share in all of the merits he gathers in the course of his work. If you ever feel resentful or displeased, I ask you to remember that your husband is busy because he is involved in saving lives."

The full impact of those few brief sentences was revealed only after Rav Shlomo Zalman's *petirah*, when the doctor's wife placed a phone call to the *askan* who had sent the *rosh yeshivah* to their home. "I must thank you for asking Rav Shlomo Zalman to visit us that day," she said with great emotion. "Our *shalom bayis* had been suffering terribly, but thanks to his visit, it was completely restored."

With his well-placed words to the doctor's wife, Rav Shlomo Zalman hinted at an important dimension of *kavod* that is often overlooked. Many of us find it relatively easy to respect people who are not close to us, yet we tend to take our own family members for granted. Rav Shlomo Zalman's words were a reminder to the doctor's wife of the importance of appreciating her own husband for his accomplishments and innate value. In his own home, too, Rav Shlomo Zalman was scrupulous about treating the members of his family with all the *kavod* they were due. In fact, until the very last day he spent in his home, Rav Shlomo Zalman even went to the effort of removing his own plate from the table after every meal, in order to spare his family members the necessity of doing so.

✒ *A Respectful Refusal*

Rav Shlomo Zalman was once visited by a journalist who wished to interview him for a newspaper article. The *gadol hador* greeted his visitor with his usual radiant smile and invited him to take a seat. After making sure that his guest was comfortable, Rav Shlomo Zalman began to explain at length that, as a matter of policy, he never granted interviews. He devoted an entire ten minutes of his precious time to explaining the matter to his visitor, making a concerted effort to spare the man even the slightest discomfort.

When the journalist left the *rav*'s home, he was met by a group of friends who had waited outside, eager to find out the outcome of his visit. Naturally, their first question was if Rav Shlomo Zalman had agreed to the interview.

"No, he did not," the journalist replied. But he quickly added, "It was still worth the effort for me to learn how to say no with a smile."

↪ Sparing a Boy from Shame

Once, Rav Shlomo Zalman received an invitation to a *bar mitzvah* that he could not attend, due to a wedding scheduled for the same night. He sent an apologetic note to the parents in advance of the *simchah*, explaining that he would be unable to attend the *bar mitzvah*. They were quite surprised, then, when Rav Shlomo Zalman arrived in the hall on the night of the event.

In response to a query from the father of the *bar mitzvah* boy, Rav Shlomo Zalman said simply, "I remembered that I had attended the *bar mitzvahs* of both of his older brothers, and I was afraid that your son would be insulted if I didn't attend his *bar mitzvah* as well. For that reason, I felt that I had to be here."

On another occasion, Rav Shlomo Zalman was approached by the parents of a fourteen-year-old boy who was mentally disturbed and was causing great hardships for his parents and neighbors. The famed *rosh yeshivah* managed to convince the boy's parents to place him in a specific institution, but then he surprised them by asking to speak with the boy himself. He insisted that it was crucial for the boy's emotional well-being for him to go willingly to the institution, rather than being forced into it. Rav Shlomo Zalman met with the boy and cleverly offered him a "position" as the "rabbi" of the institution. The boy enthusiastically accepted the offer, proud to be playing such an important role. Long after that conversation, he was still performing the functions of a rabbi, monitoring the *kashrus* standards in the institution and helping others with their *tefillin*, while his own mental health steadily improved.

Every human being, young or old, has a deep-seated desire to feel important. When we show respect to others, regardless of who they are, we are essentially giving them the most valuable gift they could possibly receive: the priceless sense of self-importance that brings out the best in every individual. Ultimately, this will play a major role in promoting the revelation of Hashem's honor as well.

Takeaway

Giving kavod generously to other people is a powerful means to increase kevod Shamayim. When people are treated with respect, it is like oxygen for their souls, and it makes it possible for them to realize their full potential.

Making It Practical

- Make someone close to you feel important, whether it is your own children, your spouse, or someone who works with you. Be generous with compliments and be vocal about the positive qualities of the people around you.
- Be present for your children by listening attentively when they talk to you, entering their fantasy worlds, and celebrating their successes
- Know who your children's friends are, what they are learning in school, and what they enjoy doing in their free time.

Rav Mendel Kaplan — Bearing the Torah's Imprint

In *Parashas Yisro* (*Shemos* 19:5), the Torah gives us a brief description of the Jewish people's role in the world: "You shall be a treasure to Me from among all the nations, for the entire land is Mine." Why does the Torah mention in this *pasuk* that the entire world belongs to Hashem? The *Keren Orah* (*Taanis* 20a) explains that this indicates the ultimate purpose of *talmud Torah*. When a Jewish person learns Torah, his learning should not merely be something that shapes his own personality; rather, the Torah should impact him in such a way that its light will radiate to everyone around him. Hashem tells us, "The entire land is Mine" in order to indicate that our learning must perfect the entire world, not just ourselves. If a person who learns Torah does not exert a positive impact on others, then it means that there is something lacking in his own learning.

Rav Mattisyahu Salomon explains that this is the basis of the famous adage that "*derech eretz* precedes Torah." If the people who learn Torah do not demonstrate *derech eretz* — basic courtesy and consideration for others — then the purpose of their Torah learning will not be realized, for they will fail to have a positive influence on other people.

❧ *Mentschlichkeit — A Ben Torah's Top Priority*

In a story related by Rabbi Paysach Krohn, Rav Yisroel Salanter alluded to this idea when a *shidduch* was suggested between his granddaughter and a young Rav Chaim Ozer Grodzensky. Rav Yisroel had met Rav Chaim Ozer years earlier, when the future *gadol* was a child and approached Rav Yisroel after a *derashah* to offer a brilliant answer to a question he had raised. At the time, Rav Yisroel kissed the young child and offered his *berachah* for a good *shidduch*. When the *shidduch* was *redt*, though, Rav Yisroel insisted on investigating more than Rav Chaim Ozer's brilliance and knowledge. To those who praised Rav Chaim Ozer for his greatness in Torah, Rav Yisroel responded, "I knew that he was a *talmid chacham* when he was ten years old, but the Torah describes marriage with the words 'I have given my daughter *to this man*.' In order to be fit for marriage, a person must be a 'man'; he must be a *mentch*. If he is not, his Torah learning is not worth a thing!"

Rav Mendel Kaplan, a legendary educator in his time, was known for constantly stressing to his *talmidim* the importance of *mentschlichkeit*. A renowned *rosh yeshivah* once commented, "I make *talmidim*, but Rav Mendel makes *mentschen*." Rav Mendel's entire life was dedicated to instilling sensitivity and caring for others in the hearts of his students, and the ideal of *derech eretz* was exemplified by his own behavior as well.

✎§ *A Mother's Pain*

Rav Mendel once had an unusual — and highly illuminating — reaction to an article describing the *teshuvah* movement in Eretz Yisrael. The article related that the phenomenon had grown to the point that many irreligious parents had banded together in an effort to stifle it. It went on to describe an exchange between two secular mothers: a woman whose son was returning from a trip abroad, and another whose son had become religious. "Your son is coming back to you," the second woman told the first in a pained tone, "but I will never have my son back, because he has become a *baal teshuvah*." The tone of the article was triumphant; the religious writer seemed to be taking pride in the anguish caused to the parents of so many *baalei teshuvah*. But Rav Mendel's reaction was the exact opposite. His eyes filled with tears as he exclaimed, "Can you imagine the sorrow a mother must feel when she thinks that she has lost a child? When we serve Hashem, we must do so in a way that is good for everyone; it should be good for the entire world!"

On another occasion, Rav Mendel was approached by a recent *baal teshuvah* who was returning home to visit his parents. The young man wanted to know the nature of his spiritual obligations during his visit, and Rav Mendel replied, "Your mitzvah while you are at home is to honor your parents . You must find things to do that they will appreciate, such as washing and waxing your father's car."

✎§ *"You Don't Speak with a Horn"*

Rav Mendel was once approached by a wealthy man who was seeking advice on how to formulate his will. He wanted to know how money he should leave to his children, who were not religious, and how much he should leave for charity. "Leave the majority of your assets to your children," Rav Mendel advised him. "If you leave too much money to charity, it will cause your children to feel ill will toward Yiddishkeit. On the other hand, leaving most of your money to them will cause them to look favorably on your beliefs. They may even begin observing Shabbos as a result."

When Rav Mendel drove a car, he sounded the horn only when it was absolutely necessary for safety. "You don't speak to a person with a horn," he would often say.

Shortly after his passing, someone else brought his car to his usual auto shop for repairs. One of the non-Jewish workers recognized the car and asked, "Where is the rabbi?" When he was told that Rav Mendel had passed away, the man began to weep. "I know I am a simple mechanic," he said, "but the rabbi always treated me like a special person. He would take interest in my life and would make me feel like a million dollars. No one in the world made me feel as good as he did."

⤳ The Supremacy of Torah

I am often asked how it can be said that kiddush Hashem is the central mitzvah of the Torah, when *Chazal* (*Shabbos* 127a) state clearly that *talmud Torah* is "*k'neged kulam*" — the equivalent of all the other precepts of the Torah combined. The answer to this question is that Torah is the most powerful means of bringing about a kiddush Hashem, and that is the reason for its supremacy; however, kiddush Hashem itself is the ultimate goal even of Torah study. At the same time, we must keep in mind that the Torah achieves its goal only when it leaves an imprint on the person who studies it: when he embodies the Torah ideal of being a *mentsch*.

Takeaway

The Torah we learn should leave an imprint on us; it must imbue us with mentschlichkeit. This is the only way for it to have its powerful effect on the world.

Rav Yaakov Kamenetsky — Committed to Truth

⋙ *The Borrowed Pen*

Rav Yaakov Kamenetsky was known for his unyielding commitment to honesty in all areas. When he was at an advanced age, Rav Yaakov was once asked how he had merited such a long life. He answered simply, "I have never told a lie."

Rav Yaakov's showed unfailing integrity when handling others' belongings, even with items of negligible value. Once, Rav Yaakov encountered a *yungerman* whom he hadn't seen since his wedding two years earlier, and promptly handed him a pen. "This pen is yours," the *gadol* explained. "I borrowed it to fill in the details on the *kesubah* at your wedding, and I forgot to return it to you."

The meticulous avoidance of dishonesty was a trait that Rav Yaakov sought to instill in his children as well. One of Rav Yaakov's sons once returned home from Yeshivas Ner Yisrael after borrowing a book from the yeshivah library to read on the train. At the train station, as soon as Rav Yaakov saw the book, he questioned whether his son had been given explicit permission to borrow it. When the son admitted that he had not, Rav Yaakov admonished him, "You will soon be receiving *semichah*, but if this book is lost or ruined before you return it, you will be *pasul* to serve as a witness in any *beis din*, or for a *kesubah* or *kiddushin*. As soon as you get home," he added, "you must mail the book back to the library immediately." This was despite the fact that Rav Yaakov's son estimated the value of the book at less than one dollar.

◄§ Respecting the Law

Rav Yaakov was also adamant about the proper observance of *dina d'malchusa dina*, the requirement for a Jewish person to abide by the laws of the country in which he lives. Naturally, he forbade people to make false statements about their household income in order to qualify for food stamps or other government programs. Once, a woman challenged him to explain his position. Numerous families of other ethnicities lied in order to obtain government benefits, she argued; why shouldn't her family do the same? Rav Yaakov's reply was terse and to the point: "They did not stand at Har Sinai; you did."

He also spoke strongly about the necessity for yeshivos to be absolutely truthful in their applications for government aid, pointing out that the children who attend a yeshivah are bound to absorb the example of their teachers. Rav Yaakov once rebuked a yeshivah principal for raising money through bingo games, of which he disapproved because they were too similar to gambling. Rav Yaakov was quick to set the record straight on the proper priorities in this instance: "You are not obligated to see to it that a yeshivah will exist," he explained to the principal. "If Hashem wishes for there to be a yeshivah, then there will be one. But you must not do something improper in order to maintain it."

Rav Yaakov was once approached by a young woman whose family had been awarded a large sum of money in a lawsuit when she was a child. The money was due to be given to her upon her marriage, she told him, but she knew that the lawsuit had been won on the basis of a false statement she had made at the behest of her parents' lawyer. Now that she was an adult, she regretted her childhood actions and wished to know what to do with the funds she had received. Rav Yaakov agreed that it was not acceptable for her to keep the money, yet he also recognized that returning it to the defendant in the lawsuit could be highly problematic. Instead, he advised her to give it away, but instead of donating the money to help other Jews, he suggested donating it to a non-Jewish charity, so she never justified her false statement by saying that it has helped other Jews.

⋙ Confidential Number

When Rav Yaakov's wife was about to undergo a serious operation, he wished to receive a *berachah* for her well-being from Rav Moshe Feinstein. His numerous attempts to reach Rav Moshe, though, met with no success, as the phone line was consistently busy. Although Rav Yaakov was privy to the number of Rav Moshe's other phone line — which was an unlisted number — he did not feel justified in using it. That number, he explained, had been given to him to reach Rav Moshe about matters concerning Klal Yisrael; for a personal matter, he was not permitted to use it.

When a person has zero tolerance for even the slightest trace of *sheker*, and when he lives with *emes* as his top priority, his actions will affect his children, his *talmidim*, and everyone else in his life. The impact of such a life — like that of Rav Yaakov Kamenetsky — can last for generations, creating ripple effects that can reach thousands or even millions of people.

Takeaway

When a person lives with emes as his top priority, when he refuses to compromise on the truth regardless of the reason, his integrity can have an eternal impact.

The Chofetz Chaim — Constant Awareness of Hashem

Ayei Elokecha — Where is your G-d?" According to David HaMelech (*Tehillim* 42:11, as explained by the *Radak*), this was the question with which the enemies of the Jewish people taunted them after the destruction of the *Beis HaMikdash:* "Where is your G-d? How could He have allowed these tragedies to befall you? Isn't He watching over you?"

But the question of *"Ayei Elokecha?"* is not one that should be asked only by our enemies. This is also a question that we must direct to ourselves: Where is our *fear* of G-d? How can we claim to fear Hashem, when we do not always observe His mitzvos? A Jew should live with the constant awareness that Hashem is watching all of his actions, and that should lead him to fear committing even the smallest transgression.

✒ *The Chofetz Chaim's Burden*

The Chofetz Chaim, Rav Yisroel Meir HaKohen Kagan, exemplified this sense of responsibility. He often remarked, "I have been afflicted doubly for my sins. I know that I am an ordinary, small person, but there are people in the world who mistakenly think that I am a great man. Since the sin of chillul Hashem is measured by the view of the world at large, this means that I am punished for my actions in accordance with the way a great man would be expected to act. That is a much greater responsibility than I am able to bear!"

All of us are responsible for the way the world perceives our actions, simply by virtue of the fact that we are visibly dressed as Jews. The presence of a *yarmulke* on a man's head marks him as a person whose actions reflect the dictates and values of the Torah and of Hashem Himself. As a result, that *yarmulke* makes a man responsible to live up to the values and standards that it represents.

In a similar vein, the Chofetz Chaim made certain to celebrate his birthdays in his old age, so that it would be evident that he had lived a long life. In *Sefer Tehillim*, David HaMelech states, "Who is the man who desires life, who loves days to see good? Guard your tongue from evil." This clearly indicates that a person who abstains from *lashon hara* will be rewarded with a long life. The Chofetz Chaim, who was known for his scrupulous observance of the laws of *lashon hara*, felt that if he did not emphasize his age, others might think that the promise of the *pasuk* had not been fulfilled. As a result, he felt obligated to raise awareness of his age by publicizing his birthday every year.

✑ A Free Herring for Everyone

The same sense of responsibility drove the Chofetz Chaim to take extraordinary measures in all his business dealings, both with Jews and with non-Jews, to avoid the smallest trace of chillul Hashem.

The Chofetz Chaim owned a grocery store for a period of time, and he once discovered that a non-Jewish customer had accidentally left behind a herring that he had purchased. The Chofetz Chaim struggled to figure out which customer had forgotten his purchase, but he could not determine the purchaser's identity. The possibility that he would somehow be guilty of even the tiniest trace of wrongdoing gave the Chofetz Chaim no rest. Finally, he came up with a solution: On the next market day, he gave a free herring to every non-Jewish customer.

On another occasion, the Chofetz Chaim discovered that a small quantity of salt had become stuck to the scales in his store. He quickly concluded that it was part of the measure of salt purchased by his last customer, a non-Jewish woman from a village several miles away from Radin, which meant that the customer had not received all the salt for which she had paid. After searching in vain for her in the marketplace in Radin, the Chofetz Chaim concluded that she had returned home. Once again, he could not tolerate the possibility that one of his customers had been shortchanged, even by mistake and by such a small measure. The Chofetz Chaim therefore prepared numerous small packages of salt and hired a wagon driver to distribute them to all the women in the village in question, thereby ensuring that the woman who had bought the salt would receive the full amount for which she had paid.

~§ Curbing the Cow

Once, when the Chofetz Chaim was learning in a nearby town, he asked a wagon driver who was traveling to Radin to deliver a letter to his wife. The Chofetz Chaim stressed that the letter contained a very important message.

Overcome by curiosity, the wagon driver opened the letter on the way to Radin, expecting it to contain some valuable secrets. He was shocked to read that the Chofetz Chaim was reminding his wife not to allow the cow that they owned to wander outside on market day. "There will be many wagons passing by that belong to non-Jews," the great sage explained, "and the cow might eat a bit of hay from a wagon that pulls up alongside it. Even though it is generally assumed that a Jew does not mind a loss of less than a *perutah*, the same presumption does not apply to a non-Jew. Thus, even taking a small quantity of hay from a non-Jew would be tantamount to theft."

The Chofetz Chaim's example should be thought-provoking to all of us. We should always ask ourselves if we are acting in a way that brings honor to Hashem, or, chas v'shalom, we cause others to wonder, "Where is your G-d?" Are we scrupulous in our business dealings, or do we sometimes come across as underhanded or conniving? Are we careful not to allow ourselves to take advantage of others even for the tiniest gain? If we truly mourn for the destruction of the Beis HaMikdash, then that sorrow should lead us to make this reckoning and work to improve ourselves in this area.

Making It Practical

- During the many *tefillos* that we recite for the *geulah* and Mashiach, try to feel the pain of chillul Hashem in *galus* and the hope that a time will come when Hashem will reign supreme, and there will be kiddush Hashem in the world.

- Learn to be pained by chillul Hashem. Think about the devastating effects of a decrease in Hashem's honor, and you will learn to change your own behavior accordingly.

- Remember the Chofetz Chaim's example and be extremely cautious to avoid the slightest possibility of chillul Hashem. This means communicating clearly with others so that they do not suspect you of wrongdoing. Don't allow people to be left with the impression that you have done something improper, even if you know it isn't true. Make a concerted effort to clear your name: for the sake of kiddush Hashem!

Rav Yechezkel ("Rav Chatzkel") Levenstein — The Jewish Reality

✍ Living in an Invisible Reality

I was once walking to *shul* when I noticed a small group of people gathering on a street corner and behaving in a very strange fashion. Every person in the group was holding a phone and seemed to be diligently searching for something, pointing or gesturing meaningfully every few moments. As I approached them, they were so absorbed in their activity that they did not seem to notice my presence at all. Finally, I asked one of them if I could help them find something. "No, thanks," he replied curtly, with his gaze remaining fixed on his phone.

That was my introduction to the game of "Pokemon," a craze that swept through modern society several years ago. Pokemon is a new type of video game that projects imaginary cartoon characters into a person's actual surroundings, using the screen of a smartphone or other gadget to make it appear as if the characters exist in the world around them. The object of the game is for players to find and capture those characters using their phones. These animated figures may appear anywhere; look out for drivers swerving erratically on the road in a frantic attempt to capture one of these critters!

Observing the Pokemon phenomenon has led me to an interesting observation: The people who play this game are actually living in and perceiving a different reality than the rest of us. They live in a world in which the reality has merged with an imaginary realm and is populated by all sorts of invented creatures. Watching a Pokemon player walking down the street, intent on his phone and racing to catch up with some invisible object, you can be certain that he is living in a reality that is very different from your own.

In a sense, this is how we, as practicing and believing Jews, appear to outside observers. When we fulfill the dictates of ha-lachah, our actions seem to be guided by an invisible force. When we allow *emunah* to guide us, our words and deeds indicate our awareness that we are serving a Higher Authority. When a per-son feels truly connected to Hashem, his perception of the real-ity of Hashem's existence will be so intense that others will sense that reality as well; it will be clear to anyone who observes him that he is living in a different, more sublime reality. That reality, however, will be derived from the holy Torah, not from some sort of animation program on a cell phone.

The Jewish people are often described as *"eidim"* ("wit-nesses") to Hashem's existence and sovereignty over the world. The *Sfas Emes* points out (*Succos* 5641) that we are also consid-ered the children of Hashem, and children are halachically dis-qualified to testify on behalf of their parents. How, then, can we be the *"eidim"* who give testimony to the world about Hashem?

The answer to this question is that we are not considered "witnesses" in the classic sense: people who deliver verbal testi-mony to back up a claim. Rather, we bear witness to Hashem's existence *through our actions*. When the world sees that the Jewish people perceive reality through a different lens, that their actions are guided by subservience to a higher Being, then the world will recognize that there is a Creator Whom they serve. We "attest" to the existence of an invisible G-d by living in our own invisible reality.

⚜§ *Visualizing Emunah*

Our task, then, is to develop our *emunah* to the point that it is as real to us as our physical surroundings. We must believe in the reality of Hashem's existence to the same degree that we believe that all the trappings of our physical environments are real. This is an ideal that was embodied by Rav Yechezkel ("Rav Chatzkel") Levenstein, the legendary *mashgiach* of the yeshivos of Mir and Ponovezh, who mastered the ability of concretizing *emunah* to the point that it became part of his reality.

Rav Chatzkel was once seen dancing between two rows of chairs in his small room above the *beis medrash*. It did not take long for the observers to realize that he was reenacting the experience of *Kerias Yam Suf*, as he sang the *Shiras HaYam* while walking between the chairs. On another occasion, the *mashgiach* was seen in the same room early one morning, pounding loudly on a *shtender* and exclaiming, "This is a loud noise, but the sounds at Har Sinai were much greater than this!" With many such tactics, Rav Chatzkel rose above the limitations of his senses, making his *emunah* just as much a sensory experience as the physical world around him.

◆§ The Yetzias Mitzrayim of the Mirrer Yeshivah

Rav Shlomo Wolbe referred to Rav Chatzkel as "the last of the Jews who came out of Mitzrayim." With that statement, Rav Wolbe was not referring merely to Rav Chatzkel's practice of visualizing the miracles of *Yetzias Mitzrayim*. Rather, he was referring to another ideal promoted by Rav Chatzkel: that every Jew should find the *"Yetzias Mitzrayim"* within his own life.

In *Sefer Tehillim*, David HaMelech states, "Give thanks to Hashem for He is good, for His kindness is eternal." Rav Chatzkel explained that this means that any kindness that Hashem performed for the Jewish people throughout their history is eternal and ongoing, and that anyone who achieves the proper level of *emunah* will be able to experience that kindness within his own life.

Rav Chatzkel found a very real illustration of this concept within his own life: He lived through the miraculous escape of the Mirrer Yeshivah from Europe during World War II, and he once wrote that it was a manifestation of the same miracles that occurred during *Yetzias Mitzrayim*. He illustrated this point with a number of examples: In Mitzrayim, Pharaoh himself ultimately gave permission for the Jews to leave; likewise, it was the Soviet secret police who permitted the yeshivah to leave Russia, in violation of the government's standard policy. Furthermore, the Jews in Mitzrayim came to be treated with great respect by the very people who had enslaved them; likewise, the yeshivah students from Mir were placed in the best hotels in Russia and were even taken on a sightseeing tour of Moscow, all as part of the travel package provided by their tickets. Additionally, just as the Yam Suf split so that the Jewish people could escape their pursuers, the *bachurim* and faculty of the yeshivah were transported to safety across the Sea of Japan. That alone was a miraculous trip, for the rickety boat that took them did not seem capable of making it across the sea. In fact, the boat sank on its very next voyage, with only a minimal complement aboard. Finally, just as Hashem provided for the Jews in the Wilderness over the next 40 years, the yeshivah students somehow received everything they needed — including food, shelter, and medical care — during the seven years they spent in Japan and China.

Rav Chatzkel demonstrated that it is not sufficient for a Jew merely to speak about the miracles of *Yetzias Mitzrayim*. Every person experiences his own *Yetzias Mitzrayim* and can identify plenty of *hashgachah pratis* in his own life. A person who succeeds in finding that *hashgachah* and recognizing Hashem's kindnesses will exist in a different reality, thus serving as a living testimony to the Divine Presence. We yearn for the day when millions of people will live this way: sensing the existence of a spiritual reality that is invisible to the human eye, and feeling a connection to Hashem and His Presence everywhere they go.

Takeaway

When we allow Hashem's Will to dictate every move we make, then we become a living testimony to His existence.

Making It Practical

- Search for the *hashgachah pratis* and the miracles that are part of your life. Contemplate the events of your life and try to see the instances when Hashem's guiding Hand was apparent. When you notice overt *hashgachah pratis* in your life, write it in a special notebook.
- At your Pesach Seder, tell your family about the *hashgachah* in your own life.
- Make *emunah* real in your own life. Talk to Hashem with silent prayer before starting any sort of endeavor.

Discussion Points

❖ *In what ways have the gedolim of our times stressed the mitzvah of kiddush Hashem?*

❖ *In what ways are our gedolim sensitive even to the feelings and perceptions of non-Jews?*

❖ *Do different gedolim display specific, unique roles in kiddush Hashem?*

❖ *There are many stories about our gedolim's brilliance and dedication to learning that seem to be beyond our abilities to emulate. But what about the examples they set in their interactions with others? Is it possible for us to reach the same level?*

CHAPTER 18

INTERVIEWS

Kiddush Hashem
in the Halls of Government —
An Interview with Rabbi A.D. Motzen

I once took a group of students to a rally supporting the Ed Choice scholarship program, in which the state government of Ohio awards a tuition voucher of up to $6000 to private school students. Obviously, this is a huge benefit for the parents of yeshivah students, as well as for the schools themselves. The herculean efforts of Rabbi A.D. Motzen, national director of state relations of Agudath Israel of America, were instrumental in the creation of this program. When I arrived at the rally, I found that it was attended by a crowd of thousands of schoolchildren and teachers. Up front were five people; four were high-ranking government officials, and the fifth was Rabbi Motzen. I took pride in the respect he was shown at the rally; his efforts had not only helped thousands of Jewish children, but had benefited many non-Jewish students as well.

As a person who is very much in the public eye, and whose work involves interacting with many prominent officials to have an impact on the lives of thousands of people, Rabbi Motzen certainly had a good deal to say about the subject of kiddush Hashem in the public sphere. I asked Rabbi Motzen to share some of his insights and experience with us.

How did you manage to have the law changed so that the government would help pay the tuitions of students in private schools? That was certainly a major achievement!

"Actually, it wasn't my achievement," Rabbi Motzen replied. "It was a group effort. The legislators are the ones who actually pass the bills, but together with a few other groups, we worked to expand the existing Cleveland voucher program to encompass the entire state. Since then, the program was expanded several times, and more recently, thanks in part to the efforts of our

Ohio director, Rabbi Yitz Frank, the scholarship amounts were increased. Agudah has become one of the main voices promoting school choice in Ohio and across the country, and lawmakers will often call for our input and support before they even draft a bill."

How do you lobby for the interests of the Jewish communities without giving the impression that Jews care only about themselves?

"There is nothing wrong with promoting your own interests; everyone understands that. Nevertheless, the best thing is to advance causes that are good for you and for others as well; you need to promote a win-win situation. We often form coalitions with other groups that share our interests. The issue of school choice is a good example of this, because scholarships are a great benefit to all low and middle income families."

Have any politicians lost regard for us because of the behavior of individual Jews?

"Unfortunately, whenever there is a scandal concerning Orthodox Jews, it has the potential to cause major harm to our efforts, even if the people involved aren't *chareidi* and have nothing to do with Agudah. We have been told by elected officials that certain scandals made them reluctant to come to events in the *frum* community, or to publicly associate with us or help us on our issues. At the same time, when members of our community make headlines because of their integrity or acts of charity, then the politicians seek out opportunities to be seen with them.

"I was once lobbying for private schools to be excluded from a bill that would have made it illegal for any school, even yeshivos, to end school after June 10th or to begin the school year earlier than a certain date. The private school association pushed for the bill to be limited to the public school system, but they were unsuccessful. It seemed that our yeshivos were going to be placed in a very difficult situation.

"In a last-ditch attempt to have the legislation changed, I met with the senator who had sponsored the bill together with the head of the Catholic Conference. I mentioned our concerns and how it would affect our religious rights. As soon as he saw my *yarmulke*, the senator asked me if I knew a certain well-known Orthodox philanthropist and business leader. I confirmed that I knew him well, and the senator began speaking highly of him, extolling him as an 'American hero.' That particular philanthropist was a major supporter of a certain Jewish school, so the senator asked me how the bill would affect that school. 'Actually, I was speaking to the principal today, and she was very concerned about the impact on the school,' I replied."

"'What can I do to help?' the senator asked me. I suggested removing private schools from the bill, but he refused. 'I've already said that I won't do that,' he insisted.

"'It's the only way to solve the problem,' I responded.

"'In that case, please get me a memo from the principal of the school explaining why it will be problematic,' the senator said. I made sure that he received the memo, and within two hours, the principal received a message from the senator informing her that private schools had been removed from the bill, and asking her to send regards to their mutual acquaintance. For thousands of others, the senator had been unwilling to change his position, but for one highly respected Orthodox Jew, who hadn't even contacted him on his own, he had given in."

I am certain that Agudah sometimes has to adopt positions that are bound to make some enemies. Do those positions ever come back to haunt us?

"We take our positions based on guidance from the Moetzes Gedolei HaTorah, and while elected officials don't always like our positions, we don't make it personal. Most of them respect the fact that we have consistent, faith-based positions. Many years ago, the chairman of Agudath Israel of California, Dr. Irving Lebovics, was lobbying for a bill that would protect religious employees in the workplace. The chairman of the relevant committee, who was working on a different bill that involved behavior that violated halachah, made him a tempting offer: He handed Irving a pen and told him he could write the religious exemptions any way he wanted, in exchange for Agudath Israel removing its opposition to his own bill. Irving contacted Rav Elya Svei for guidance; he reasoned that the problematic bill was eventually going to pass anyway, and this was an opportunity to secure important protections for religious Jews. After careful consideration, Rav Elya told him not to accept the deal. 'He will simply end up saying that the Agudah supported this forbidden behavior,' he explained. Ultimately, the workplace bill passed, but the chairman's bill was rejected.

"Several years later, Irving encountered the former committee chairman at a political event, and the legislator asked to have a word with him. 'The last time we spoke, I was quite angry,' the lawmaker recalled. 'The entire reason that I ran for office in the first place was to have that bill passed, and I resented your refusal to support it. But I have to tell you the truth: If you had agreed to my request, I would have lost all my respect for you and for your organization.'

"Irving's story is a lesson on the importance of following *da'as Torah* and on the fact that if you stick consistently to your principles, regardless of whether the secular world shares your values, you will earn their respect."

How do you deal with issues such as the separation of men and women and the prohibition to shake hands with people of the opposite gender?

"The key is to communicate and explain the reasons for our behavior. When Nina Turner, an African-American legislator, became the state senator of the district that includes Beachwood, Ohio, I offered to give her a crash course on Jewish life and culture. I explained that there are many Jews in Beachwood, and she could expect to be attending plenty of Jewish events. When I explained that Orthodox Jewish men generally do not shake hands with women, she was visibly moved. 'Rabbi,' she said, 'you have no idea how you just saved your community. If I were walking down Green Road on a Saturday afternoon and offered my hand to a man coming out of synagogue, and he refused to shake my hand, I would never have dreamed that he does not shake hands with women for religious reasons. I would have automatically assumed that it was because I was black!'

"When I invite non-Jewish women to events, I explain to them in advance about the standards of dress at an Orthodox event. I don't tell them what to wear; I simply explain to them about what the other women will be wearing, and I let them make their own decisions. These women do not want to stand out in the crowd; they want the Orthodox community to feel that the elected official understands them. If we explain that we view *tznius* as a form of respect for women, they are not offended; they admire the idea."

What is your next project?

"I am always working on multiple projects. Together with our dedicated team of state and regional directors, we are active in nearly 30 states and Washington, DC, mainly on issues of religious freedom and education. I am currently working together with our man in Washington, Rabbi Abba Cohen, on federal initiatives that can help parents with tuition and on issues related to higher education that affect our *yeshivos gedolos*.

"In every project, I always keep in mind the words of the Rosh Agudas Yisroel, the Novominsker Rebbe. At a staff meeting soon after I began working at the Agudah, the Rebbe said, 'The Agudah does many things.' And that's true: We have Pirchei and Bnos, Torah projects, camping, social services, and advocacy, and much more. 'But no matter what you do for the Agudah,' the Rebbe added, 'you must always remember that the overall goal is to be *marbeh kevod Shamayim.*'"

Takeaway

We cannot downplay the impact of every individual Jew. A chillul Hashem committed by one person is never a private sin; it paints the whole Jewish people in a different light.

It is crucial to follow da'as Torah, even if we are afraid of the results of adopting an unpopular position. If we stick consistently to our principles, regardless of whether the secular world shares our values, we will earn their respect.

┌─────────────── **Making It Practical** ───────────────┐

• If you find yourself in a conflict or ethical dilemma, let yourself be guided by the importance of being consistent in your values. You will never go wrong by maintaining that unchanging approach.

└──┘

Chai Lifeline: More Than Just Another Organization
An Interview
with Rabbi Sruli Fried

My dear nephew Yosef Shalom Feldheim passed away at the age of three after a yearlong battle with cancer. Throughout his ordeal, I was exposed to the incredible *chessed* performed by the people of Chai Lifeline. They were there when the news of his diagnosis was first received, and they supported the family throughout the grueling period of his illness.

Chai Lifeline is an organization that is constantly creating kiddush Hashem. I was fortunate to have an opportunity to hear a bit about the organization's work from Rabbi Sruli Fried, who has served as the regional director of Chai Lifeline in New Jersey for the past 12 years.

What is unique about Chai Lifeline in contrast to the many other organizations that provide services for the ill?

"There is a tremendous amount of *chessed* for the sick and infirm in the Jewish world, and there are even organizations in the non-Jewish world that provide all sorts of services, including entertainment and medical referrals. But what is unique about Chai Lifeline, and what we consider our greatest strength, is our individualized case management. We care for all the needs of a patient and their family — not only the more obvious needs, but even the minor details that often tend to be overlooked.

"Even under ordinary circumstances, it can be quite a challenge for a family with children to function on a daily basis. There is always an overwhelming list of things that have to be done: preparing the children for school or camp, doing laundry, picking up the dry cleaning, shopping for food and other necessities, arranging babysitting when the parents have to be out, and many more details. When a child is sick, the family's life becomes vastly more complex; there are constant appointments, the parents are likely to be constantly shuttling back and forth between their home and the hospital, and everything in the household becomes topsy-turvy. Under those circumstances, having someone take care of all the ordinary details of the family's life can mean the difference between calm and chaos. There is a wide array of things that we can do to help the family: babysitting, shopping for food for Shabbos or for new clothing, driving car pool, or even having someone provide emotional support for the mother when she learns that her child has had a relapse. The case manager from Chai Lifeline functions as an adviser, a friend, a social worker, a helper, and even a cleaner, all in one."

What do you feel is the most fulfilling aspect of your job with Chai Lifeline?

"The other day, I was substituting for a case manager who was out, and I received a frantic phone call from the mother of a sick child. She explained that another child was scheduled to start camp the following morning, and she had forgotten to buy a camp bag for the child. I hurried to run that errand for her, and I brought the bag to her home. She was extremely grateful. From my perspective, that is the most meaningful part of the job. Although I spend most of my time dealing with administrative tasks such as overseeing the staff, fund-raising, and organizing school intervention, my greatest pleasure comes from managing cases, having direct contact with the people, and making a difference in their lives with the small things that we do for them."

What sort of reactions have you gotten from doctors and nurses to the services you provide?

"To give you an idea of the answer to that question, let me tell you a story. There was a very special young girl named Malky Hirth who tragically died from cancer. Shortly before she passed away, her parents were told that she had only a few days left to live. Her father immediately called his Chai Lifeline case manager and told him that his eldest son, who was learning in Eretz Yisrael, had to be brought home. The phone call took only a few seconds, and then he returned his full attention to his daughter in her hospital bed. A nurse who was standing in the room was astounded. 'This is unbelievable!' she exclaimed. 'There are so many details that have to be taken care of to get that child home — flights, rides, and other arrangements — and all you had to do was make a simple phone call! I see that Chai Lifeline is much more than just an organization,' she added with great emotion. 'It's a family!'"

I am sure that some of the cases that you encounter do not have happy endings. I have no doubt that your work brings you face to face with profound grief and heartbreaking tragedies. How do you deal with these emotions?

"We cry. If I ever stop crying and become desensitized, that will be the day I retire."

Do you find that the patients and their families have an impact on the people who work with them: the hospital staff and the staff of Chai Lifeline?

"Illness often brings out the purest qualities in a human being. We often witness incredibly inspiring displays of grace and *emunah* from families dealing with the illness of a loved one. I have often been told by doctors that they were amazed and humbled after they shared the most horrific news possible with the families of their patients, and the families responded by telling the doctors that they were grateful to them for doing their best. One doctor said to me, 'I see that these are people who constantly thank G-d in their prayers every day. That is how they are able to be grateful to the people around them, and to lead lives of gratitude.'"

Where do these families find the strength to display such nobility of character?

"The families themselves often do not believe at first that they are capable of it. You have no idea how many times fathers or mothers have told me immediately after receiving tragic news, 'There is no way we can handle this,' or 'My spouse doesn't have the emotional capacity to deal with this.' But within a very short time, they are forced to dig within themselves for the power to deal with their situations, and they discover inner reserves of strength that they never knew they had. This is a powerful message for all of us. These patients and their families are not alone; every person undoubtedly possesses reserves of untapped strengths and potential. Why should we wait for a tragedy to bring out that potential? Every one of us has the ability to extend ourselves, to step outside of our comfort zones and to surpass the limits that we have always thought confined us."

Do you have any advice for patients and their families about dealing with doctors and other hospital personnel? After all, a patient is always in a difficult situation: On

the one hand, it is important to be pleasant and to display trust and confidence in his doctors. On the other hand, it is also important to be assertive, to advocate for the patient and to ensure that he is receiving the best possible care. What is the best way to strike a balance between these two priorities?

"That is a very important question, and we could prevent much chillul Hashem by adopting the right approach. The most important guideline is this: Don't try the side door until you have first knocked on the front door. Don't use all sorts of convoluted methods to accomplish something if you could simply take the direct approach. For example, if a patient or parent feels the need to solicit a second opinion, he should be forthright with his doctor about it. It is perfectly all right to say to a doctor, 'With all due respect, I am going to get a second opinion before we proceed as you suggest.' Medical professionals understand that parents should advocate for their children. The alternative is to go behind the doctor's back, and then for the doctor to find out from a colleague that the patient has gone for a second opinion without telling him. It is important to take the straight path: to be *yashar*, to be transparent, and to be communicative. By the same token, it makes a major difference when we explain our cultural differences to the staff in a hospital, when we clarify to them why we do certain things that they may not understand. That is the sensitive and appropriate thing to do."

Sensitivity is one of the hallmarks of Chai Lifeline: sensitivity to the patients, their families, and the medical system with which they must interact. And it is clear that that sensitivity, in its many forms and manifestations, is one of the keys to the massive kiddush Hashem that the organization continues to foster.

We can learn from Chai Lifeline how to be sensitive to others who are struggling. It is often not the big things that are needed; it's the small things that count. The big things are taken care of by the big organizations. We, as individuals, can help with some of the small things. It is much better to be honest and forthright with doctors than to take action behind their backs and possibly jeopardize your relationship with them at a later date.

Making It Practical

- Volunteer to help a family in crisis. Find out if they need help with babysitting, meals, car pools, shopping, or even cleaning help. Brainstorm about the small things that might be forgotten while they are dealing with larger issues, and then offer to help in those areas.

- Communicate with nurses and doctors about your culture and religion to create mutual understanding. Be open about your personal plan for dealing with medical issues, even if it sounds as if you are questioning them.

Derech Eretz in the Sky
An Interview
with Rabbi Paysach Krohn

Derech eretz literally means "the way of the land." Every "land" — every place in the world — has its own individual norms and standards of behavior. This is true not only of different countries, but of different places within the same country or community as well. The standards of behavior on the street are different from those in a library; the rules of etiquette that govern our behavior at a *simchah* are not the same as those that apply on a shopping trip. And aside from the *derech eretz* that we must practice on the *eretz* — the ground — itself, there is a different standard of behavior that applies in the sky.

In the close confines of an airplane cabin, anything that a passenger does is bound to be noticed, and is likely to affect his fellow passengers as well. In those cramped quarters, people tend to be less tolerant of others and more defensive of their personal space. What guidelines can we follow to make sure that we always create a kiddush Hashem when we are in the air?

To answer this question, we turned to Rabbi Paysach Krohn, who has extensive experience traveling around the world for his inspirational speaking tours. Rabbi Krohn graciously shared with us some of his ideas and experiences.

Based on your travel experience, can you share with us some "dos" and "don'ts" for airplane travel?

"The first thing is to follow the rules. You may have paid a lot of money for your seat on the plane, but you are still a guest — among many other guests — and you must not make the mistake of thinking that you can do anything you want. Always remember that the plane is not your private property, and avoid being selfish or inconsiderate. That means that you should not monopolize the space in the overhead bins, and you should not be the passenger who needs a personalized reminder from the stewardess to turn off his cell phone after the general announcement has been made. When the seat belt sign is on, don't be in the aisles. That type of behavior doesn't befit an ambassador of Hashem and His Torah.

"I was once a plane, and a woman was talking loudly on her cell phone before takeoff. Even though she was seated in the front of the plane, her voice traveled all the way to the rear. At the end of her conversation, she recited her own phone number loudly to the person on the other end, and then she hung up. At that point, a man at the back of the plane punched her number into his own cell phone and called her. When she picked up, he admonished her for her behavior. 'Keep your conversations to yourself, ma'am,' he said. 'No one else is interested in them.' She was very insulted.

"As a *frum* Jew, you should never attract attention the way that woman did," Rabbi Krohn concludes.

What would you suggest to families traveling with small children, who are bound to cause some disturbances on a flight?

"First of all, parents must bring some form of entertainment for their children. It wouldn't be fair to the other passengers if the children make a ruckus throughout the flight because their parents didn't plan a way to keep them entertained. I know that it can be difficult to find room in your luggage for extra things, but this should be a priority.

"A mother who was flying with infant twins once had the foresight to bring along a bag full of individually wrapped chocolates, each with a note attached apologizing in advance for any disruption her babies might cause. She passed those chocolates around to all the passengers in the rows around her. I can assure you that she didn't receive any complaints after that flight."

How should a person *daven* on a plane without disturbing others? What is the proper protocol for joining a *minyan* on a flight?

"This is a question that every individual should ask his own *rav*. I am not a *posek*, but I heard from Rav Shimon Schwab that a passenger on an airplane should *daven* in his own seat. Certainly, one should never organize a *minyan* without permission from the flight attendants."

Do you have any tips about how to relate to the flight attendants on a plane in order to maximize kiddush Hashem?

"Always be pleasant, and never get angry at the flight

attendants. If your kosher meal is missing, it isn't the stewardess's fault, and you should not take out your frustration on her.

"I was once flying to England in first class, and the stewardess asked me if I would prefer my tea light or dark. I asked for a light tea, thinking that that meant the tea wouldn't be overly strong. When I started to drink it, though, I realized very quickly that milk had been added to the tea.

"I was in the middle of a *fleishig* meal when that happened, and I became alarmed. But I quickly calmed myself and called over the stewardess. 'Is there milk in this tea?' I asked her. When she confirmed that there was, I said, 'I just want to tell you something, so that you will know to avoid this mistake for the future. This isn't your fault, but Jews do not eat milk and meat together, so I really can't drink this tea in the middle of a meat meal.' Then, to add some humor to the situation, I added, 'That's one of our G-d's commandments. We are so close to the heavens up here that we need to be especially careful to listen to His every word.' The stewardess laughed, and the pilot himself soon came out to apologize. Because we all spoke to each other with respect, a potentially tense situation became a friendly one.

"The most important thing is to treat others with respect and dignity," Rabbi Krohn emphasizes. "There has been a lot of ugly rhetoric in recent political campaigns, and I feel that it is affecting society as a whole. People are speaking to each other with much less respect than they used to demonstrate. We have to take care not to be influenced by that culture of contempt."

Do you have any edifying stories to share about kiddush Hashem on an airplane?

In fact, Rabbi Krohn once had an experience that illustrated the powerful impact of maintaining a positive demeanor. While he was waiting at La Guardia Airport to board a flight to Toronto, he noticed a pair of security guards making their way through the terminal, apparently searching for someone among the crowds. As the other passengers grew apprehensive, the security guards spotted Rabbi Krohn himself and headed directly toward him.

"Sir, is this your cell phone?" one of the guards asked, as soon as they were within earshot.

Rabbi Krohn reached into his pocket and was surprised to discover that his cell phone was missing. Indeed, the phone in the guard's outstretched hand was his. "Yes, it is," he confirmed. "How did you find it?"

"You left it in a bin at the security check," the guard replied.

Rabbi Krohn thanked the guards profusely, but he was also puzzled. "There must be two thousand people in this terminal," he exclaimed. "How did you remember what I looked like?"

"Do you remember what you said to us when you walked through security?" the guard said. "You thanked us for being here, and you told us that you feel safer because we are here. Thousands of people walk through security every day, and no one says a word to us, but you thanked us for doing our job. When we saw that you had left your phone behind, we decided that we would have to find you, even if it meant searching the entire terminal."

Rabbi Krohn was amazed. A simple display of *hakaras hatov* to people who were doing their job had led him to recover a lost cell phone, sparing him from a significant loss. Rabbi Krohn has recounted this story in many speeches, in order to emphasize the importance of gratitude. Many people have begun following his example and thanking the security guards at airports. "In fact," Rabbi Krohn relates, "someone recently called me and said that he had thanked a security guard at JFK for keeping him safe. The guard smiled at him and said, 'Oh, did you also hear the message from the rabbi?'"

Takeaway

Air travel presents many opportunities for kiddush Hashem, but the danger of chillul Hashem is equally great. Whenever we fly, we should keep in mind that we are guests in someone else's domain, and that we must follow the rules and be sensitive to the people around us.

Selfless Giving
A Conversation with Steven Rosedale

In a famous *pasuk*, the *navi* Michah declares, "And now, what does Hashem your G-d want from you, other than to do justice, to love kindness, and to walk modestly with your G-d?" By commanding us to "*love* kindness," the *navi* seems to imply that it is not enough for us to perform *acts* of kindness; we must also develop an *attitude* of loving kindness. What is the difference between "loving" kindness and merely performing *chessed*? What is the nature of this approach to *chessed* that we are meant to develop?

Some explain that *ahavas chessed* refers to performing *chessed* selflessly; it means engaging in acts of kindness that result from altruism and from pure caring for the recipient, rather than self-interest on our part. Very often, people are motivated to perform acts of kindness by the expectation of personal gain. They hope that their favors to others will somehow be repaid, so that they will somehow benefit from their kindnesses. A person who masters the trait of *ahavas chessed* will be driven to perform *chessed* because of his innate love of kindness, regardless of whether he can expect to benefit personally from it in any way.

What motivates a person to give selflessly to others? What is the key to attaining the altruism of *ahavas chessed*?

In order to answer that question, let us examine what we can learn from a profession that revolves around giving to others: the profession of nursing.

Mr. Steven Rosedale is a prominent figure in the Cincinnati Jewish community who runs a thriving nursing-home business. In the business of nursing care, it is easy to fall into the trap of treating patients in a condescending or even dehumanizing manner. Some patients in institutionalized settings have become so dependent on their caregivers, and have lost the ability to function to such a degree, that nurses may be tempted to treat them as inferior or even subhuman, rather than giving them the dignity they deserve. Mr. Rosedale's nurses are taught to view every patient as a complete human being, and not merely an assortment of ailments and physical needs. He trains his staff to treat every patient with dignity and respect, and the results have been remarkable.

"As a teenager, I became interested in mental health, and I later studied under a professor named Morrie Schwartz, the subject of the book *Tuesdays with Morrie*," Mr. Rosedale recalls. "This was in 1970, when hospitals, old-age homes, and mental health institutions treated their patients in a terribly dehumanizing fashion. In the best scenario, these people were treated like children; often, they were viewed as subhuman. Morrie Schwartz promoted a revolutionary concept called the 'therapeutic milieu.' In simple terms, it means that if you treat others — even your patients — with dignity, they will react by acting with dignity."

The "therapeutic milieu" calls for demonstrating love and kindness toward patients simply because they are human, regardless of their physical appearance or mental faculties. It means appreciating the human spirit that exists within every person, without exception. In more familiar terms, it means appreciating that every human being deserves respect because they are a *tzelem Elokim*.

"I was very taken by this concept," Mr. Rosedale continues, "and when my father-in-law offered me a job as a nursing-home administrator, I was excited by the opportunity to put Morrie's theory into action. I decided that these values would be the basis of the nursing homes I would build, and I resolved to hire only employees who would share these values, who could see past the superficial and appreciate the *tzelem Elokim* within every patient. Every patient would be treated with dignity and respect, regardless of how much of their humanity they seemed to have lost."

As radical as this approach was at the time, it was also enormously successful. "We witnessed genuine miracles, which proved the theory completely true," Mr. Rosedale attests. "People who had given up hope because of a debilitating illness, or who had been told that they had only a few months left to live, went on to live for many joyous years after a few months of compassionate, dignified nursing care. It was all about reaching out with our hearts to touch the hearts of others."

The key to giving to others in the most ideal way, then, is recognizing the *tzelem Elokim* within every human being, the fact that every person is inherently valuable and deserving of kindness. This is the recognition that can lead a person to develop a commitment to kindness and altruism. Mr. Rosedale, who found his way back to Yiddishkeit after growing up in a secular environment, relates that this was something that he recognized in many *frum* Jews, and that sparked his own interest in Yiddishkeit. Over the years, he has found this quality to be an innate attribute of many of the Torah figures whom he respects.

"I remember that when I brought my son to be interviewed for yeshivah, it was with great reluctance," he says. "I didn't actually believe that I would send him there. But when I met the staff of the yeshivah, I was touched by how genuine they were, and how they were willing to look past the superficialities of others and connect with them on a deep level."

Today, people are often reluctant to connect with each other; relationships tend to be very casual, and there is tremendous resistance to looking past the surface and understanding the true nature of others. When people are willing to connect to others on a deeper level, it means that they are prepared to recognize the *tzelem Elokim* of other people; they are willing to see past all the minor superficialities that irritate them, and to recognize that every person is a being of immense value.

"This is what I saw in the *rebbeim* in that yeshivah, and I observed it in many other Jews as well," Mr. Rosedale recalls. "Eventually, I came to realize that it is the Torah lifestyle that gives a person the tools to develop this depth of understanding, and teaches him to recognize what it truly means to be a human being. Even at that time, my outlook was radically altered by my brief encounter with the staff of the yeshivah. Somehow, they had reached my *pintele Yid*, and I was completely sold. I turned to my son and said, 'You are going to this yeshivah, and if you don't, I will go in your place!'"

Mr. Rosedale has also seen this quality in the members of the Cincinnati kollel, of which he is a supporter. "My involvement with the kollel came because my wife said our community needed a kollel, and a local *mechanech*, Rabbi Nehemia Kibel, made a similar statement, and I said I would do it," he relates. "I realized that in my experience with Ner Yisroel, the special quality I sensed in the *rebbeim* was that they were *tocham k'baram*, they were genuine servants of Hashem, and I felt that a kollel would bring that type of people to our community. Indeed, the effects on our community were far beyond anything I could have imagined, and the kollel has brought untold *berachah* to our family. These special young men and their wives reached out with their hearts to touch the hearts of members of our community, and all of us were uplifted by their selfless giving."

We live in a world that is intensely focused on physicality and externals. As a result, our perceptions and attitudes tend to be shaped by superficialities. We evaluate ourselves and others based on trivial things such as clothes, money, and social status; we fail to look beyond the surface and to recognize the *tzelem Elokim* within every person. But even a nurse treating the most severely impaired patients must learn to appreciate the human being, the *tzelem Elokim*, within the poorly functioning bodies that rely on their aid. In a similar vein, we must look past the externals that seem to mark others as being somehow inferior to us. If we learn to respect every human being as a *tzelem Elokim*, if we learn to open our hearts to others and to touch their inner worlds, we can surely achieve incredible things.

Takeaway

If we learn to value and touch the tzelem Elokim within every individual, regardless of how they appear externally, we can help others realize their true potential.

Making It Practical

- When you interact with others, keep a mental picture of the Divine spark that exists within every individual.
- If you meet someone who is elderly or disabled, and who is dependent on others for basic human functions, close your eyes for a moment and think about the rich past that they probably had, or the depth of their inner world. Look past the surface and see them as the human beings they truly are.

The Workingman's Mission

For many men, going from full-time learning to working at a job is one of the most wrenching transitions of their lives. It is a move from a life steeped in Torah learning, a life filled with clear meaning and purpose, to a very different lifestyle, one in which the goal is still a worthy one, but the means of achieving it can be less satisfactory. Even if the typical workingman has set times for learning, and even if he understands that he is working toward the important goal of supporting his family, many men feel that a void has opened in their lives when they make this transition. Instead of spending most of their waking hours in the *beis medrash*, they are now involved in very different pursuits for most of the day. Suddenly, the deep satisfaction they enjoyed during their years of learning is no longer their focus. How can a person fill this emotional void?

Many *rabbanim* struggle to help the members of their communities with this issue. I turned to a certain *rav* with extensive experience in this area to learn about his approach to the subject. The *rav*, who asked to remain anonymous, had the following to say:

"First of all, I don't like to use the term '*baalebatim*.' It doesn't do justice to the *avodah* of a *frum* Jew in the workplace, and it has a derogatory connotation. Our workingmen are tremendous *ovdei Hashem*; they struggle with constant *nisyonos*, and they are always under scrutiny from the outside world. As a result, I prefer to call them '*mekadshei Hashem*'; they are men who are on a constant mission to promote *kiddush Shem Shamayim*."

How do you communicate this idea to your *shul* members?

"I speak about it often, and I explain that even after a person enters the working world, he should view it as simply continuing the same mission that he had during his years in the *beis medrash*, albeit in a different setting and in an entirely different way. Despite the differences, he still plays a crucial role in creating kiddush Hashem. I also urge the men to celebrate their successes in being *mekadesh Shem Shamayim* at work or in their dealings with the secular world. Just as we celebrate a kiddush Hashem in learning by holding a festive *siyum*, we should also celebrate a kiddush Hashem at the workplace with a celebration.

"One of my *mispallelim* once found a woman's purse in the street. When he picked it up, he saw that it contained 5000 dollars in cash, along with some documents indicating that it belonged to a non-Jewish woman who lived nearby. The man called a *rav* to ask what to do, and the *rav* told him that while he was technically permitted to keep the purse, it would create a major kiddush Hashem if he returned it. 'Also, keep in mind that your *parnassah* is decreed on *Rosh Hashanah*,' the *rav* reminded him. 'Regardless of whether you keep this money or return it, your bank balance will end up exactly the same.'

"After a difficult internal struggle, the man decided to return the money. The woman was deeply moved when she saw that there wasn't a single dollar missing from her purse; she told him that her father had just passed away, and she had been planning to use the cash for his burial expenses. She graciously offered the finder 1000 dollars as a reward, and showered him with blessings.

"The very next week, the man received a phone call from his health insurance company, informing him that the company had decided to pay a 4000-dollar bill that they had been refusing to cover. The *hashgachah pratis* was unmistakable; he had received exactly the amount of money that he had chosen to return, and he had gained the merit of a major kiddush Hashem as well. I shared this story with my congregation, and I made it clear that this kiddush Hashem was a reason for celebration, and an example that everyone can emulate."

That is certainly a wonderful story, but how often does the average person have an opportunity to make a kiddush Hashem of that nature? Most people spend hours every day working at jobs that offer little to no opportunity for an achievement of that nature. How can they carry out their mission of kiddush Hashem?

"Actually, a working person's interactions with the outside world offer many opportunities for kiddush Hashem. Even small, seemingly insignificant things can make a major difference. There is a doctor in my *shul* who told me that his staff is heavily influenced by his personal refinement. He has several dozen employees, and he was once surprised when one of his staff members informed him that another woman was using inappropriate language at the workplace. 'I have never heard that,' he told her. Her response was: 'That's because no one would ever speak that way in your presence. They respect you; they know that you are genuine, and they appreciate your standards.' That was enough for these women to keep their tongues in check. In fact, one of his employees related to him that when she was tempted to use inappropriate language at home, she would repeat his name to herself in order to remind herself to speak properly."

But what about the people who do not have much interaction with others at work? What about the people who spend their days sitting at a computer and working in solitude? How can they consider themselves to be involved in a mission of kiddush Hashem?

"Those people are the modern-day manifestations of the kiddush Hashem of Yosef *Hatzaddik*. Yosef resisted his temptations and refused to commit an *aveirah* even though he was far away from his family and support system. The *Rambam* teaches that when a person performs a mitzvah or desists from an *aveirah* solely for the purpose of serving Hashem — not because he is being watched by others — it creates an immensely powerful kiddush Hashem. That is precisely what these men accomplish in the privacy of their offices, at their own desks and on their own computers, where no one will ever know if they have given in to temptation."

What are some of the traits that a person should develop in order to create a kiddush Hashem at his workplace?

"There are a number of attributes that are very important for this purpose. First and foremost, there is integrity; that is the most important quality to master. A person must also have a good work ethic and should be friendly to his co-workers in a professional way. It is also important to be forgiving rather than being rigid, to always speak in a pure and refined fashion, to avoid belittling or denigrating others, and to have a positive attitude at all times. Of course, a person must also be consistent in following the laws of *bein adam laMakom*, and he must abide by the guidelines for separation between the genders. All of these things will earn the respect and admiration of one's co-workers and employers."

For those of us in the workplace, whatever our professions may be, there is always a way to turn our jobs into a quest for kiddush Hashem. If we keep this lesson in mind, we will surely excel at transforming our workaday pursuits into the greatest accomplishment possible: serving Hashem by bringing honor to His Name.

Takeaway

A person in the workplace can serve Hashem in an immensely powerful way. Every day presents an opportunity to turn a mundane job into an incredible enhancement of kevod Shamayim. Working Jews are not merely "baalebatim"; they are part of the army of mekadshei Hashem.

Making It Practical

- Strive to be the most pleasant person at your workplace, and avoid an aggressive approach to your business dealings.
- Regardless of the circumstances, try to keep a positive attitude at all times, and greet your co-workers with a smile.

The Workingman's Mission, Part 2

I n his introduction to Rabbi Pinchas Bodner's book *Halachos of Other People's Money*, Rav Mattisyahu Salomon comments that the fact that Jews must interact with non-Jews for business purposes was part of Hashem's master plan for the world. These dealings give the Jewish people an opportunity to demonstrate their honesty and integrity, thus promoting kiddush Hashem, which is the purpose of the world's creation. In this section, we continue our discussion with the same *rav*, who has some more surprising insights to share with us about a Jewish person's mission in the working world.

I understand that you stress the importance of maintaining proper *middos* and *derech eretz* in the workplace as part of the mission to promote kiddush Hashem. But how do you inspire your congregants to maintain their commitment to the *mitzvos bein adam laMakom*? How does their sense of mission extend to those mitzvos as well?

The *rav* has a surprising answer to this question: The *mitzvos bein adam laMakom* are an integral part of the same sense of mission. "I conducted a survey among my *mispallelim*," he relates, "and I asked them what areas of *avodas Hashem* they have found make a difference to the people around them. Surprisingly, many of the answers had to do with *mitzvos bein adam laMakom*. Those are the practices that show the outside world that the Jews are unique, and that we are servants of Hashem.

"For example, one of my *mispallelim* said that when he returned to work after a three-day Yom Tov, one of his co-workers turned to him and demanded, 'How could you do that?' He didn't understand the question, and the man said, 'We were in the middle of preparing for a very important presentation to an executive, which is due tomorrow, and you disappeared and were unavailable for three days. I understand that it was your holiday, but don't you even check your email?' The *frum* employee explained a little bit about the halachos of Shabbos and Yom Tov, adding that he reports to a higher "Executive" than any of his superiors at work, and that the Torah's laws take priority over any workaday concerns.

"With that, his co-worker's anger immediately gave way to admiration. 'I wish I could disconnect and recharge like that,' he said. 'You are truly blessed to have this in your life.'"

Many of our *mitzvos bein adam laMakom* seem bizarre or old fashioned to people in the secular world. Aren't your *mispallelim* afraid to stand out or to be seen as strange?

"Actually, the opposite is true: Many of them have found that their observance of these mitzvos has a profound impact on their co-workers, and that it often protects them from the pitfalls of being in a secular environment. One man told me, for instance, that he always feared that wearing a *yarmulke* at work would put him at a disadvantage, and that in his first two jobs in the corporate world, he did not wear one. In retrospect, he feels that he did not progress in his career at that time as much as he could have. Fifteen years ago, he began wearing a *yarmulke* at work, and the effects have been incredibly positive, as he has become highly respected by his peers. The *yarmulke* also protects a person from falling prey to the corporate shenanigans that are so tempting in the work world; it reminds a person that he represents Orthodox Jewry, and that makes him much more careful about his behavior.

"Another man once went to a meeting in the south, in an area where he generally removes his *yarmulke* before meeting with prospective clients. After giving a lengthy presentation with a financial plan for a firm, he asked if there were any questions. No one had anything to ask, which was very unusual for his line of work. When he returned to his car and went to retrieve his *yarmulke* from the glove compartment, he realized that he had never removed it from his head! At that point, he realized that there had been no questions because they had seen that he was a religious Jew, and he assumed that the deal would not materialize. A few weeks later, he was surprised when he received a call informing him that they wished to proceed with the plan. He commented that it was unusual for a client to commit to a plan without asking any questions, and they replied, 'We could see that you are a man of G-d, so we trust everything you said!'

"One final story actually happened in a private home," the *rav* concludes. "A *frum* family was remodeling their home, and as they were planning the renovation, the contractor repeatedly discussed arranging the electric system to accommodate televisions. Each time, the couple told him that they weren't interested in that. When they reached the master bedroom, the contractor raised the same issue and they repeated that they had no need of a television. The contractor said, 'I can understand that you don't want it for your children, but don't you want it at least for yourselves?' They explained that they were not interested in having a television at all, and he grabbed the man's hand and gave him a hearty handshake. 'That is really impressive!' he exclaimed."

What are some of the greatest challenges your congregants encounter in this regard?

"One of the main challenges is the casual atmosphere in today's corporate world, which makes it very difficult to maintain proper *gedarim* between genders. A working person has to find ways to be cordial to his co-workers, colleagues, and customers while still maintaining a proper degree of separation. Business contacts often engage in small talk, asking about a person's family, personal background, and so forth, and that atmosphere can make it much more difficult to maintain the appropriate boundaries. One businessman tells me that he has his wife run his office and deal directly with the female customers who tend to be overly casual.

"Another major challenge, which is really a general issue in every area of life, is to make sure that one follows the halachah in every circumstance. There is a tremendous amount of ha-lachah that a person needs to know and follow in the course of his business dealings; often, people aren't even aware of the *she'eilos* that they should be asking."

Do you have any suggestions to help make the transition to the workplace easier for people who are accustomed to being in yeshivos and kollelim?

"One thing is for certain: It doesn't help when they hear only that the outside world is totally devoid of morals and decency. It's true that there is plenty of immorality and unpleasantness out there, but many people work in places where the standards of behavior and moral values are much higher. They meet people from the secular world who are very decent and honest, often with fulfilling family lives and moral principles of their own, and they begin to wonder what makes the Torah lifestyle better."

How do you respond to that type of question?

"We need to recognize the importance of mitzvos and learn-ing Torah for our *neshamos*. We have to recognize that our unique-ness lies in our relationship with Hashem and the connection we achieve through serving Him. We can't deny that a non-Jew may be personable, witty, and even happy and well mannered. The dif-ference is that a Jew achieves a connection to eternity by serving Hashem and performing His mitzvos. Every thought and action of a Jew is connected to *Shamayim* and influences all of creation; that is a connection that is unique to us. I encourage my congre-gants to think about this connection and to work on developing it. I advised one man, for instance, to start writing a *sefer*.

"This is a message that every *rav* can impart to his *mispalle-lim*. A person can transform himself from a 'simple' working man into a *mekadesh Shem Shamayim* through all the mitzvos of the Torah: both those that are *bein adam lachaveiro* and those that are *bein adam laMakom*. When people recognize this tremendous power that they possess, it can fill them with a profound sense of meaning, and they will recognize the major difference that they can make in the world."

Takeaway

In today's workplace, it is a major challenge to remain properly sheltered and observe the boundaries required of us by the Torah. In order to achieve this, we must remember that being unique and standing out is an integral part of our role as mekadshei Hashem. A working person must remember that succeeding in his mission benefits the Jewish people!

Making It Practical

- Make sure that the way you dress and act in your workplace marks you as a religious Jew. That in itself will protect you from the spiritual pitfalls of the working world. Your co-workers will act differently in your presence, and they may even treat you with more respect and dignity.
- Whenever possible use your free time to learn Torah, even in your office. When you do that, you will mark yourself as an *eved Hashem*, and you will feel more responsibility to live up to the standards of the Torah.

Living for Others
A Conversation with Talmidim of Rav Shmuel Kamenetsky

Once in a while, I have occasion to attend a *chasunah* where Rav Shmuel Kamenetsky, the venerated *rosh yeshivah* of the Philadelphia yeshivah, is present. Rav Shmuel is hailed as one of the *gedolim* of our generation, and whenever I see him, I am mesmerized by the sight of this great man greeting everyone who crosses his path, regardless of their backgrounds. It has struck me that while Rav Shmuel's stature is far beyond us in many ways, and many of us cannot hope to attain his lofty level of Torah knowledge or *avodas Hashem*, we can all certainly learn from the way he interacts with others. In many ways, Rav Shmuel Kamenetsky's interpersonal conduct can serve as a model of dedication to kiddush Hashem.

Over the course of a 25-year period, four of my brothers learned in the Yeshiva of Philadelphia at various times. In order to gain some insight into this aspect of Rav Shmuel's greatness, I turned to them to develop a better picture of the *rosh yeshivah*'s attitudes and *hanhagos*.

Rav Shmuel is known for noticing everyone around him, greeting everyone he encounters, and showering attention even on the people that others might ignore. Is this something that he has taken upon himself as his personal mission as a *gadol b'Yisrael*, or is it also a type of behavior that he expects of his *talmidim*?

"There is no question that the *rosh yeshivah* teaches us to look past ourselves and to think about others," one of my brothers replied. "In almost every *shmuess* he delivers, he urges us to contemplate what we are able to do for other people and to keep the needs of others in our thoughts. We have all had experiences in which we were walking down the hall when the *rosh yeshivah* suddenly stopped us and asked, 'What are you thinking about?' We have learned to be prepared for that question in advance. I never understood it to mean that the *rosh yeshivah* expected us to be thinking about the *sugya* we were learning at all times; I felt that he didn't want us to feel that we were isolated, in our own individual bubbles, but rather to be thinking about the people around us."

"I had a different understanding," another brother interjected. "I thought it means that the *rosh yeshivah* just wants his *talmidim* to be thinking at all times, regardless of what they are thinking about. That is what it means to be an *eved Hashem*."

Do you feel that the *rosh yeshivah*'s unique conduct has filtered through to the *bachurim*? Would you say that there is anything about the *bachurim* in the yeshivah that stands out as a unique attribute?

"As a former Philly *bachur* myself, I would say there are many special things about the *bachurim*," one brother said. "There is one thing, though, that stands out in my mind: Whenever we went to the washing station in the yeshivah, we always found that the cups were already filled. The *rosh yeshivah* always appreciated when the *bachurim* would make sure that they refilled the cups after they used them, as a *chessed* for the next people who would use the sinks. That eventually became the standard conduct in the yeshivah. Recently, I visited the yeshivah and I checked if this was still happening; sure enough, all the cups were still full."

What other expectations does the *rosh yeshivah* have of his *talmidim*?

"He always asks the *bachurim* in the yeshivah to dress neatly and to maintain a dignified appearance. He tells his *talmidim* to make sure that they do not appear unkempt when they walk in the streets. He even insists that the *bachurim* wear their hats with the brims down, which is considered more dignified. In addition, he teaches his *talmidim* to wear their hats and jackets whenever they are outdoors, even on the short walk from their dormitory rooms to the *beis medrash*. He also teaches the *bachurim* other *hakpados*, such as avoiding walking on grass and ruining its appearance, whether it is on yeshivah property or their own lawns, and putting away *sefarim* after they are used, rather than leaving them scattered throughout the *beis medrash* in a disrespectful fashion."

What is the underlying message of all of this?

"The *rosh yeshivah's* message is that we represent the Torah, and that is a major responsibility and our sacred mission at all times."

My brothers echoed my observation that Rav Shmuel treats every human being with respect, regardless of the person's origins or status in society. On that note, they had several stories to tell.

Rav Shmuel was once visiting a camp, where the counselors brought a group of campers with special needs to meet him. As the campers were introduced to the *rosh yeshivah*, one of the girls proudly announced, "My brother's name is also Shmuel!" Her counselor was horrified at the comment, which was out of place when directed at one of the greatest men of our generation, but the *rosh yeshivah* did not miss a beat. "Yes, isn't it a beautiful name?" he replied.

The *rosh yeshivah*'s interactions with non-Jews are also remarkable. He was once walking in the street with a *bachur*, after a snowstorm had left a thick blanket of snow on the streets of Philadelphia. When a large snow plow began making its way down the street, the *rosh yeshivah* turned and waved to the driver, gesturing to express his thanks.

On another occasion, he noticed an African-American girl shoveling the snow around a fire hydrant. The *rosh yeshivah* approached her and asked, "Did anyone ask you to do this?"

"No," she replied.

"It's very kind and thoughtful of you to be doing it," the *rosh yeshivah* complimented her.

"Once, he was walking in the street with a *bachur*, and there were two black teenagers having a boxing match further down the road," one of my brothers related. "The teens had removed their shirts for their fight, and had left them on the ground a few feet away. When they noticed Rav Shmuel approaching, they respectfully stopped their fight and hurried to gather their shirts, which were closer to the *rosh yeshivah*. Rav Shmuel told the *bachur* who was accompanying him to bring the shirts to the teenagers in order to spare them the extra effort of retrieving them. Then he greeted them and made small talk, asking them about their families and jobs."

Has the *rosh yeshivah* ever made any explicit comments regarding the importance of greeting non-Jews?

"I was once learning *Orchos Chaim L'HaRosh* with the *rosh yeshivah*," one brother replied, "and when we reached the subject of greeting others, he asked me, 'Do you say good morning to everyone?'"

"'I try,' I replied.

"'You must do it all the time,' he said, 'even to non-Jews.'"

"In advance of every *bein haz'manim*," my brother added, "Rav Shmuel delivers a *shmuess* about the importance of increasing *kevod Shamayim* at all times. He always reminds the *bachurim* that Rav Boruch Ber used to tell his own *talmidim* to be very careful not to create a chillul Hashem. Rav Boruch Ber's *talmidim* were men of tremendous stature in their own rights, and if even they had to be warned about this, then we must certainly be very cautious."

What aspect of being a *talmid* of Rav Shmuel do you feel has had the greatest impact on you?

"Much more than the *shmuessen* that the *rosh yeshivah* delivers, it is the fact that he teaches by example," my brother said. "Everything he teaches us is reflected in his own conduct. Just as he admonishes us to think about others, he himself does the same. I have seen him approach a singer at a wedding to ask for his business card, simply to make him feel good about himself. His actions speak to me even more than his words."

Takeaway

We might not be able to reach the level of Torah knowledge that Rav Shmuel Kamenetsky possesses, but we can definitely learn from the way he acts toward every individual, regardless of who they are. Every person he meets is warmed by the kindness with which he speaks to them.

- If you notice a neighbor working on his garden or shoveling the sidewalk, comment on how nice his garden looks or how considerate he is for clearing the sidewalk.
- When you are walking down the block or driving in the street, give some thought to the people around you, and try to take notice of any favors you might be able to do for them.

Working on the Internal
An Interview with Rabbi Levi Lebovits

In the passage of *Shochen Ad*, which is recited at the end of *Pesukei DeZimrah* on Shabbos and Yom Tov, we find the words *"b'kerev kedoshim tiskadash"* — within the holy ones You will be sanctified." The simplest way to understand these words is as a statement that Hashem will be sanctified among the people who are *kadosh*. Rav Shimon Schwab, however, explained the phrase to mean that Hashem is sanctified by the *inner essence* of those who are holy. When a human being attains a status of *kedushah*, it represents a change within him, a core of righteousness that exists within his very being, and that is the key to creating kiddush Hashem.

Achieving this internal sanctity and connection to Hashem is a goal that every Jew should take on as a priority. Unfortunately, it is also a goal that has eluded many people in today's *frum* society. In the first issue of *Klal Perspectives*, Rabbi Chaim Dovid Zwiebel, the executive vice president of Agudath Israel of America, was asked to identify the greatest challenge facing the Orthodox community today. His response: "The increasing number of people from across the spectrum who feel no meaningful connection to Hashem, His Torah, or even His people."

Internalizing a connection to Hashem is the focus of the *mussar vaadim* delivered by Rabbi Levi Lebovits in Denver, Colorado. These *vaadim* are well attended by groups of *baalebatim*, *rebbeim*, and *yeshivah bachurim* alike. In his pursuit of this work, Rabbi Lebovits is actually following in the footsteps of his own *rebbi*, Rav Reuven Leuchter, one of the foremost *talmidim* of Rav Shlomo Wolbe. Rav Leuchter, who had the good fortune of learning *b'chavrusa* with Rav Wolbe for nearly 25 years, has spent over two decades delivering his own unique *vaadim* to American and Israeli *bachurim* and *yungerleit*, all for the same purpose. One of Rabbi Lebovits's first *vaadim* was a weekly *vaad* with the *mesivta rebbeim* of Yeshivas Toras Chaim of Denver. One of those *rebbeim*, Rabbi Eli Krausz, who saw great benefit and potential in Rabbi Lebovits's approach, partnered with him in sharing its success with other communities and yeshivos as well. In order to explore the nature of these *vaadim* and to gain some insight into how to develop an internal connection to Hashem and to Yiddishkeit, I spoke with Rabbi Levi Lebovits to learn more about his work.

How are your *vaadim* different from typical *mussar vaadim*?

"A typical *mussar vaad* focuses on motivating the participants to feel accountable to follow through on personal *kabbalos*. The *vaadim* are based on action; the goal is for the members to begin doing things that they hadn't done before, and their success is measured by the degree to which they accomplish that. The focus of our *vaadim* is different; it is on developing a personal connection to Torah and mitzvos. We spend months delving into a mitzvah, and at the same time delving into ourselves, and this leads us to develop a new sense of the meaning of the mitzvah and to identify with it in ways we never did before. The process can yield tremendous results, as a person can not only gain renewed *cheshek* to fulfill a mitzvah, but can also experience the impact that each mitzvah can have on his life in general."

Can you give us an example of this contrast between the two approaches?

"Let us take *teshuvah* as an example. The usual approach to *teshuvah* is to work on improving our actions; we seek to identify the areas where our observance of the mitzvos is lacking, and then we try to fill in the gaps. That is very commendable, but it deals only with the symptoms of our behavior, not the root causes. In reality, though, *teshuvah* must affect much more than our actions; it should deal with the essence of our relationship with Hashem. If we strengthen our bond with Hashem, then our actions will evolve to become products of that relationship, rather than merely a means of fulfilling obligations.

"The word '*teshuvah*' is derived from the root '*shav*,' meaning 'to return.' A return is a transition; it is a shift from one place to another. Changing our actions alone will not take us to a different 'place,' but if we change our entire outlook and value system, then we will have achieved the true meaning of *teshuvah*."

What does this mean in practical terms? What sort of *kabbalah* should a person accept in Elul, the month of *teshuvah*?

"Let us look at this in light of the contrast we were discussing. If we view *teshuvah* as a process of repairing our actions, then a *kabbalah* for Elul might be an effort to minimize an *aveirah*. For instance, a person might commit to avoid speaking *lashon hara* during a specific time every day. But if *teshuvah* is the means through which we strengthen our relationship with Hashem, we would have to choose an action that would lead to a deeper relationship. In this case, refraining from speaking *lashon hara* wouldn't be enough. Of course, it would be a tremendous accomplishment in its own right, but a person should do more than that; he should also commit to becoming more aware of the severity of the sin of *lashon hara*, or becoming more loving toward others. In that way, he will fulfill Hashem's intent in the mitzvah and will thereby deepen his relationship with Hashem."

Why do you feel that there is a need for these *vaadim*? Have you noticed a void in our society in this respect?

"This is a crucial weapon in our battle against the temptations of the outside world, which are constantly becoming more alluring. Our Torah and mitzvos can help us resist the outside world only to the extent that we identify and connect with them. A person is automatically drawn to the things to which he feels a connection, and the world around us is filled with so many things in which we can easily become caught up. We need to hone our senses of the pleasure and satisfaction that we can derive from the Torah and mitzvos, in order to avoid being trapped by the allure of the outside world."

At what age do you find this approach to be effective?

"I have seen the most *hatzlachah* working with people who are at the age of *beis medrash* and older. The more life experience and maturity a person has, the more we can discuss in a *vaad*. That being said, it is possible to influence younger *bachurim* and children as well, but it should come through modeling the ideals of a mitzvah rather than working together with them on developing appreciation for it. A *rebbi*, for instance, can give his own personal insights and express excitement over the things that he teaches in class; this will show his students that the *rebbi* isn't merely giving over information from *sefarim*, but is actually drawing on his own inner passion."

Have you found that the yeshivos are interested in this approach?

"I have given *vaadim* to the *bachurim* of Yeshiva Toras Chaim of Denver for five years now, and I have heard from other *roshei yeshivah* that they are working on implementing the *mehalach* of these *vaadim* in their own yeshivos."

What are some of the results that you have seen from these *vaadim*?

"I have found that people experience Torah in a completely different way than they had previously. The *vaadim* make a difference in their *davening*, their learning, their Shabbosos and Yamim Noraim, and many other things. They recognize that Torah is real, and it becomes a more central part of their lives."

What final suggestion would you give to the readers as a worthwhile endeavor for personal growth?

"Start a *vaad* with your friends! *Daas Chochmah U'Mussar* and *Alei Shur* are *sefarim* that are very helpful in beginning the process. And I am available to help with the rest!"

Takeaway

Yiddishkeit is a relationship with Hashem. The mitzvos and Torah are the tools that have been given to us to build an intimate connection to Hashem. A person who uses these tools to develop a strong connection to Hashem will be a true ambassador for Him in the world.

Making It Practical

- Find ways to use the mitzvos to build a relationship with Hashem. Think of a mitzvah not just as an obligation or ritual, but as a way to connect to Hashem.

- Experience the closeness with Hashem that Shabbos creates. The Shabbos day is a special rendezvous with Hashem, which we honor by partaking in special meals and wearing special clothes, and when we are free of all distractions. It is possible to learn to enjoy Hashem's presence on Shabbos.

- Take a minute before you *daven* to think about the fact that you are about to communicate with Hashem, and that your daily *davening* is part of an ongoing dialogue with Him.

Connecting Through Chessed
An Interview with Rabbi Benzion Klatzko

We are all familiar with the Torah's description of the *chessed*, and particularly the *hachnassas orchim*, of Avraham Avinu; with these stories, the Torah teaches us that *hachnassas orchim* is an incredibly powerful means of promoting *kiddush Shem Shamayim*. One of the most well-known practitioners of *hachnassas orchim* today is Rabbi Benzion Klatzko, who hosts a minimum of 65 guests every week in his home in Monsey. With his prolific hospitality, Rabbi Klatzko has certainly been responsible for an exceptional kiddush Hashem, and I spoke to him to gain some insight into his extraordinary pursuit of *chessed*.

First, I would like to understand how you began hosting so many guests every week. Most people can't even fathom having 50 guests every Shabbos. How are you able to do it?

"My wife and I both come from families that practice *chessed* and *hachnassas orchim* on a very high level. My own parents have an extra table for guests every week, and their kindness goes beyond providing a meal. When they host *meshulachim* or other guests with limited means, my father always makes sure to look at the guests' shoes. If a guest has shoes that appear to be worn out, my father invites him to the basement, where he has a large stock of new shoes bought specifically for this purpose, and he tells the guest to choose a pair as a gift. Whenever someone tells my parents that he is collecting for *hachnassas kallah*, my mother gives him a wedding gift for the *kallah*; she, too, has a large collection of gift items on hand for these occasions. She also gives every *meshulach* a gift to bring home for his wife.

"My in-laws, the Juravels, used to run a veritable *chessed* industry out of their home. Their kitchen functioned as a soup kitchen in the most literal sense. Every morning, trays of chicken and a huge pot of soup would be placed on the counters of their kitchen. They left their front door unlocked, and many people came to their home to partake of the meal every day. This went on for three or four decades. They also used their basement for a 'store' that we called the 'Juravel Boutique.' It was filled with clothes, baby items, and all sorts of other necessities, and anyone in need was invited to take the items for free. Over the years, word spread about this endeavor, and people donated items all the time. In recent years, they moved to a different community and these activities came to an end, but you can see that my wife and I both grew up internalizing the idea that there is much more to *chessed* than simply inviting a few guests for an occasional meal."

I believe that some people are afraid of becoming too heavily involved in *chessed*; they are concerned that others may end up taking advantage of them. How would you react to that concern?

"It does happen," Rabbi Klatzko admits, "but Hashem also showers us with boundless *chessed*, and we also make the mistake of taking advantage of His kindness. We shouldn't allow that concern to limit our *chessed*. Most people are genuinely grateful and would not exploit someone who helps them. On those rare occasions when it does happen, a person can change his approach for those specific individuals, recognizing that his *chessed* doesn't actually help them."

You have been inviting dozens of guests to your Shabbos table every week for years. In your experience, what is it that makes the greatest impact on the guests? Is it the food? The *divrei Torah*? The family atmosphere?

"None of the above. If a guest feels that he is merely another face in a crowd, just a nameless body at the table, then the impact of the meal is very limited. I remember that when I was a *bachur*, I was once a guest at someone's home, and the host didn't say a single word to me throughout the meal. I was very deflated by the experience. The most important thing to give a guest is personalized attention. When a guest feels that someone has noticed him, when he receives even a small amount of *kavod* — something that every human being needs — it creates a wonderful feeling. It makes him feel special, and it makes him feel connected. In our home, we give every guest his own time in the spotlight."

How do you manage to do that, if you have 65 guests every week?

"We have a special practice: At every meal, we pass around a *l'chaim*, and we ask every guest to come to the front of the room, to introduce themselves, to tell us something special about themselves, and to give a *berachah* with their *l'chaim*. Even the more timid guests agree to do this after they are prodded, and they feel very good about it afterward."

Don't your children resent having to compete with 65 guests for their parents' attention? How do you prevent them from feeling that your hospitality comes at their expense?

"First of all, my children sit next to me at every meal. Regardless of how important our guests are, I never give them those seats. The children also get their moments in the spotlight, although that is certainly not enough for them, and that is why we have 'family time' after every Friday-night meal. I make sure to end the meal with my guests at a reasonable time, and while the guests are told that they are welcome to stay and continue socializing, I take my family upstairs for some private time. That is when my children have an opportunity to talk to me about anything that is on their minds."

How do you handle the preparations for all of your guests?

"We all have our individual jobs, and we try to make it fun and enjoyable for the children. The children who are in charge of setting the table for dozens of people have come up with an innovative game: They rollerblade around the table, placing the napkins, plates, and cutlery in front of each seat."

What about all the logistical arrangements? How do you keep track of how many guests are coming each week and who was invited? It seems like a job for a full-time secretary.

"That is actually one of the functions of my pet project, the website 'Shabbat.com.' This website is a massive network that is used for matching potential hosts with Shabbos guests. A guest can use the website to find a host, or a host can use it to look for a guest to invite. We ask all of our guests to sign up on the website, and the system records every request for a meal, keeping us updated as to whether the guests have decided to come, have canceled, or are still undecided. Everyone who registers on the site also provides some basic background information, and we can see who has hosted them in the past as well. That way, we can look at the list for any meal and see whether the guests will be a good mix, or it would be better to rearrange the schedule. We can also send an email that is automatically delivered to all the guests registered for a particular meal, containing information about *davening*, parking, or other things that may be important for them to know. And if someone inadvertently leaves something behind in our home, we can use the website to find a list of the guests at any meal, which can help us reunite the object with its owner."

I imagine that you have met many diverse people through your incredible acts of hospitality. Do you have any dramatic stories to share?

"There is a feature on my website called a 'proximity invite,' which automatically sends a private invitation to every registered individual within a predetermined distance from my home. One week, I used this feature to send an invitation to everyone within five miles of my house; I wanted to see if any new guests would sign up. Sure enough, a young woman came to the meal and asked me, 'Who told you to invite me for Shabbos?' I told her that no one had said anything to me about her, but she insisted that there must have been someone. I explained the concept of a proximity invite, and then she revealed her story to me: Her personal life was in shambles; her father had been imprisoned, her mother was suffering from depression, and her siblings had taken to the streets in order to escape from their problems. 'I decided that I was going to end my miserable life this Shabbos,' she said, 'but when I got your invitation, I decided to wait until after Shabbos.'

"'Are you still thinking about taking your life?' I asked her.

"'If you invite me again, I will wait,' she said. We began inviting her to our home every Shabbos thereafter, and she became very close with our family. Today, she is married and has a home and children of her own."

Do you have plans to expand your activities beyond hachnassas orchim?

"We have already done that, and we hope to continue expanding our ventures even further. Shabbat.com is already used not only for hospitality, but for making *shidduchim* and matching *chavrusas* as well. On average, our website has been making one *shidduch* a week! We are now working on a new feature: a comprehensive job list, to help job seekers find *parnassah*.

"All of these things revolve around the same idea: making connections," Rabbi Klatzko concludes. "That is obviously the basic idea of pairing *chavrusas*, making *shidduchim*, and finding jobs for people who are unemployed, but it is also one of the foundations of *hachnassas orchim*. When you make a person feel special and connected, that is when your act of *hachnassas orchim* becomes a true *chessed*."

Takeaway

Providing for others' physical needs is one level of chessed, but an even higher level is to provide for their emotional needs as well. A host should show interest in his guests' personal lives, relating to them through dialogue and connecting with them emotionally. The impact of that kind of hospitality can be incredibly profound.

Making It Practical

- When you have guests or *meshulachim* at your table, take an interest in them by asking about their families or other details of their lives. Make a point of getting to know them a bit better.
- Put every guest in the spotlight at some point during a meal, giving them an opportunity to make their presence felt.

The Contagious Spirit of Shabbos
Rabbi Warren Goldstein

Shabbos is described as *me'ein Olam Haba* — a taste of the World to Come. On Shabbos, we are given a preview of the world as it will appear in the future, when Hashem's sovereignty is recognized by the entire world and His kingdom is complete. In fact, Shabbos is more than just a glimpse of the future; it is actually a means of bringing that future closer, for Shabbos itself has the power to bring about kiddush Hashem.

The Shabbos Project is an incredible initiative that demonstrates the inspirational power of Shabbos. I am not aware of any other campaign that has achieved the same degree of explosive growth. In the fall of 2017, I had the honor of speaking with Rabbi Warren Goldstein, the chief rabbi of South Africa and founder of the Shabbos Project. Rabbi Goldstein revealed that when the project was first launched in South Africa in 2013, it had the participation of 70 percent of the country's Jewish population, which stands at 75,000 Jews. In the year 2017, the program took place in over 1300 cities in 95 countries around the world.

How did this initiative spread throughout the world so quickly?

"After the impact the Shabbos Project had in South Africa, we received emails from people all over the world who wanted to learn more about the project and how they could bring it to their own cities. In response, we released a video online that captured the beauty and power of the Shabbos Project and invited the rest of the world to join. The following year, South Africa was joined in the Shabbos Project by communities in 460 cities. Over the years, the project has continuously expanded to include more individual participants and participating cities."

What is the main goal of the Shabbos Project?

"As you know, *Chazal* teach us that when all of Klal Yisrael observes two Shabbosos, it will bring the *geulah*. There is actually a passage in the *Yerushalmi* that states that only one Shabbos is required. Nevertheless, we are not emphasizing that our goal is to bring Mashiach; we leave that up to Hashem. What we see from *Chazal* is that Shabbos has a tremendous power to create *kevod Shamayim*, to transform people and communities, and that it is the source of all *berachah*. Our goal is to spread recognition of the beauty of Shabbos, to do our part in enhancing *shemiras Shabbos* and connecting people to the tremendous gift of Shabbos.

"Our second goal is to foster *achdus*. When so many people come together from so many different backgrounds and from all walks of life to fulfill the Will of Hashem, it leads to a tremendous kiddush Hashem. The sheer volume of participation makes people feel that they are part of something very special and important."

What do you feel is the cause of the project's resounding success?

"The unique thing about this campaign is that it is not run by an organization; it is a movement of the people. Individuals from all over the world volunteer to participate, out of a passionate desire to bring the project to their communities. Each of those individuals then taps into their respective communities' resources, *shuls*, and organizations to help make it happen. Shabbos is a gift to every Jew, and it seems to have a natural energy that draws people in. It has motivated people to take responsibility in their own communities, and thousands of people have been stirred to be a part of it.

"The power of modern communication has also played a major role in making this happen. When a movement of the people is combined with a tool such as the Internet, the sky is the limit. We have reached millions of people through social media. Even in Pakistan, a Jewish person discovered the project and decided to keep Shabbos. In Nevada, there was a woman who was so isolated that her granddaughter had asked her if they were the only Jews in the world. When she discovered our project on social media, she decided to put out a message asking if other Jews in the area were interested in participating. This led to six families coming together to keep Shabbos."

Your project aims to foster Shabbos observance among people who have never kept Shabbos before. What resources do you provide them to help with that?

"With the help of *poskim* such as Rav Yitzchok Berkowitz, we have created materials that provide direction and guidance for people who are not used to keeping Shabbos. These materials have been translated into many languages. During the three months before *Parashas Lech Lecha*, we open a call center in Tel Aviv where our operatives are available to answer questions in multiple languages; they guide over 7000 volunteers who are working on the ground in their respective cities to make the Shabbos Project a success. That network continues to grow.

"For people who have little or no experience with Shabbos, we provide two different versions of instructions for keeping Shabbos, one short and the other long. In the short version, which we have drawn up in consultation with *poskim,* the idea is to give the readers a feel for Shabbos by focusing on three goals: not going to work, not using electronic devices, and not driving.

In the longer version, which we call the Shabbos Map, there are many practical applications of the laws of Shabbos, in areas ranging from food preparation to *muktzeh* and *hotzaah*.

"Nevertheless, it is important to emphasize that this is not an outreach project. Our vision is to bring *all* Jews together to participate, including those who are already *shomer Shabbos*. All of us can take steps to enhance our Shabbos observance; the Shabbos Project is for everyone, ourselves included. In May, I met with the Novominsker Rebbe to ask his advice on how we can encourage more Observant Jews to participate in the Shabbos Project. Based on that discussion, we have launched a campaign that will involve *shomer Shabbos* communities around the world learning *perek shloshim* of the *Rambam's Hilchos Shabbos*, which discusses the laws of *kavod* and *oneg Shabbos*.

What about the *challah*-baking events? How do they fit into the mission of the Shabbos Project?

"In addition to the observance of Shabbos and all its benefits, we wanted to introduce people to the joy and pleasure of Shabbos. We wanted to create excitement about Shabbos, especially among the women, and the *challah* baking has become an eagerly anticipated event. In Johannesburg alone, which is home to 50,000 Jews, 6000 women came together last year for this event. In Argentina there were 8000 participants, and there were 3000 in Mexico City. One woman from Scottsdale, Arizona, was so moved by the *challah*-baking event that she kept Shabbos that week along with her non-Jewish husband. They continued keeping Shabbos, and he eventually became a *ger tzedek*. We hear about many stories like this. Of course, there are other organized events, such as communal Shabbos meals and *havdalah* events, which add to the spirit of excitement."

What guidance would you give to a person who is involved in the project and is hosting guests for the Shabbos meal?

"It is important to treat everyone as an equal, regardless of the level they are on. It's important to reach out to family, friends, and neighbors — not in a condescending manner, but by supporting them and offering to help them feel like part of the project. We are not patronizing other Jews; Shabbos is Hashem's gift to the Jewish people, and we are introducing other Jews to their share in this priceless treasure."

Let us hope that the Shabbos Project continues to succeed in increasing the scope and quality of Shabbos observance throughout the world, and that its efforts lead to the ultimate kiddush Hashem.

Takeaway

Shabbos has an immense power to create a sense of connection. It is a tremendous gift to the Jewish people, and can offer any Jew a taste of the beauty of Yiddishkeit.

Making It Practical

- Think about what you can do in your community to build on the successes of the Shabbos project. Make phone calls or send emails to people with whom you come in contact, notifying them about the annual experience.

- Try to use your own Shabbos table as a force to create kiddush Hashem throughout the year. Ask around in your community if there are any people who need a meal for Shabbos, and make your Shabbos table a special experience that is available to guests.

Project Inspire —
Awakening the Sleeping Giant

Akiddush Hashem, as we have learned, is a powerful force that can have an impact on Jews and non-Jews alike. But is there any advantage to performing a kiddush Hashem in the presence of another Jew, as opposed to a non-Jew? The *Meshech Chachmah* says that a kiddush Hashem witnessed by a Jew is a more significant accomplishment. When a non-Jew observes a kiddush Hashem, it increases his faith in Hashem, but the effect ends there. When a Jew witnesses a kiddush Hashem, it inspires him to improve himself, and the observer himself then becomes a vehicle for further *kiddush Shem Shamayim*. His own future actions, the mitzvos that he is inspired to perform, will bring honor to Hashem time and again. Thus, the initial kiddush Hashem serves as the catalyst for many more actions that continue to increase Hashem's honor.

Kiddush Hashem is not the exclusive domain of professionals. On the contrary, it is the mission of each and every Jew. It stands to reason, then, that every Jew should feel an obligation to influence other Jews to draw closer to Yiddishkeit, even more than he feels responsible to sanctify Hashem's Name among non-Jews. In fact, the Chofetz Chaim lists a number of mitzvos that obligate us to strive to influence other Jews, including the mitzvos of *hashavas aveidah* and *tochachah*, as well as the concept of *arvus* (responsibility for other Jews). That is precisely what the field of *kiruv* is about.

Project Inspire is an organization that was created to raise awareness of the duty of every individual Jew to be *mekarev* his nonreligious brethren, and to help ordinary Jews understand how they can influence and inspire others. I spoke with Rabbi Chaim Sampson, the founding director of Project Inspire, to gain some insight into the organization's work.

How was Project Inspire born and what is its mission? Is it different than a standard *kiruv* organization?

"Project Inspire was created to fulfill a dream of Rav Noach Weinberg," Rabbi Sampson explained. "There are millions of nonreligious Jews in the world, and Rav Weinberg felt that it is impossible for all of those Jews to be reached by *kiruv* professionals. We can approximate that there are about 1,500 *kiruv* professionals in North America, and in the best possible scenario, each of them might be *mekarev* 100 Jews. That would mean that only a total of 150,000 estranged Jews would be brought back to Yiddishkeit, which is just a tiny fraction of the total nonreligious population. Rav Weinberg knew that it was necessary to harness a much more powerful force in order to reach all of the Jews in the world.

"Rav Weinberg saw the entire religious sector of Klal Yisrael as a powerful army with the potential to accomplish this. He referred to the half-million religious Jews in North America as a 'sleeping giant,' and he felt that we had to 'awaken' that giant by inspiring religious Jews to recognize their responsibility. He personally tried to establish five different organizations — even before he started his yeshivos for *baalei teshuvah* — to achieve this purpose, but he was not successful at that time. Project Inspire was established to carry out this vision.

"As an organization, Project Inspire is less focused on its staff doing direct *kiruv*; our aim is to train religious Jews to reach out to those who are not religious, and to equip them with the tools they need to be *mekarev* others. In a nutshell, instead of teaching students, we are training the teachers."

What are your techniques for waking up that "sleeping giant"?

"We began by distributing prepared *mishloach manos* that we encouraged religious Jews to send to others who are not religious, along with meaningful cards. We went on to provide small, simple gifts for Pesach and Rosh Hashanah as well. These are simple ways to reach out to nonreligious Jews and inspire them. In addition, we have *kiruv* training programs geared for laymen, which have been attended by 10,000 people. We also run large conferences attended by thousands of people on the theme of inspiring oneself to inspire others, and we distribute Tishah B'Av videos with the stories of laymen who have been successful in *kiruv*. This conveys the message that any Jew can succeed in these efforts. It doesn't take a professional."

Can you share a success story with us?

"One of our famous stories is about a *chassidishe* woman from Boro Park who came to one of our training programs. Shortly after she attended the program, she was returning to America after a visit to Eretz Yisrael, and a nonreligious actor from Israel was seated beside her on the plane. At one point in the flight, he became bored and began peppering her with questions about Yiddishkeit. She used her training to the best of her ability to provide him with intelligent answers. One of our main messages is that a person should never let an opportunity for *kiruv* pass him by. With that in mind, she ended the conversation with an invitation for Shabbos. A couple of weeks later, he called to accept her invitation. When he arrived, she gave him a gift: a leather-bound *siddur* with his name inscribed on the cover. By the time Shabbos was over, he was in tears; he had been surrounded by religious Jews his whole life, but never understood how beautiful it truly was. They kept in touch, and she treated him as if he was part of their family. Eventually, he returned to Eretz Yisrael to learn in Aish HaTorah, and he now lives and learns full-time in Monsey, is married to a *frum* girl, and is beginning his own family."

Is there a specific type of person who is naturally better equipped to succeed in *kiruv*? What would you say is the key to success for a layman?

"I asked my friend Steve Eisenberg, one of the most successful people in *kiruv* in our times, to explain the secret of his success. He told me, 'When I meet someone, I always ask myself what I can do to help him with any need he may have. I have many resources available to me, and if he is looking for a place to rent, a job, or a *shidduch*, I can help him connect to all sorts of resources. I don't have any ulterior motives for doing this. It is all about helping another Jew with anything he needs.' The reason he is successful is that people sense that he cares about them for who they really are. No one will be influenced by a person who only wants him to become religious; he needs to sense that you care for him as an individual and that means being interested in helping him for who he is. We can all do this, and this is truly our greatest tool. If we care for people sincerely, they will be open to who we are and the Yiddishkeit that we represent."

What is the greatest obstacle to success in *kiruv*?

"No one wants to be the object of your mitzvah or the vehicle for you to earn *Olam Haba*. People feel used and distrustful when they sense that that is someone's mindset. I remember that when I was in yeshivah, I was once sick and hoping for visitors to come. Finally, my friend arrived and I thanked him excitedly for coming. He replied, 'Don't worry about it. I will get *s'char* in *Olam Haba*.' I was very dismayed by that response. It created a very bad feeling. Hashem wants our interactions with other people to stem from feelings of true caring and love, not from self-interest. That is one of the rules that we teach in our training programs: You must develop a relationship before you can even try to influence someone.

"The Mishnah says that a person should be '*oheiv es habrios umekarvan laTorah*' — he should love people and draw them close to the Torah. You cannot skip the first step. You must love them *before* you try to be *mekarev* them. And it is important to realize that the Mishnah doesn't say that one should love people *in order* to bring them close to the Torah. Your love for others cannot be dependent on their becoming fully Orthodox. They must feel appreciated as individuals.

"Another major obstacle to the success of *kiruv* is the 'all or nothing' syndrome. There is a common misconception that *kiruv* is considered successful only when an irreligious Jew becomes completely observant. This hurts everyone: The laymen do not even wish to try, because they feel that it will take too much time and effort to achieve that goal, and the nonreligious Jews feel too discouraged to begin the process because they cannot imagine transforming themselves in that way. We can't expect perfection of everyone. We must appreciate even the tiniest steps. Even if a person begins keeping only one mitzvah or some part of Shabbos, that is also considered success. Every mitzvah or part of a mitzvah is a precious jewel, worth more than any amount of money."

What are some of the unique difficulties involved in kiruv today?

"For one thing, people are no longer moved by intellectual arguments. In the recent past, we were able to run Discovery seminars, and 10 percent of the participants would realize that they could not ignore the blatant truths that were presented to them. Today, though, our society is driven by the pursuit of pleasure. That is all that people desire, and in order to influence anyone, we must expose them to the pleasure of the Torah lifestyle. When they experience the beauty of Torah, the delight of having a life with real meaning, and the wonderful experience of Shabbos and spending time with their families, that is what inspires them to change."

What is the most effective kiruv tool?

"Taking people on educational trips to Israel is very powerful. Those trips allow them to remove themselves from the distractions of their daily lives and the influences around them. That opens them up to the kedushah of a Shabbos, the power of a Friday night at the Kosel, and a glimpse into the meaning of Yiddishkeit, which can be a profoundly moving experience."

What are Project Inspire's plans for the immediate future?

"We will continue working to awaken the 'sleeping giant': to train ordinary Jewish laymen and develop their interest and ability in kiruv. We have also begun working on connecting the giant to the kiruv organizations, building a partnership that will allow the organizations to tap into the power of the volunteer population. For instance, if an organization is running a trip to Israel, they can solicit volunteers to recruit people to be leaders on the trip. These volunteers can then follow up with the participants after the trip, offering to learn with them and helping them maintain their inspiration. Our third objective is to help the *frum* population themselves feel inspired; a person can influence others only when he feels passion for his own Yiddishkeit."

What can we do on a practical level to become involved in this initiative?

"Have your *shul* bring in a *kiruv* training program for its members, or set up a committee in *shul* to focus on this sort of effort. Additionally, we all know people we can reach out to: friends, neighbors, co-workers, relatives. Why not try to reach out to them with sincerity and caring, and share the beauty and joy of their heritage with them — one step at a time!"

Rabbi Sampson ended our discussion by noting that Rav Noach Weinberg, the man whose vision sparked the establishment of Project Inspire, was driven by a single objective: creating kiddush Hashem.

"I once asked Rav Noach what would happen if we managed to get everyone involved but it still wasn't successful," Rabbi Sampson recalled. "He told me that if that happened, Mashiach would come. All that Hashem wants is for us to care enough to take action for *Acheinu Bnei Yisrael*. Once we have reached that point, He will do the rest."

Takeaway

We can make a difference only if we care about others for who they are and if we are concerned about their overall well-being, not if we are merely targeting them to make them religious. We must also realize that kiruv is not an "all or nothing" proposition; even the tiniest amount of progress has extraordinary value.

- Create or be a part of a welcoming committee in your *shul* or community to embrace newcomers and provide support for any of their needs. Make sure that your help is offered without a trace of judgment and without seeming to be driven by ulterior motives.

- If you know of someone who might benefit from a trip to Israel, take the initiative to make it happen; help them get in touch with the proper organization.

A Convert's Challenges

For millennia, the Jewish people have been exiled among the nations of the world, driven from country to country and from society to society. The Gemara (*Pesachim* 87b) teaches us that this is part of a Divine master plan, and that Hashem exiled us from our land in order to attract converts to our nation. Of course, we don't seek converts; in fact, we are required to try to discourage potential *geirim*, in order to weed out those who are more likely to fail. But those *geirim* who do become part of our nation are people from whom we have much to learn, and whose life decisions truly add to Hashem's honor.

The journey of a convert to Judaism can be very difficult, and there is much that we can do to see to it that *geirim* receive the support they need. In order to learn more about this subject, I spoke with a woman who converted to Judaism and is familiar with the experiences of many other *geirim* as well.

Can you describe some of your experiences integrating into the Jewish community after your conversion?

"My own experience was actually very positive. The families in my community accepted me warmly, and the rabbi was very supportive, always available, and very sensitive to my journey and to my progress. I lived in a *frum* community that was very secure and very mature; it was the perfect 'incubator' for me. There were about eight or nine families who made sure that I was always taken care of for Shabbos, and who made themselves available at all times to help me.

"My personal challenge came about seven or eight years after I converted. This experience might have been unique to me, as a single person, but I learned that when you become established in a community, people tend to think of you less often. My advice is to always remember the singles in a community, whether they are young or old. Continue inviting them even if they turn you down; your invitations will let them know that you are thinking of them, and they will appreciate that immensely."

What was the hardest aspect of integrating into the community?

"The disillusionment. This is an experience that others have described to me as well: A *ger* comes to Yiddishkeit with excitement and idealism, ready to embrace the beautiful message of the religion and the ideals that it represents. Judaism embodies everything we have spent our lives seeking. But then, at some point, we are confronted with the reality that the lifestyle does not work perfectly, or that it has completely broken down in some areas. The people who live this lifestyle are flawed human beings, just as we are. We might have seen some isolated flaws while we were preparing for *geirus*, but we were too excited to pay much attention to them. But then, as full-fledged Jews, we suddenly see a chillul Hashem, and then another one, and so forth. *Geirim* don't necessarily expect perfection, but when we are disappointed time after time, it causes us to struggle with our commitment."

Do you have any specific examples of things that disillusioned you?

"Sometimes, the disillusionment comes from seeing other Jews failing to live up to Torah values. They may be following the letter of the law, but they ignore its spirit. We may also feel confused when we see religious Jews disregarding the laws of the land, or rationalizing breaking the law.

"Still, to paraphrase an old idiom, I believe in the message of Hashem even if His messengers fall short. I have found Hashem and His Torah to be a source of vitality and security for me. If His messengers are not ideal, that doesn't detract from the importance of the message."

What else causes challenges for *geirim*?

"Sometimes, people are suspicious of *geirim*, and that makes us very uncomfortable. Of course, if there is evidence that a specific person might be problematic, then the community should beware of that person. But if there is a pervasive sense in a community that *geirim* are a burden or possible source of trouble, a *beis din* should not recommend that community for a *ger*. Every *ger* should seek rabbinic advice in order to select an appropriate community where he can live and learn."

What would you want other Jews to understand about *geirim*?

"*Geirim* are not people who have reached the pinnacle of knowledge and perfection. Even though we have accepted the Torah, it doesn't mean that we already know everything; it means only that we have committed to continue learning and to strive to keep whatever we have learned. Be patient and informative to *geirim*, and treat them in a nurturing way. Some of us are not very good at communicating and are fearful of saying things that are wrong; we may also be embarrassed to appear ignorant. Do not judge us for the things we don't know; remember that we are people who are filled with idealism and zeal for the truth we have learned, but that it takes time to master living as a Jew."

How does converting to Judaism affect a *ger*'s relationship with his family?

"It changes the relationship drastically. Even if a *ger*'s family is respectful and doesn't criticize his choice to convert, the very act of converting changes the way the family interacts with each other. As time goes on, all *geirim* feel a certain erosion of their closeness with their families. They are now different from their parents and siblings, and the relationship will never be the same. This can be very painful, even if the *ger* realized in advance that it might happen, and it is very helpful that the Jewish perspective today does not call for *geirim* to completely sever all ties with their families. This is another area where it is very important to have the support of a *rav*. As an only child who grew up with a very loving mother, I was shocked when I learned that I could not be buried with her, and I thank Hashem that I had a *rav* by my side at that time."

What other areas come as a surprise to some *geirim*?

"The financial challenges! Potential *geirim* should be told about the huge financial burden that comes with a religious lifestyle. A profession that could allow a person to live comfortably in the secular world may leave them in poverty when they adopt a Jewish lifestyle. There are suddenly higher food bills, tuition bills, and other expenses that the *ger* may not have considered."

What are some specific sensitivities that other Jews should have in their dealings with *geirim*?

"Be sensitive and do not use the term '*goyim*.' It often sounds derogatory or condescending, and *geirim* have families who are not Jewish. The correct term is 'gentile.' And this is not just a matter of terminology; a person should not show contempt for non-Jews in any way. *Geirim* love their families and are pained to see them denigrated; we simply understand that we have been given a different mission in life."

Do you have any messages for other *geirim*?

"Throughout the year, especially around the Yamim Tovim but at other times as well, there are beautiful *shiurim* and other classes that are available in many communities, often at no cost to the attendees. I feel that *geirim* should take advantage of these opportunities to gain a greater depth of understanding of the

Jewish faith and its mitzvos. I am often shocked at how few people attend these *shiurim*; these are great opportunities that many people are missing."

Is there anything that can be done during the conversion process to help ensure long-term success for *geirim*?

"In addition to a sponsoring rabbi, every *ger* should have a sponsoring family. Most Jews who are *frum* from birth are fortunate to have large families serving as their support systems, but we do not have that benefit. The sponsoring family can function like actual relatives; they can offer friendship and support to the *geirim*, and invite them into their homes. *Rabbanim* are too busy to give *geirim* everything they need, and it would make sense to have laypeople involved as well."

What do you feel are some of the things that ordinary Jews could learn from *geirim*?

"*Geirim* tend to have a powerful emotional attachment to Hashem, and perhaps a greater appreciation for the joys of Yiddishkeit. *Geirim* can serve as a reminder of how precious, exciting, and inspirational the truth of Torah really is."

Takeaway

Every convert to Judaism can be credited with accomplishing an amazing feat. Any person who becomes a ger has demonstrated tremendous emotional strength and the courage to change his entire way of life. We all find it difficult to change ourselves and our lives; geirim serve as an example of the fact that major transformations are possible. In return for this inspiration, we must respect their sensitivities and make sure that our own dealings with converts always create kiddush Shem Shamayim.

- Avoid talking in a derogatory way about non-Jews, especially in the presence of a *ger*.
- Offer to be a surrogate relative (sponsoring family) to a *ger* in your community
- Talk to your children and students about the admiration that we should have for *geirim* and *baalei teshuvah*.
- Don't expect perfection from *geirim* or *baalei teshuvah* (or, for that matter, from anyone else).

The Attachment Theory

In 1958, a British psychiatrist by the name of John Bowlby introduced a revolutionary theory, which eventually transformed the approach to child-rearing practiced in America. Bowlby posited that children, after their birth, form an initial attachment with their mothers, and that relationship gives them the security they need in order to explore the world. The mother-child bond also serves as a prototype for all future relationships. Disrupting an infant's relationship with a mother, Bowlby concluded, can lead to severe, lifelong emotional damage.

Bowlby's theory suggests that a child must develop an attachment with a mother figure within a critical period of up to five years after birth, and that the failure to create such an attachment during this period will lead to irreversible developmental damage. Bowlby's theory has been expanded over time, and psychologists now recognize that attachment to other human beings is an indispensable part of an adult's life as well. Scientists now recognize that in order to be stable, resilient, strong, and happy, every human being must have a sense of attachment to others. This is a marked departure from the mindset that prevailed before this theory was developed; in earlier years, it was widely believed that maturity entails emotional independence, and that a craving for human relationships was a sign that one lacked maturity.

There is plenty of evidence that relationships with others can be critical for a human being's emotional and physical health. Research has shown that the survivors of the Nazi death camps during the Holocaust typically made it through the war in pairs; people who were alone were far less likely to survive. It has also been established that married men and women typically live longer than those who are unmarried. Loneliness can have negative medical consequences; it tends to elevate blood pressure to the point that the risk of heart attack or stroke is doubled. James House, a sociologist at the University of Michigan, has stated that a lack of companionship is a greater health risk than smoking or high blood pressure.

When I learned about Bowlby's theory, I began to wonder if the natural human need for attachment can be satisfied with a relationship with Hashem. Is it possible for a human being to develop such a close relationship with Hashem that he will derive a sense of security and calm –and, in fact, his entire emotional stability — from that bond? Certainly, this seems to describe the level of *bitachon* that we associate with outstanding *tzaddikim*, but can ordinary people such as ourselves achieve such a relationship? Scientists believe that the need for attachment is a function of evolution, but we understand it as an emotional need programmed into the human mind by Hashem Himself. In that case, it would make sense that the ultimate purpose of that need is to foster *deveikus* to Hashem. But is that something that we can truly attain?

I have come to believe that in this area in particular, the *geirim* who have joined our nation can serve as a powerful example of the degree of attachment every Jew can achieve. I have had the pleasure of meeting many *geirim*, and I have seen that many of them derive their main emotional stability from their relationships with Hashem. They actually sense His caring and love, and He seems to be their primary "attachment figure" in life.

This emerged most strikingly from a conversation I had with

one specific *giyores*, who described the final stages of the conversion process. She related that when she was questioned by a *rav* before her conversion, he asked if she understood that the Jews are a persecuted people; she acknowledged that she did. "Why do you want to be Jewish?" he asked.

"We looked each other in the eye," she told me, "and I answered, 'I am seeking the closest relationship possible with the Creator of the universe. If you know of anyone closer to Him than the Jews, send me there!'" With that, the *rav* approved her conversion.

When I asked how she had developed a personal relationship with Hashem, the woman replied that it had developed gradually. "First, I recognized that Hashem was my Creator. Then I knew Him as my King, and then He became my personal Father. I eventually came to know Him as my Teacher, my Mentor, my Encourager, my Sustainer, my Corrector, my Provider, and my constant Companion. He knows me better than I know myself," she added, demonstrating that her relationship with Hashem had become a tangible part of her world. "He never pushes me too hard or too fast; His dealings with me are always just right, and I try hard to please Him. I don't like disappointing my Father and King. This is a one-on-one relationship that He offers to anyone who desires it.

"I trust Him completely with my thoughts; after all, He knows them anyway," she said. "We speak throughout the day; I talk to Him verbally, and He communicates with me through His written words and through my heart."

Realizing that I was speaking with a person who had mastered a sense of closeness with Hashem, I asked her what methods she recommends to build a relationship with Him. "Talk to Him as you would talk to anyone else in a close relationship," she said. "Be aware of His *hashgachah pratis*, and thank Him for it. Don't just shrug off simple coincidences as things that happened to you by chance. Even if you find the perfect parking space, don't dismiss it as luck; thank Hashem verbally and recognize that He is looking out for you. You simply have to desire that personal relationship," she added, "and I highly recommend it."

Many people have occasional feelings of emptiness and anxiety, with the sense that something is missing in their lives. This woman attested that her relationship with Hashem fills that void, but she added that one must be fully committed to the relationship in order for it to work. "It's impossible to be a fair-weather friend," she said. "A person must commit to the relationship for the long haul. I always keep in mind that Hashem never promised me a rose garden, but He did promise to walk with me through the thorns. I hold on to that thought and keep my hand outstretched."

This conversation left me with the powerful sense that true *deveikus* to Hashem is possible even for the average person. But I was left with one uncertainty: Perhaps it was only natural for a *giyores*, who has given up a certain degree of connection with her family and her entire world, to turn to Hashem for closeness. But what about those who have spouses and families, and who do not necessarily feel that something is lacking in their lives? Are they also capable of feeling such closeness with Hashem?

Of course, I understand that this might well be what the Torah expects of us, but I was curious if there was any research that had verified the possibility. Sure enough, I soon discovered that a major research paper had been written on this subject. The researchers analyzed whether it is more likely for a person to connect to G-d if he lacks healthy attachments to other human beings, and they concluded that the opposite was actually true: A person who has healthy attachments is *more* likely to develop and maintain additional attachments, and thus is more likely to develop a lasting relationship with his Father in Heaven.

It should be clear, then, that *deveikus* to Hashem is not just a lofty ideal attained by the greatest *tzaddikim*. On the contrary, it is something that is accessible to every one of us. At the same time, we must be aware that *deveikus* will not develop on its own; we must work on building and developing that relationship. If we truly apply ourselves to it, we will certainly reap the fruits of our labors.

Takeaway

There is much we can learn from a ger's emotional connection. A person who has converted to Judaism does not go through the motions of observance by rote. On the contrary, every single religious act is meaningful to him, and is part of a real relationship with Hashem.

┌─────────────── **Making It Practical** ───────────────┐

• Concretize your relationship with Hashem by truly talking to Him, in the form of an actual conversation, once a day.

• Visualize yourself leaning on Hashem for support, or Hashem leading you by your hand through the obstacles and challenges of life.

└──┘

A Law-Enforcement Liaison
Mrs. Fraida Balaban

Mrs. Fraida Balaban, a resident of Staten Island, New York, works as a liaison between Jewish communities and the police. In that capacity, she tries to communicate the needs of Orthodox Jews to the police and to build trust, mutual respect, and understanding between the authorities and the religious public. She is passionate about helping the police better serve our community, and she values a working relationship with the police force. Naturally, this makes her a prominent representative of the Jewish community, and the type of person who can teach us a lot about dealing with the non-Jewish world.

How did you become involved in this work?

"When I was growing up in Denver, Colorado," Mrs. Balaban recalls, "I became aware of the things that were happening in the neighborhood where I lived. There was some criminal activity in the area, and I tended to notice certain houses that seemed suspicious. One day, the police made a drug raid near my home. I went over to thank the officers for their hard work, and I told them that their job wasn't finished yet; I knew that there were many more dens of crime in the area. The police officer handed me his card and said, 'Call anytime if you have a lead.' That is precisely what I did, and many criminals were arrested with my help. Some of the houses that were cleared of drug dealers were later purchased by Jewish families. That marked the beginning of a partnership that has continued to this day."

Mrs. Balaban's partnership with the police reached a new level after a certain distressing incident. "There were three innocent young sisters who were traveling in their parents' car in a city near Denver. The car was being driven by an 18-year-old girl, and two of her younger sisters, one of them below the age of 12, were her passengers. The car caught the attention of a couple of police officers, and when they looked up the license-plate number, they found that the car was registered as a stolen vehicle. The girls were pulled over, and a frightening scene began to unfold. The girls were separated from each other, handcuffed, and placed in different police cars; they were held at gunpoint and treated like hardened criminals. The police suddenly realized that they had made a terrible mistake; the car had been identified as stolen because of a computer error.

"The police apologized profusely, but the damage had been done. I became involved in the situation, and I explained to the police that the girls led extremely sheltered lives and were shocked and traumatized by the way they had been detained. 'If you knew more about our lifestyle and our community, you would have reacted differently,' I told them. 'You would have been much gentler with the girls, and they would not have suffered all of that needless trauma.' The police were very receptive to being educated about our culture. I brought them to religious schools and *shuls* and introduced them to our *rabbanim* and community leaders. We worked together to develop a pamphlet about the Orthodox Jewish community, which is now distributed to every police officer as part of their training in understanding Jewish culture."

Did the incident with the three girls lead to any changes?

"That story is now used to illustrate the concept of 'critical thinking,' which is taught to the police in their yearly in-service training. The officers are taught to look past the protocols and to evaluate every situation independently, to allow common sense to tell them when the ordinary procedures are out of place. A police officer needs to understand that when he finds himself dealing with an old lady or a young Jewish girl, he should act differently than when he confronts a tough criminal."

How did the police react differently after they had learned more about the Jewish community?

"The fact that they understood Jewish law and culture helped resolve some thorny situations. For instance, a Jewish man once parked his truck in an illegal spot outside a *shul* just before Shabbos. A neighbor called to complain, and a couple of police officers entered the *shul* and asked the truck's owner to move his vehicle. Of course, the man said that he couldn't do that, since Shabbos had already begun. The police warned him that he would have to pay a large fee if they were forced to tow the truck, but the man insisted that there was nothing he could do about it. Fortunately, one of the officers had read the pamphlet about Orthodox Jewish life and understood the issues involved, and he volunteered to take the keys and move the truck to an acceptable spot. That is certainly not the standard procedure, but it is the type of thing that can result from respect and understanding."

In addition, Mrs. Balaban adds, whenever an Orthodox Jewish person in Denver is suspected of a crime, the police make sure to contact her before taking action. And then there is the respect that the Jewish community as a whole has earned in the eyes of the police. "A police officer once remarked to me that the best way to decrease crime in a neighborhood is by increasing the Jewish population," she relates. "In one particular neighborhood, we urged the police to track down a certain criminal, whose activities were scaring away potential Jewish home buyers. The police took the threat very seriously because they wanted the Jewish population to grow; they appreciate having a larger percentage of Jewish residents, which causes the crime rate to drop."

As a resident of Staten Island, have you interacted with the police in New York? Have you noticed any differences between the NYPD and the police force in Denver?

"My experience in Denver equipped me with some valuable connections, which I can use to influence the police. I was quite surprised to discover that, in spite of the large Jewish population in New York, the police officers do not receive much formal training to educate them about our culture. They are expected to learn about *frum* Jews from experience on the job, and select staff meets with *rabbanim* twice a year, but that is not enough. There are constant misunderstandings, which create ill will between the police and the *frum* community. I am working to bring the formal training and methods we used in Denver to New York, so that the police here can become much more educated about Jewish culture."

Is there anything specific about our communities that the police find impressive?

"They are impressed by our sense of community and the support we give each other. In many other communities, people do not even know the other residents of their own blocks; they would never know if anything suspicious or dangerous was taking place even in the homes next door. In our communities, there is much more interaction between neighbors. I once asked a police officer if he felt that he should introduce a 'neighborhood watch' campaign in our community, which would encourage residents to remain alert and report any suspicious activities. 'Are you kidding?' he replied. 'Your communities are the epitome of a neighborhood watch! You don't need a special program; you are always looking out for each other anyway!'"

Mrs. Balaban notes that the favorable impression created by Jewish communities can have a far-reaching impact. "For instance, the police identify areas that they consider 'friendly territory.' When they are on duty but not responding to a call, they often sit in their cars in areas where they feel welcome, and where the residents will not glare at them with hostility. The police often spend time in *frum* areas, and that can be a major benefit for a neighborhood."

What message do you think the police would want our communities to hear?

"Never hesitate to call the police if you notice something suspicious or fall victim to a crime, even a minor one. People are often hesitant to call the police when they are uncertain if there is actual danger, but the police want to be kept informed. If you spot a stranger taking pictures in your neighborhood, or even sitting in his car and appearing to be staking out the area, the police would prefer that you take precautions by informing them of what you saw. Even if the person turns out to be harmless, it is always preferable to err on the side of caution and to report what you see."

What important insights have you gained from your years of experience?

"In the course of my work, I have had many occasions to make special requests of the police, to ask them to provide special services or to set aside their ordinary protocols. But these requests could not have been made without a relationship, and I built that relationship by offering my own help to the police. In my early years, I helped the police organize several drug busts in my neighborhood, and I am employed as a volunteer in the Special Operations Unit of the Denver Police Department. Every community must recognize that it takes an investment of time and effort to earn the respect and appreciation of the police. It needs to be a two-way street, a situation of give and take. If a community succeeds in building that type of relationship, it can be extremely valuable."

Takeaway

A relationship with the police force can be very valuable. Proper communication and training can help the police understand our communities. Every relationship is a two-way street; the police should be made to feel comfortable in our neighborhoods, and we should show appreciation for their hard work and service to our community. If we do not give them something in return, we should not expect to be accommodated when we ask for favors.

Making It Practical

- Show appreciation to the police officers who keep our streets and neighborhoods safe. Wave to them, greet them, and thank them for their service.
- Honor the police when you can, and develop a working relationship with them. If you build a rapport with your local police, it will benefit both you and them.
- In some communities, hundreds of people show up at the local police station every year on Thanksgiving to present a lavish meal to the officers as a sign of appreciation. Try to think of something that you or your community can do to show your gratitude to the police.

In Conclusion

We have seen that the mitzvah of kiddush Hashem is an integral part of the purpose of our lives, that we were sent into the world on a quest to bring about *kevod Shamayim* and that the Torah and mitzvos are the tools that were given to us to carry out that mission. The purpose of this book is to help every person explore his own unique, personal mission and ability to generate kiddush Hashem.

With enough effort and thought, all of us can become vehicles for bringing honor to Hashem. We can make kiddush Hashem our top priority in life by being constantly concerned about Hashem's honor, by dedicating ourselves to His Torah and mitzvos, and by scrupulously avoiding anything that even remotely resembles a chillul Hashem. If we succeed in this mission, perhaps the light of Mashiach will finally shine throughout the world.

Join the movement to help spread these sensitivities, by starting a *chaburah* or class in your *shul* or community with this *sefer* or the Hebrew version, or bring a kiddush Hashem curriculum to your schools, by contacting LivingKiddushHashem@gmail.com or (303) 335-8968. For other ideas of what you can do, and free resources visit LivingKiddushHashem.com.